American Fancy

Exuberance in the Arts 1790–1840

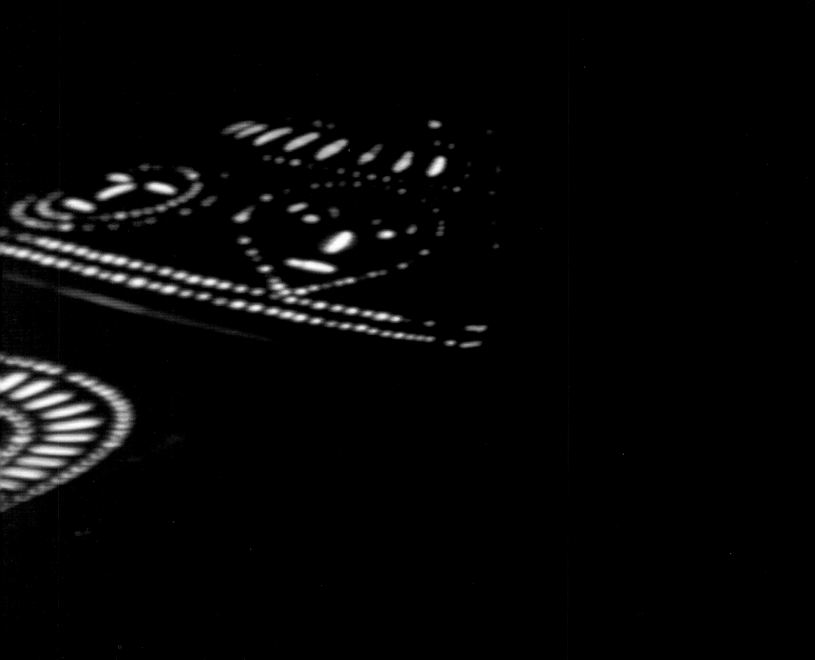

American Fancy

Exuberance in the Arts
1790–1840

Sumpter Priddy

Published by the Chipstone Foundation

Milwaukee

Milwaukee Art Museum

To an English teacher named Rosalie
and an avid antiquer called "Chips"

Published by the Chipstone Foundation
7820 North Club Circle, Milwaukee, Wisconsin 53217

Distributed by
D. A. P.
Distributed Art Publishers, Inc.
155 Sixth Avenue
New York, New York 10013
www.artbook.com

Printed and bound in England   5 4 3 2 1
ISBN 0-9724353-9-5

Design: Wynne Patterson, Pittsfield, Vermont
Copyediting: Alice Gilborn, Mt. Tabor, Vermont
Typesetting: Aardvark Type, Hartford, Connecticut
Printing: Balding + Mansell, Norwich, Norfolk, England

This book has been published by the Chipstone Foundation in conjunction with the exhibition *American Fancy: Exuberance in the Arts, 1790–1840,* organized and circulated by the Milwaukee Art Museum:

Milwaukee Art Museum
Milwaukee, Wisconsin, April 3–June 20, 2004

Peabody Essex Museum
Salem, Massachusetts, July 14–October 31, 2004

Maryland Historical Society
Baltimore, Maryland, December 3, 2004–March 20, 2005.

The Chipstone Foundation also plans a full virtual exhibit of this pioneering installation that will be accessible on chipstone.org in the fall of 2004.

Library of Congress Cataloging-in-Publication Data

Priddy, Sumpter T., 1953-
    American fancy : exuberance in the arts, 1790-1840 / by Sumpter T. Priddy III and the Chipstone Foundation.– 1st ed.
        p. cm.
    Includes bibliographical references and index.
    ISBN 0-9724353-9-5 (hardcover : alk. paper)
    1. Decorative arts–United States–History–18th century–Themes, motives. 2. Decorative arts–United States–History–19th century–Themes, motives. 3. Fantasy in art. 4. Emotions in art. 5. Imagination (Philosophy) I. Chipstone Foundation. II. Title.
    NK806.P75 2004
    709'.73'09034–dc22

                                                                    2003028173

Contents

Preface

*F*ancy. Few would guess today that such an archaic sounding word was central to the tastes and perceptions of early nineteenth-century American society. But words, like styles, are transitory. *American Fancy: Exuberance in the Arts, 1790–1840* is a book about a specific group of objects that are spiritually linked through their association with an early nineteenth-century cultural phenomenon known then and now simply as "Fancy."

As a student of the decorative arts, I am instinctively motivated to identify and describe artifacts, especially those that have not yet received their due recognition. In a slightly more dogmatic vein, I believe that Fancy should be seen as a noteworthy American style, no less significant than other established decorative arts styles—whether expressed in the baroque, rococo, or neoclassical tastes. Yet Fancy was not merely a specific style in the arts. It is therefore not readily described using the conventional methodologies of the decorative arts field. For early nineteenth-century Americans, the word Fancy expressed far more, for it reflected a progressive cultural attitude born out of new and enlightened ways of seeing, understanding, and responding to the surrounding world.

Due to the breadth of the subject, this study leaves a number of stones unturned. In the end, I am more interested in the meaning and effect of Fancy objects than in most other issues. Methods of production and use, as well as descriptions of stylistic variations—often considered cornerstones for decorative arts books—are less important than how these artifacts helped to shape the visual world by which early Americans defined themselves. Furthermore, I have not attempted to provide an encyclopedic overview of Fancy. I have tried to illustrate objects from different regions of early America, as well as imported goods that satisfied popular tastes, and have resisted attempts to record their endless variations or to categorize them according to specific regional characteristics—my intent being to suggest that the core physical and emotive attributes of Fancy transcend geographic and social boundaries alike.

A brief word on the word itself: in this book, you will see both "fancy" and "Fancy." The lowercase spelling connotes the word as it is conventionally used as a noun and as it is defined in any English language dictionary. Often, however, Fancy will be capitalized to convey there was a time when it was more than just a word—when its use as a noun and an adjective represented the dynamic early American cultural outlook and style that serve as the focus of this book. Fancy can be seen as a style in the arts, but also as a distinctive attitude and novel way of perceiving the material world. Fancy's usage in this book might be compared to such terms as "Modern" or "Postmodern," which are usually capitalized and bring to mind not only a certain aesthetic taste, but are accompanied by their particular attitudes, emotions, and perceptions.

Also, a brief note on the sources: many of the concepts related to Fancy came to America from Great Britain, and therefore the work of British writers contributes significantly to the study, particularly in the examination of concepts prior to 1815. Eighteenth- and nineteenth-century aesthetic theories depended on a network of assumptions and a body of writings about perception, the importance of the visual arts, and the role of reason and emotion in aesthetic experience—ideas that cannot be divorced from the story of Fancy in the decorative arts. Literary and philosophical sources effectively lay the groundwork for and justify this novel interpretation of Fancy, and are explored in greatest depth in the chapter entitled "A Brief History of Fancy." Occasional references are made to continental sources, although exclusively to ones translated into English during the period. This study does not consider the impact of Fancy upon the decorative arts of Britain or continental Europe, although it does survey some wares produced abroad and defined as Fancy upon their arrival in America. Rather, the focus is on American makers and users of Fancy goods, and the impact of Fancy upon craft traditions as they merged with vernacular or regional expressions.[1]

Whatever its limitations, I hope that *American Fancy: Exuberance in the Arts, 1790–1840* provides a useful framework for exploring the relationship between human behavior and the goods we produce and use. Although this book concerns the products of a time long since past, contemporary readers should find many aspects of this story relevant, as our material world reflects our thoughts and feelings in the same way that Fancy goods reflected the outlooks of the late eighteenth and early nineteenth centuries. Old things often have the power to awaken new insights, and in looking to the past we sometimes discover new ways of seeing the present. In this, I hope, is the lasting value of this delightful thing called Fancy.

Acknowledgments

*There is no man whose imagination does
not sometimes predominate over his reason.*

Samuel Johnson, *History of Rasselas,* 1759

Many friends and colleagues have contributed in bringing this project to fruition. I am greatly indebted to Jonathan Prown, Executive Director and Chief Curator of the Chipstone Foundation, for his role as both administrator and scholar. His relentless advocacy made both the book and the exhibition a reality, and his provocative intellectual challenges have helped tremendously in shaping the concepts. Glenn Adamson, Chipstone Curator, was a crucial voice in identifying and refining the subtle intellectual theories that originally underlay the Fancy style, and made numerous, and substantive contributions to chapter 1 and chapter 4. Jeffrey Plank of the University of Virginia shared important observations on the relationship between the history of ideas and the history of things, and contributed illuminating passages to the preface, chapter 1, chapter 2, and chapter 4. Alice Gilborn, who served as general editor for the project, has worked with extreme diligence to provide order and clarity to my oft-befuddled manuscript. The finished product is testimony to her perseverance and dedication. Designer Wynne Patterson has done a brilliant job working against an extremely tight schedule to design this stunning book and had vital impact upon some of the most significant images within. I also am extremely grateful to the Chipstone Foundation for its confidence in this project, and specifically to President and Chairman of the Board David Knox, former Chairman Allen Taylor, and to the entire Board of Directors. In a more tangible way, I have benefited from the tireless efforts of Nancy Sazama, Registrar and Executive Assistant, and Sarah Fayen, Charles Hummel Fellow at Chipstone, who have overseen many of the crucial responsibilities that have made the book and exhibition realities. Robert Hunter, editor of Chipstone's *Ceramics in America,* has been of invaluable assistance in providing photographs and bibliographical citations.

The Milwaukee Art Museum likewise has offered considerable support and assumed a tremendous responsibility in sponsoring and mounting the accompanying exhibition. Director David Gordon, past Director Russell Bowman, and former Assistant to the Director Brian Ferriso were vital in moving the exhibition forward. In addition to playing a valuable role in shaping the look and concepts of the show, Eleanore Gadsden, Associate Curator of American Decorative Arts, has overseen the monumental task of coordinating loans, organizing grant proposals, and serving as a liaison between the museum, Chipstone, the author, and the sponsors. Designer Lou Storey has brilliantly interpreted the concepts from the manuscript and the exhibition proposal and distilled them to create a beautiful and powerful exhibition. Installation expertise also came from Mike Mikulay, who played a crucial role in executing the many details that fine-tuned the exhibition presentation and heightened its impact.

Likewise, I am tremendously grateful for the confidence shown by Dean Lahikainen, Curator of the Peabody Essex Museum, and Dennis Fiori, Director of the Maryland Historical Society, for two other venues for the show. Many people at both institutions have been of great help, notably in providing numerous photographs for the book. Among those who have committed important resources and staff time to this project are Kristen Weiss, Mark Tatum, and Christine Michelini of the Peabody Essex, and Nancy Davis, Jeannine Disviscour, and Ruth Mitchell of the Maryland Historical Society.

Throughout the years, many friends associated with the Winterthur Museum have played major roles in the project. The idea was first conceived in a class with Kenneth Ames, who was, and remains, a significant influence on my approach to the arts. Professor James Curtis, former Winterthur Director Charles Hummel, and former Winterthur classmates June Sprigg, Becky Lehman, Susan Scholwer, Donna Braden, Michael Brown, as well as former students Michael Ettema, Peter Hammell, Becky Hammell, and guide specialist Carol Baker assisted over the years. Curators Nancy Goyne Evans, Sue Swann, Arlene Palmer Schwind, and, more recently, Wendy Cooper and Linda Eaton contributed significant scholarly insights and recommended pieces for consideration; Winterthur Furniture Conservator Michael Podmanizcky provided valuable information on Samuel Gragg and the Buttre eagle chair. Susan Newton proved endlessly, and cheerfully, helpful in her doggedness and incredibly efficient pursuit of photography, both old and new. Stunning photographs were composed by George Fistrovich and, more recently, Laszlo Bodo and Jim Schneck. Librarians Neville Thompson, Kathryn McKenney, Dot Wiggins, and Bert Denker of the Winterthur Museum Libraries endured more questions and provided virtually as much assistance as anyone.

Ronald Hurst of the Colonial Williamsburg Foundation has provided critical support by lending to the exhibition and, like Graham Hood before him, committing significant staff time to queries and photographic requests. Among those who have repeatedly given expertise and support are John Austin, Linda Baumgarten, Gail Berger, Cary Carson, John Davis, Barbara and Charles Driscoll, Eunice Glosson, Kim Smith Ivey, Jane Mackley, Anne Motley, and Janine Skerry. Mildred Lanier, Mack Headley, and Kathleen Smith generously provided helpful citations from their textile research, and Margie and Harold Gill fielded an endless barrage of queries over the years. Photographer Hans Lorenz long ago set a high standard for the images and, with his assistant Craig McDougal, was crucial to the success of the project. Cathy Grofils has borne the task of providing dozens of images with tremendous efficiency and commitment. A trusted core of close friends and colleagues at Williamsburg has long believed in the project and lent strong emotional and professional support. Special thanks are due to Margaret Pritchard, Barbara Luck, and Laura Pass Barry for their commitment to help with virtually every aspect of the undertaking, and to Susan Shames, whose quiet nature gives discreet hint of a deeper wisdom.

Gerald Wertkin of the American Folk Art Museum has played an equally important role by providing a significant core of photographs and loans to the exhibition. Stacy Hollander has been of great assistance with curatorial decisions, Janey Fire and Anne-Marie Reilly came to the rescue for photography and numerous queries, and Lee Kogan has been an unstinting advocate for the project. The museum's former photographer, John Parnell, took many of the images in this book while still on staff.

Numerous photographers, both private and institutional, have further contributed to the book. Gavin Ashworth, whose creativity and long hours produced a remarkably strong group of images, provided the largest number of these, and I am grateful for his tremendous assistance and remarkable artistic ability. The book is far better thanks to his creative input. Astorino PhotoGraphics, Inc., Thomas Crane, and my good friend Katherine Wetzel took other fine views. Dave Burgevin of the National Museum of American History made a great effort on our behalf.

Many museums and individuals have been helpful in answering queries concerning their collections and providing photography and/or permission: Sarah Bennett, Albany Institute of History and Art; Terri Tremblay, American Antiquarian Society; William Hosley, Antiquarian and Landmarks Society; Joe Williams, Appomattox Court House National Historical Park; Caroline Nutley, Art Institute of Chicago; Athenaeum of Philadelphia; James Abbott and Beth Ryan, Baltimore Museum of Art; Ruth Janson, Brooklyn Museum of Art; Gary Baker and Sarah Beth Walsh, Chrysler Museum of Art; Cornell University Library; Richard Malley, Connecticut Historical Society; Jane Spillman and Jill Thomas-Clark, Corning Museum of Glass; Olive Graffam, Diane Dunkeley, Patrick Sheary, and the late Michael Berry, DAR Museum; Carol Lee, Denver Art Museum; Dale Couch, Georgia Department of Archives and History; Donald Roan and Abe Rowan, Goschenhoppen Folklife Museum; Greater Milford, New York, Historical Association; Guilford Courthouse National Military Park; Hancock Shaker Village; Donna Braden and Jim

Orr, Henry Ford Museum & Greenfield Village; High Museum of Art; Phil Zea, Peter Spang, Amanda Lange, Edward Meader, Penny Leveritt, and Susan McGowan, Historic Deerfield; Christina Bolgiano, James Madison University Library; Deborah Lambeth and Avis Heatherington, Historical Society of Early American Decoration; Peter Baldaia, Huntsville Museum of Art; Mohammed Rajaii and Chris Phillips, Indiana University Library; Lilly Library, Indiana University; Elizabeth Gusler, Kenmore; Landis Valley Museum; David Barker, Leeds City Museums; Susan Walker, Lewis Walpole Library, Yale University; Library of Congress; Barbara Batson, Library of Virginia; Earl Shettleworth and Deanna Bonner-Ganter, Maine State Museum; Maine Charitable Mechanics Association; Peter Kenney, Metropolitan Museum of Art; Christopher Monkhouse, Minneapolis Institute of Art; Minnesota Historical Society; Susan Stein, William Beiswanger, Diane Ehrenpreis, Robert Self, and Carrie Taylor, Monticello; Linda Ayers and Carol Borchert, Mount Vernon Ladies' Association; Lorelei Eurto, Munson-Williams-Proctor Arts Institute; Deborah Waters, Museum of the City of New York; Martha Rowe, Jennifer Bean, and Wes Stewart, Museum of Early Southern Decorative Arts; Lizabeth Dion, Museum of Fine Arts, Boston; Bayou Bend, the Museum of Fine Arts, Houston; Fine Arts Museums of San Francisco; Nassau County, New York, Division of Museum Services; James West and J. Carter Harris, National Association of Clock and Watch Collectors; Barbara Goldstein Wood, National Gallery of Art; National Library of Medicine; William Jedlick, National Park Service; Ulysses Dietz and Scott Hankins, Newark Museum; Richard J. Koke and Eleanor Gillers, New-York Historical Society; New York Public Library; Shelley Stocking and Kathleen Stocking, Fenimore Art Museum, New York State Historical Association; New York State Library, Albany; Christina Phillips, New York State Museum; Suzanne Flynt, Pocumtuck Valley Memorial Association; John Holverson, Portland Museum of Art; Jack Lindsay and Stacy Bomento, Philadelphia Museum of Art; Thomas Michie, Museum of Art, Rhode Island School of Design; Science Museum, London; Jean Burks, Polly Darnell, Marge Serisky, Julie Yankowsky, Shelburne Museum; Bonnie Lilienfeld, William and Jane Yeingst, Shannon Perich, and the late Rodris Roth, National Museum of American History; Richard Sorensen, National Museum of American Art; Jane and Richard Nylander, Society for the Preservation of New England Antiquities; Strawbery Banke Museum; Margaret Woodbury Strong Museum; Donna Baron, J. Edward Hood, and the late John O. Curtis, Old Sturbridge Village; Abbie Ferrie-Calkins and Clarita Anderson, University of Maryland; Suzanne Savery, Colleen Callahan, and Teresa Roane, Richmond History Center, Valentine Museum; Julius Barclay, Alderman Library, University of Virginia; Washington Street United Methodist Church, Petersburg, Virginia; the late Christopher Gilbert, Victoria and Albert Museum; Danielle Mann, Wadsworth Atheneum; the late Charles and Florence Montgomery of Yale University; York County Heritage Trust.

Many scholars generously contributed their special expertise, and many also provided illustrations. Alexandra Alizavatos Kirtley has been a dedicated colleague and frequently shared her astounding insights into the Fancy era; Cozy Baker and Caroline Davidson have assisted with the history of the kaleidoscope; Charles Brownell of Virginia Commonwealth University shared his knowledge of B. Henry Latrobe; Stiles Colwill provided critical information on Francis Guy and sent me a copy of his book on the artist; Davida Deutsch cited important documentation regarding schoolgirl art and assisted with illustrations; Nancy Carter Crump reviewed numerous early texts for references to Fancy cooking; Ellen Denker assisted with queries concerning rocking chairs and the Anna Pottery; Ed Polk Douglas recalled references concerning Fancy wallpapers; Tori Eberline shared notes on women's education; Elaine Eff talked with me about painted window shades and screens; Oscar and Toby Fitzgerald shared thoughts on quilt designs; Larry Gobrecht forwarded information on Fancy literature; the late Milton Grigg wrote me about painted interiors; Elaine Hawes sent references to the first kaleidoscopes in Alexandria; Paige Inslee cited kaleidoscopic quilts in Britain; Peter Kinney provided sources for transparent painting on glass; Frank Lynch of www.SamuelJohnson.com helped with citations for the great lexicographer; Candace Metallick made introductions in Cooperstown, New York; Mark Matz introduced me to *The Idiot* and *The Boston Kaleidoscope and Literary Rambler*; Robert Mussey provided information regarding early Fancy chairs in Boston and Philadelphia; Chris Ohrstrom assisted with documentation and images of Fancy wallpapers; Jonathan Rickard cited period sources for Fancy mocha wares and sent numerous images of pieces in his remarkable collection; Betty Ring assisted with Fancy needlework and provided illustrations; Jane Webb Smith clarified research on ornamental painters John and Hugh Bridport; Don Walters has shared numerous insights over the years; Camille Wells recommended a bibliography on early stores; Frank S. Welsh shared insights on Fancy painting; Martha Willoughby assisted with research in the New York Public Library; Trisha and Don Herr helped with a variety of questions concerning textiles and printed fabrics; Melinda and Laszlo Zongor forwarded citations on overshot coverlets; Elle Shushan of Augustus Fine Arts sent me an early history of mourning and mourning jewelry; Robert Trent assisted with numerous queries over the years; and Taylor B. Williams was extremely helpful on the subject of enameled snuffboxes and in providing illustrations.

Other friends and associates made special efforts on behalf of the project. Revelle Gwyn and Meyer Dworsky provided a haven for writing; Robert Bardwell safely transported many of the objects for photography; and Pat Sykes assisted with an endless array of details in New York. Many gallery owners have shared their expertise, generously provided contacts with collectors, or sent transparencies for the text. Their intellect and generosity have contributed significantly to the success of the final product: Marna Anderson; Sandra Crowther, Kentucky Hotel; Stuart Feld, Hirschl and Adler; Wayne Fisher's American Design; James and Nancy Glazer; Sam Herrup; Alan and Penny Katz; Jolie Kelter and Michael Malcé; Kate and Joel Kopp; Thurston Nichols; Marguerite Riordan; Stephen Score; David Schorsch; Elizabeth Stillinger and William Guthman; Edwin Hild and Patrick Bell, Old Hope Antiques; Alan Kaplan, Leo Kaplan, Ltd.; Betty Ann Morgan; Frank and Barbara Pollack; Deanne Levison, Levison and Cullen; Paul Vandekar, Earl Vandekar of Knightsbridge; Susan and Jim Widder; Kimberly Washam and Don Heller. I am also indebted to Nancy Druckman, Leslie Keno, John Nye, and Tom Savage of Sotheby's and to Dean Failey, John Hays, Margot Rosenberg, and Andrew Brunk of Christie's for their help in securing illustrations.

I am equally indebted to those in the private sphere who also have contributed to the book and exhibition and helped to shape the intellectual content of the project. I am extremely grateful for the kindnesses extended to this project over the years by Mrs. George M. Kaufman and the late Mr. Kaufman, who shared their knowledge, their enthusiasm, and their collection. Helaine and Burt Fendalman have assisted in so many ways over the last two decades that it is difficult to recall them all. A host of collectors enthusiastically permitted photography of pieces in their collection for the book, and many have also lent to the exhibition: Elizabeth Beebe; Kenneth W. Coker; Claiborne and Charlie Dickinson; William K. du Pont; Ellen Glennon; Mr. and Mrs. Alexander H. Galloway, Jr.; Holcombe T. Green, Jr.; Julie Hunter; Paul Johnson; Susan Doherty and Syed Ali; the late Bert and Nina Little; Eric Maffei and Steven Trombetti; Robert and Mary Matthews; Roddy and Sally Moore; Betsy Bobbitt Nicholson; Elbert Parsons; Gordon Plotkin and family; William and Joyce Subjack; Mrs. R. Carmichael Tilghman; Anne Timpson; Marshall Goodman; Tom Gray; Bob and Jo Wagner; Michelle and Robert White; and Mrs. Joseph M. Winston. Tinsmiths Robert Cukla of Hammersong and Chuck Baker generously provided reproduction lighting devices that could be illustrated when lit. John Rison Jones made introductions at the Huntsville Museum of Art.

A variety of talented individuals associated with my office over the years deserve a special, and belated, thanks. Sarah Cantor, Elsie Klumpner, Jonathan Woods, Joshua Criswell, Jill Kent, and Mariano Kanamori played particularly important roles securing and managing the seemingly endless photographs, captions, and permissions needed to illustrate the book. Martha Vick and Winfrey Wright undertook research and checked many, many footnotes. Ed Chapman, Dywana Saunders, and Russell Bernabo each contributed in a myriad of ways.

I am especially indebted to a core group of personal friends who lent critical moral support during the long period when this project was finished but lacked institutional sponsorship. Peggy Scholley and Luke Beckerdite, Clifford Dunlap and Ralph Harvard, and Grace and Don

Friary were tremendously important in those often discouraging times. Betsy Garrett buoyed me greatly by going to bat when the odds were unfavorable, and Wendell Garrett devoted significant energy and good-will to the project. More recently, Charlene Johnson served as a trusted friend and has advised me in more ways than one can imagine, as well as performed the thankless task of overseeing business during my extended absence to refine the project. Milly McGehee, the late John Bivins, Jr., and Anne McPherson all provided essential friendship at critical times. To my siblings Rives, Bruce, John, and Tim—and their families—I also owe a debt. To my way of thinking, each listed here deserves wings.

FIGURE I   Alexander Jackson Davis,
Grecian Interior, New York City, ca. 1830.
Watercolor on paper. 13¼" x 18⅛". (Collection of the New-York Historical Society,
1908.28.)

Introduction

About 1830 Alexander Jackson Davis (1803–1892), one of America's leading architects, sat in a New York studio and admired his recent sketch of an idealized classical interior (fig. 1).[1] Exquisitely done, the drawing depicts a level of style confined to exceptionally few American homes during that era. Each architectural detail, each furnishing, represented a pure manifestation of the "Grecian" taste so popular after 1800. Pervading Davis' imagined architectural space is a sense of cool repose and decorative restraint communicated through the artist's cautious use of tempered Grecian designs. Only one color ideally suited this austere style, "the whitest of the white," as Charles Dickens observed of the houses that dotted America's landscape.[2] "There are pleasant associations in that word," wrote another early nineteenth-century observer praising the color of the President's House in Washington. "It breathes an innocent purity and a spotless virtue."[3]

As Davis was completing his ideal Grecian interior, another aspiring artist was creating a watercolor image that depicted a very different type of American interior, one that was significantly different in scale and in character. This artist's name, coincidentally enough, was Joseph H. Davis (active 1832–1837), an itinerant painter who traveled the roads of rural New England where he found sitters for his portraits (fig. 2). This Davis had no formal training in architecture or the fine art of painting, and although his technique left much to be desired from an academic standpoint,

FIGURE 2   Joseph H. Davis, *Sylvanus C. Foss and Mary Jane Foss*, probably Strafford, Strafford County, New Hampshire, 1836. Watercolor, pencil, and ink on paper. 10¾" x 15" (sight). (Collection of the American Folk Art Museum, New York. Promised gift of Ralph Esmerian, P1.2001.34; photo, © 2000 John Bigelow Taylor, New York.)

FIGURE 3 Chest, Rhode Island or coastal Connecticut, ca. 1825. Yellow pine and painted decoration. H. 23", W. 41½", D. 17". (Courtesy, Elbert H. Parsons, Jr.; photo, Gavin Ashworth.)

FIGURE 4 Fire bucket, Massachusetts, ca. 1800. Leather, iron, and painted decoration. H. 12¾", Diam. 8¾". (Courtesy, Peabody Essex Museum.)

his images possessed a magnetic appeal that attracted people everywhere he visited. This man's work was touched only peripherally by the time-honored tenets of formal classicism, yet the evocative settings for his portraits were no less idealized than those created by his New York contemporary.

Joseph Davis and his sitters were captivated not by the Grecian taste, but by an unrestrained sense of decoration, one that infused vivid colors and boldly ornamental patterns into their household furnishings. Minor allusions to classicism appear discreetly in the picture—principally in the shape of the Grecian "klismos" chairs—but its dominant style expresses a sensibility that is quite exhilarating. In this portrait, Sylvanus and Mary Jane Foss are presented in a brightly painted interior with an eye-catching carpet. Mr. Foss wears a richly patterned waistcoat that echoes the visual liveliness of Mrs. Foss' embroidered scarf and long apron. The couple faces one another in front of a painted table with an ornamental vase of flowers and colorfully bound books. On the wall, ornamental trappings enliven a landscape painting. Davis created variations of this idealized setting for dozens of New Englanders, indicating that this portrayal not only pleased him but also delighted his clients, who imagined themselves recorded for posterity in such lively surroundings.[4]

The Fosses made their home in Strafford, New Hampshire, but their tastes were no different than those of millions of middle-class Americans who lived throughout this nation in the early nineteenth century. Had they lived in downtown Philadelphia, in a Connecticut village, on a farm in Ohio, or on a Carolina plantation, the Fosses would have encountered similarly exuberant expressions of Fancy. The Fosses represent the mainstream of early nineteenth-century American society, a group commonly thought to have found its primary aesthetic inspiration in restrained classical taste. If Joseph Davis' portrait is an accurate indicator, however, mainstream

America was only partially touched by classical style. Instead, people like the Fosses lived in a vibrant world that was filled to capacity with colors and patterns, with visual excesses and superfluities, and with lively furnishings that matched the lively details of their clothing.

How did the Fosses perceive this new and delightful world that surrounded them on all sides? And what were the means by which they understood its contrast to other, more austere tastes derived from classical art and thought? The answer resides in the simple word "Fancy." Davis' watercolor offers a tantalizing glimpse into that evocative world, which brought together novel attitudes and spirited artistic expressions to offer pleasure and meaning to countless Americans.

FIGURE 5   J. M. Davidson, coverlet, Lodi, New York, 1837. Wool. H. 87¾", W. 82¼". (Courtesy, Denver Art Museum Collection. Gift of Mary Willsea, 1962.37; photo, ©2003 Denver Art Museum.) The coverlet bears the woven inscription "J. M. / DAVIDSON / FANCY WEAVER."

FIGURE 6   Trade sign, Massachusetts, 1840–1860. Pine and painted decoration. H. 17½", W. 27⅜". (Courtesy, Hancock Shaker Village, Pittsfield, Massachusetts.)

Like many New Englanders of the era, the Fosses may have possessed a Fancy sleigh in which they rode to church, or attended Fancy balls dressed in Fancy clothing. Mr. Foss was probably a part-time farmer by occupation and may have owned a Fancy horse that grazed upon Fancy grass. When Mrs. Foss caught a cold, she sniffled in a Fancy handkerchief, while on fine summer days she might wander into her garden and pick purple fancies—violets—from its borders. When they journeyed out to shop, Mr. Foss likely purchased goods at the Fancy Hardware Store while his wife sampled specialties at the Fancy Bakery or browsed at the Fancy Millinery Shop. After returning home and consuming supper, perhaps at a Fancy table set with Fancy china, they may have retired to the parlor to sing a rousing chorus of "Tell Me, Where Is Fancy Bred?" or "Delighted Fancy Hails the Hour" around their decorated piano.[5] When their ornamented clock struck eight, Mr. and Mrs. Foss sent the children upstairs to their rooms, spent time together in their parlor fit with Fancy carpets and Fancy wallpaper, then walked upstairs by the flickering light of a Fancy lantern. They pulled back their Fancy coverlet, climbed into their Fancy bedstead, read briefly from the most recent Fancy literature, and then dreamt the night away (figs. 3–8).

FIGURE 7   Coffeepot, attributed to James Fulivier, Pennsylvania, ca. 1825. Sheet iron, brass, and painted decoration. H. 10½", D. 16¼". (From the Collections of Henry Ford Museum & Greenfield Village.) The coffeepot is signed on the base "James Fulivier 75 cts is the price of this" and "Jared H. Young."

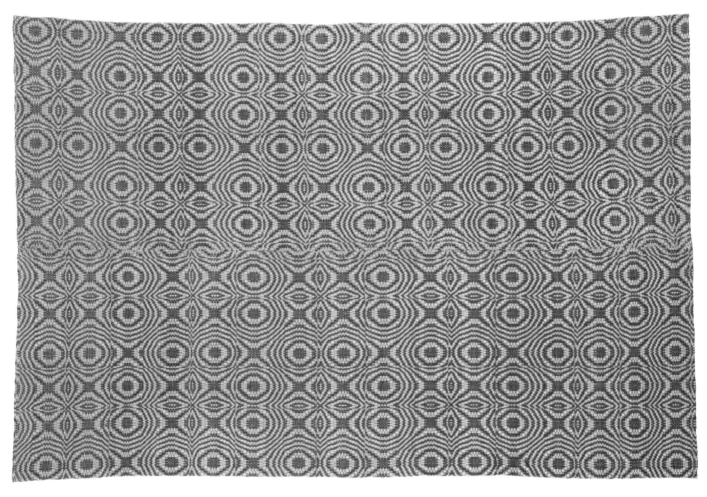

FIGURE 8 Overshot coverlet, America,
1820–1830. Cotton warp and wool and cotton
weft. H. 94", W. 65¼". (Courtesy, The Art
Institute of Chicago, 1967.18; photo, Bob
Hashimoto, © The Art Institute of Chicago.)

AMERICAN FANCY

To modern Americans, Joseph Davis' depiction of the Fosses' Fancy world may seem neither familiar nor comprehensible. If asked to define "fancy," today's audience might associate it with excessive decoration or purposeful aloofness. The current definition, however, is one of many to have evolved over time, and gives little sense of the word's rich heritage. In 1750 the average American or Englishman would have equated fancy not with ornamentation or snobbery, but with imagination and creativity. By 1820 the response would have expanded to encompass such a broad range of definitions as to suggest the era was captivated by the concept, as indeed it was. Understanding this evolution and discovering the meaning of the early nineteenth-century phenomenon popularly known as Fancy are essential to understanding the American experience emotionally, artistically, intellectually, and socially.

Between 1790 and 1840, Americans eagerly participated in the celebratory and progressive spirit of Fancy, which was intimately linked to a growing receptivity to virtually every form of creativity rooted in the imagination. During that period, Fancy came to signify almost any activity or object that delighted the human spirit or stirred the imagination—it occupied people's minds, pervaded their homes, and shaped their perspectives on the world (fig. 9). Just about everything that pleased the senses fell within Fancy's realm, whether a colorful array of household objects or such imaginative creations as fine art and sculpture, music, literature, and dance (fig. 10).

FIGURE 9   Enoch A. Titus, *Fancy Parrots,* America, March 10, 1835. Ink on paper. 9⅝" x 7⅝". (Private collection; photo, Gavin Ashworth.)

FIGURE 10   James Hewitt, sheet music, *Delighted Fancy Hails the Hour,* New York, 1807. (Courtesy, New York State Library, Manuscripts and Special Collections.)

Yet, if Fancy things were generally colorful and boldly patterned, the style possessed no single identity. Rather, it was best identified by intangible means, by the wide range of emotional responses it was able to elicit—delight, awe, surprise, and laughter. These were triggered not just by the stunning nature of the objects, but also by a dynamic combination of images and allusions that connected the viewer's imagination to the larger world which he or she shared with these engaging material objects.

The decorative expressions of the Fancy style—whether painted surfaces, kaleidoscopic quilts or imaginary landscapes—were never considered the most significant aspect of the style. Rather, they served to fuel the storehouse of the memory and functioned as reference points that elicited strong emotional responses because of their implicit connection to people, things, and ideas beyond the objects. Most nineteenth-century viewers did not passively receive information from these decorative goods but actively participated in an intellectual and emotional process, centered on absorption and response, allusion and association.

America's artisans augmented this process by creating an astonishing range of Fancy artifacts that helped to meet the public's rising desire to respond imaginatively to the surrounding world: brilliantly colored fabrics, vividly painted furniture, boldly patterned wallpapers, and whimsical ceramics, to name but a few (figs. 11 and 12). Some of these artifacts had their greatest impact when viewed from afar; others, when carefully inspected in detail. Yet all employed ornament intended to elicit emotions and to expand the imagination—in short, material expressions of Fancy expressed

FIGURE 11   I. Scott, parlor wall, Alexander Shaw House, Wagram, North Carolina, 1836. Wood and painted decoration. (Courtesy, Abby Aldrich Rockefeller Folk Art Museum, Colonial Williamsburg Foundation, Williamsburg, Virginia.)

AMERICAN FANCY

the core attributes of human fancy. They reflected the essential powers cited by the eighteenth-century Scottish philosopher Thomas Reid when he observed that "Fancy may combine things that never were combined in reality. It may enlarge or diminish, multiply or divide, compound and fashion."[6] To understand Fancy today, we must try to imagine the intense visceral and visual response early nineteenth-century Americans must have felt when they first walked into a Fancy room filled with Fancy things, for this look and this response were the aspirations of many during the era, and achieving them must have been an awe-inspiring experience (fig. 13).

To rediscover this lost sensibility, traditional approaches to the decorative arts do not, alone, suffice. Rather, just as imaginative literature, poetry, and music were intended to engage the beholder and to arouse emotional responses, so too were objects inspired by Fancy. Traditional modes of furniture analysis place the greatest emphasis upon style, history, and construction, yet these are usefully balanced by a careful consideration of the perceptual and emotional responses through which the

FIGURE 12   Chest, New England, ca. 1825. White pine and painted decoration. H. 41⅛", W. 38¼", D. 18½". (Private collection; photo, Milly McGehee.)

FIGURE 13   Joseph Warren Leavitt, *Interior of John Leavitt's Tavern*, Chichester, Merrimack County, New Hampshire, ca. 1825. Watercolor, ink, and pencil on paper in original maple frame. 6½" x 8⅝" (sight); 8⁹/₁₆" x 10½" (frame). (Collection of the American Folk Art Museum, New York. Promised gift of Ralph Esmerian, P1.2001.18; photo © 2000 John Bigelow Taylor, New York.)

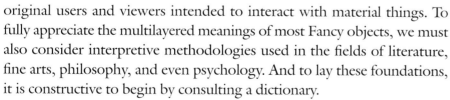

original users and viewers intended to interact with material things. To fully appreciate the multilayered meanings of most Fancy objects, we must also consider interpretive methodologies used in the fields of literature, fine arts, philosophy, and even psychology. And to lay these foundations, it is constructive to begin by consulting a dictionary.

According to *The Oxford English Dictionary*, "fancy" is a contraction of "fantasy." This is the equivalent of the ancient Greek noun *phantasia*, derived from the verb *phantasier*, meaning "to make visible." *Phantasier* referred to the mind's capacity to recall images from the memory exactly as they were originally seen, or to combine the images and create new, or

FIGURE 14 Detail, *A View in Medford, America,* ca. 1830. Oil on board. 22½" x 19½". (Courtesy, Marguerite Riordan.) See fig. 213.

imaginative, syntheses. The Romans adopted the noun *phantasia,* but they also created another term that was nearly identical in meaning. This was the Latin *imaginatio,* or, in English, imagination—and it was employed almost synonymously with *phantasia.* Both words were incorporated into the emerging French and English languages and continued in use largely unaltered throughout the medieval period. On occasion, however, the English contracted their word "phantasy" to form "phantsy" or "phansy." By Shakespeare's time, the spelling of phantasy and its contraction phansy had evolved into "fantasy" and "fancy" or "fancie" and had diverged enough to acquire separate identities. Both words were still related to creativity, although fancy usually was confined to imaginary creations that contained enough reality to remain believable. The meaning of fantasy, on the other hand, moved beyond the realm of reality into a capricious or dreamy world. The exact demarcation between fancy and fantasy was not always clear, although their extremes left little doubt there was a difference.[7]

In his monumental *Dictionary of the English Language* (1755), the first dictionary based on the historical usage of words, the British lexicographer Samuel Johnson (1709–1784) offered a series of provocative definitions for the noun fancy.[8] This brilliant man of letters and social commentator observed no less than nine distinct meanings that had evolved over time:

1. Imagination
2. An opinion bred rather by the imagination than reason
3. Taste; idea; conception of things
4. Image; conception; thought
5. Inclination; liking; fondness
6. In Shakespeare it signifies love
7. Caprice; humor; whim
8. False notion
9. Something that pleases or entertains without real use or value

Johnson's list effectively indexes many of the conceptual and aesthetic attributes that eventually coalesce to define the Fancy style in America and offers a useful starting point for charting the concepts (fig. 14). We will return to these definitions periodically throughout the book, but we can begin by observing several trends.

The first four meanings link fancy with creativity or imagination—a meaning echoed in other early dictionaries. Thomas Dyche and William Pardon, who published *A New General English Dictionary* in 1740, similarly defined fancy as "that internal sense, power, or faculty of the soul that is sometimes called imagination."[9] Other dictionaries did the same. Two centuries ago the British and Americans alike viewed the fundamental power of imagination much as we do today—as the mental power or "faculty" responsible for creativity. But their exploration of its powers often delved much deeper than ours, for in their heightened desire to reap the rewards of imagination, they also sought to nourish it by providing the memory a wealth of images that served as the storehouse of the mind. Feeding the imagination required the gathering of experiences from the surrounding world: the human senses of taste, smell, hearing, touch, and sight all contributed to this process. Writers frequently acknowledged the importance of the senses to creative endeavors, and artists sometimes portrayed them whimsically in print (fig. 15). The images and experiences thus gathered by the senses provided the building blocks for imagination. They prompted a fruitful participation in the imaginative processes essential to the development of the Fancy style and a heightened awareness of the key visual and emotional attributes of Fancy.

Johnson's third definition stands out for its association of fancy with "taste," which echoes the words of another eighteenth-century cultural observer who noted that "Fancy forms the pictures which affect taste."[10] However, not everyone of the era agreed upon the character of taste. The

FIGURE 15   Louis Boilly, *The Five Senses,* France, ca. 1825. Lithograph. 8¼" x 7". (Courtesy, National Library of Medicine, History of Medicine Division, Bethesda, Maryland.)

great French philosopher Voltaire associated the fine arts of painting and sculpture with higher learning and true taste. However, he attributed ever-changing preferences for the useful arts of everyday life, and particularly for dress, to the whimsical powers of the mind.[11] Voltaire specifically acknowledged the arbitrariness of expression rooted in fancy, and he emphasized dress as a prime example of this "low sphere." Yet, even by acknowledging fancy's role in this realm, he reflected changing outlooks, both in the arts and in literary and philosophical circles, where fancy and imagination were gaining credence. Moreover, that fancy inspired "new and contradictory modes" became an alluring selling point. In the eyes and minds of a growing number of thinkers and consumers, expressions drawn from the creative consciousness were not only valid, but also essential, exciting, and enriching.

Johnson's other definitions suggest even more immediate or tactile links to the material world of Fancy and help us better to understand its basic attributes. For instance, the "caprice; humor; whim" that he observed bring to mind a stoneware jar of the 1820s (fig. 16) which features a deliberately capricious dancing figure holding a jug in his hand. Even seemingly utilitarian devices such as candle-powered lanterns and sconces

FIGURE 16   Storage jar, New York, ca. 1820. Salt-glazed stoneware and incised and cobalt decoration. H. 12". (Private collection; photo, David Schorsch, American Hurrah Archive, New York City.)

(fig. 17) were fashioned in the early national period to produce ever more lively geometric patterns of light, to create lively images of shadow and light, and to complement the already lively look of Fancy decorated interiors. Similarly, the engaging surface of a chest (fig. 18) painted in New England during the 1830s evocatively demonstrates another important early belief, that expressions of Fancy were most effective when they literally painted themselves onto the audience's collective memory.

FIGURE 19 Overmantel painting, attributed to Winthrop Chandler, McClellan House, South Woodstock, Connecticut, 1785–1790. Oil on panel. 27" x 58". (Courtesy, Shelburne Museum, Shelburne, Vermont.)

Both in form and decoration, Fancy goods elicited surprise and delight, often through the illusion of decoration that was greater or lesser than, or whimsically imitative of, reality. Such is the case with a Fancy overmantel from the McClellan House of South Woodstock, Connecticut (fig. 19). Decorated by the imaginative New Englander Winthrop Chandler, the false image engages the viewer in a delightful visual trick through its imitation of a bookshelf surmounting the fireplace, a common New England architectural convention. The viewer's mind instinctively churns in response to the experience, perhaps considering the real bookshelves that exist in other houses, wondering why they are not here, contemplating the intent of the maker, or weighing alternatives for improving the deception. In early America, where life was ruled by long hours of work and few individuals were formally educated, such expressions provided a desirable opportunity to invigorate the mind. A stoneware jug made in New York about 1825 reflects a similar artistic approach (figs. 20 and 21). It presents two different faces for the devil: one, grotesquely human in character, facing to the right; and the other, in the form of Beelzebub, the devilish biblical goat, gazing to the left. The faces on the jug are linked in the center

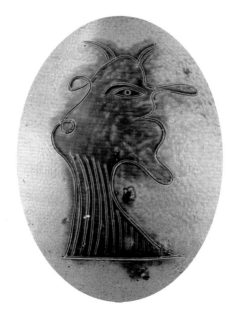

FIGURE 20 Jug, New York, ca. 1825. Salt-glazed stoneware and incised and cobalt decoration. H. 15¼". (Courtesy, Elbert H. Parsons, Jr.; photo, Gavin Ashworth.)

FIGURE 21 Detail of the two faces of the devilish figure on the jug illustrated in fig. 20.

FIGURE 22 Chest with drawer, Rhode Island, ca. 1830. Pine and painted decoration. H. 37⅞", W. 45¾", D. 19¼". (Private collection; photo, Gavin Ashworth.)

by shared horns and a shared eye—and by their common symbolism, presumably intended for the "demon rum" inside the jug. The layering of imagery and meaning creates a complex maze of illusion and allusion in which the imagination can freely wander.

Another key attribute of Fancy was its spontaneity. Unlike the broader mental faculties of judgment and imagination, the fancy was thought to act quickly. Its purpose was not to guide deliberative action, but rather to whip the mind into a dynamic froth of volatile impressions (fig. 22). This effect is perhaps clearest in the case of trompe l'oeil paintings, but all expressions of Fancy were meant in one way or another to manipulate the viewer's perceptions and activate the sense of wit and whimsy. The effect of the faculty of fancy was held to be a worthy end in itself. Leigh Hunt,

AMERICAN FANCY

an enthusiastic observer of the powers of fancy and of the wit that contributed to it, noted that "Wit does not contemplate its ideas for their own sake . . . but solely for the purpose of producing an effect by their combination." He added that we laugh "not to anyone's disadvantage, but simply to our joy and reassurance." For Hunt and others, the joy of fancy came from the surprise of finding similarity in dissimilarity, or from the delight in recognizing an irreconcilable double meaning. And the degree of delight usually depended upon "the vivacity of the surprise."[12]

Johnson's last two definitions of "fancy"—as being a "false notion" or "something that pleases or entertains without real use or value"—reintroduce the duality of fancy versus reason. Johnson lived in a time when highly imaginative modes of expression were often dismissed as frivolous, before the stylistic rise of Fancy. The early association of the word "fancy" with the superfluous is evident in the observations of one Bostonian in 1719:

> The Carpenter who builds a good House to defend us from the Wind and Weather, is more serviceable than the curious Carver, who employs his Art to please his fancy. This condemns not . . . Carving, but only shows that what is more substantially serviceable to Mankind, is much preferable to what is less necessary.[13]

That conservative outlook toward ornamentation and emotion would eventually change.

Few individuals captured the spirit of Fancy better than the artist, inventor, and ornamental painter Rufus Porter. The author of a popular booklet entitled *Curious Arts,* Porter provided instructions for fashioning a wide array of decorative household goods—transparent window shades, painted floorcloths, and grained woodwork, to name but a few. He also included a recipe for making "exhilarating gas," a period term for nitrous oxide, or laughing gas. This bit of chemistry may seem a far cry from his other directions for making eye-catching material goods. Yet, like most of his contemporaries, Porter was not just interested in the appearance of Fancy objects, he was also interested in their psychological impact. Porter prepared his readers for the unexpected recipe with an explanation that could apply equally well to his Fancy decorations:

> The effects . . . are in general, highly pleasurable, and resemble those attendant on the agreeable period of intoxication. Exquisite sensations of pleasure; an irresistible propensity to laughter; a rapid flow of vivid ideas; . . . are the ordinary feelings produced by it. And what is exceedingly remarkable, is, that the intoxication thus produced, instead of being succeeded by the debility subsequent to intoxication by ardent spirits, does, on the contrary, render the person who takes it, cheerful and high spirited for the remainder of the day.[14]

During the age of American Fancy—from 1790 to 1840—Americans saw artistic expressions of fancy and imagination in an appreciative light, viewing them as essential to the development of the mind and character.

FIGURE 23 Cup and saucer, Staffordshire, England, ca. 1840. Earthenware and polychrome decoration. Diam. 6" (saucer); H. 2½", Diam. 4½" (cup). (Private collection; photo, Gavin Ashworth.)

At the same time they embraced a cultural phenomenon that coalesced into a vision and a style with far-reaching implications. Fancy was a concept that helped to define that era in unprecedented ways, and no term better captures its spirit. Understanding that fascination opens up an entirely new view of early nineteenth-century America and its material goods—an awareness that rekindles the long-forgotten perspective in which objects and experiences are tied inextricably to the imagination of their creators and to the delight and response of their beholders (fig. 23).

Today the uninitiated can gaze upon a Fancy chair or quilt or painting and appreciate its dynamic visual energy and emotional delight. This accessibility doubtless accounted for Fancy's success during its heyday as well. On an immediate level all of us can understand and delight in Fancy, and we can make many of the same multifaceted associations that once made this phenomenon so exciting and new. Indeed, as this book will suggest, the sensual appeal of these objects is not only timeless but also primal. Yet a comprehensive examination of the Fancy world must go beyond an appreciation of the essence of the style, and attempt to reconstruct both the background and the precise tenor of the excitement that nineteenth-century Americans must have experienced whenever they saw Fancy's innovative expressions.

American Fancy

1 A Brief History of Fancy

The fancy runs from one end of the universe to the other collecting . . . ideas, which belong to any subject.

David Hume, *A Treatise on Human Understanding*, 1739–1740

Fancy began in Great Britain. Before appearing in material form in early America, fancy was viewed principally as a function of the mind. In the late eighteenth and early nineteenth centuries, Americans embraced the material culture of Fancy as a result of new understandings of creativity and emotion derived from eighteenth-century investigations into the nature of the human intellect. In fact, at its height Fancy was less a mode of decoration, a class of music, or a subject of literature than it was a larger philosophy or attitude toward life. Progressive ideas about the meaning of the word coalesced with great clarity about 1760. Thereafter, British writers and artists, and their colonial counterparts, made a conceptual leap that brought fancy from the realm of abstract philosophy to the tangible objects that constitute the main subject of this book.

For our purposes, literary historian William Park admirably summarizes the crucial eighteenth century:

> However one regards history, the eighteenth century appears as the time of crisis, a time of extraordinary transformations, probably the most extraordinary that have ever taken place—feudal to bourgeois, classic to romantic, aristocratic to democratic, hierarchic to egalitarian, agricultural to industrial, religious to secular, from God the creator to man the creator. Even among the religious thinkers, the concept of God shifted from transcendent to immanent, from the God without to the God within, from God the father to the human divine.[1]

The evolution toward a secular society described by Park brought with it the need to explain the breadth of human experience in terms other than religious ones. As the reliance on church and faith shifted toward a new

FIGURE 24   Charles-Louis Clerisseau, *View of the Exterior of the Maison Carrée,* in the second edition of *Antiquities of France,* Paris, 1804. (Courtesy, The Winterthur Library: Printed Book and Periodical Collection.) Ancient architecture symbolized the durability of classical thought and society to Britain's eighteenth-century intellectual and political leaders, who widely promoted the *antique* style.

emphasis on science and knowledge, Europe and its New World colonies experienced a parallel transition away from the need to accept and believe and toward the desire, in eighteenth-century terms, to know and to understand. One of the central aspects of this transition was an intense effort to decipher the workings of the human mind, identify its component "faculties," and weigh their relative merits. This exploration came to revolve around a careful consideration of two contrasting mental faculties: reason and imagination, the latter also known as fancy.

Reason and fancy were seen to encompass mental powers so different, and to respond to outside stimuli so dissimilar, that they were held to confer distinct perspectives on the world, to mold separate attitudes toward right and wrong, and to impart differing outlooks in matters of creativity and taste.

Eighteenth-century thinkers viewed reason as the force essential to knowledge and understanding. It encompassed the skills fundamental to logic and philosophy, as well as the fields of science and mathematics. Reason processed solid facts from the surrounding world and reached conclusions that would stand the test of time. Hailed as mankind's highest and most defining power, reason separated humans from beasts and, faith not discounted, made it possible to aspire to the wisdom and moral-

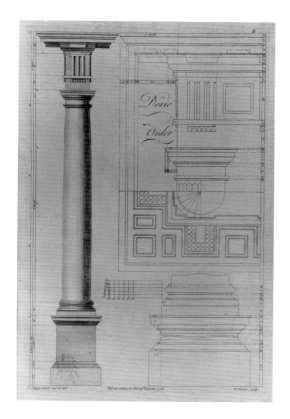

FIGURE 25 Doric order illustrated on pl. 2 in the third edition of Thomas Chippendale's *The Gentleman and Cabinet-Maker's Director*, London, 1762. (Courtesy, The Winterthur Library: Printed Book and Periodical Collection.) During the eighteenth century, classical architecture provided British and American artisans one of their principal sources for scale and proportion and often inspired even the smallest details of buildings and furnishings.

ity of the Creator. "Reason is the great distinction of human nature," Samuel Johnson wrote, "the faculty by which we approach the same degree of association with celestial intelligences."[2]

Eighteenth-century attitudes toward reason reflected an intellectual tradition that was inherited from the ancients and reemphasized during the Renaissance. In looking to the ancients for inspiration, the eighteenth-century British affirmed their commitment to permanence and stability, the importance of reason in the fulfillment of human potential, and the pursuit of time-honored principles that remained constant through history (figs. 24–26). Any man who ascribed to such high ideals should, according to Johnson, "divest himself of the prejudices of his age and country; he must consider right and wrong in their abstracted and invariable state." Above all, "He must disregard present laws and opinions and rise to general and transcendental truths, which will always be the same."[3]

FIGURE 26 Tall case clock, southeastern Pennsylvania, 1740. Walnut and mixed wood inlays with oak, pine, and poplar; brass and iron works. H. 89½", W. 20⅜", D. 13⅛". (Private collection; photo, Gavin Ashworth and Philadelphia Museum of Art.) The impact of classical proportion and detail is particularly evident in this Pennsylvania tall clock. Such classical inspirations, although frequently expressed more subtly than here, were the foundation for eighteenth-century architecture and furniture.

Opposite reason stood imagination or fancy. For most eighteenth-century thinkers, this faculty embraced virtually every aspect of mental creativity beyond the scope of reason. On an elementary level, imagination employed the senses to gather experiences from the surrounding world and provide stimulus to the emotions. The imagination stored these experiences in the memory, from which it could later recall them individually or recombine them into distinct new images.

Although frequently defined as synonyms, the words fancy and imagination were often used in slightly different ways. Most notably, there had long been a propensity, crossing a broad spectrum of disciplines, to employ the word fancy when addressing subjects of a lighter nature. The term imagination, in contrast, was generally reserved for topics that bore greater weight. Although a formal distinction between the two terms did not emerge in literature until the early years of the nineteenth century, these tendencies reflected a tradition both in spoken English and in British psychology and literature from a much earlier date. As early as 1582, the British poet Nicholas Bretton acknowledged fancy's lighthearted nature:

Why, Fancie, is a frende,
    to every curteous Knight;
Why, Fancie, is the chiefest thing,
    that doth the mind delight.[4]

The distinction conferred a hierarchy upon the terms and often created a prejudice against the whimsical nature of fancy. Ironically, this prejudice was vital in paving the way for a cultural shift in which society eventually conceded to fancy not only tremendous power, but also a vital role in shaping the material world. The rise of fancy emerged from a debate that involved many of Britain's leading thinkers and centered upon the surprisingly contentious issue of the merits of reason and imagination. The debate reflected changing perceptions of the mind and eye and established new standards for creativity and style.[5]

At first, many of the leading figures in Britain's highly literate culture did not endorse the belief that attributes of spontaneity or emotion were desirable ends in themselves. For the pragmatic British, this sentiment was grounded in practical concerns, for a proper balance between mental faculties was, to them, instrumental for building a stable society and a culture that would avoid frivolous expenditures of time and effort that accomplished little of lasting merit. Those who weighed the virtues of the mind did not espouse subjugating imagination entirely, therefore, but rather directing it—assuring that it remained always subordinate to the guidance of reason. As Samuel Johnson observed: "Fancy is a faculty bestowed by our Creator, and it is reasonable that all his gifts should be used to his glory. . . . We may take Fancy for a companion, but must follow Reason as our guide."[6] Johnson and his contemporaries feared that unbridled imagination would divert humans from rational pursuits, and that the pursuit of momentary notions would shortchange social stability and

FIGURE 27   Matthew Darly, detail showing *The Antique Architect*, from *Dr. Forceps, The Antiquarian*, and *The Antique Architect*, London, 1773. Black and white line engraving on paper. H. 6⅝", W. 4¾". (Plate). (Courtesy, Colonial Williamsburg Foundation.) In the eighteenth century, the term *antique* identified anything of ancient origin, or inspired by ancient prototypes—whether in architecture, furnishings, or philosophy. The word implied stability and permanence and was often contrasted with the word *modern*.

AMERICAN FANCY

time-honored ideals. If British society saw reason as an impartial judge, it considered the careless exercise of imagination to carry the risk of moral compromise. John Dryden put it concisely: "A man is to be cheated into Passion, but to be reasoned into Truth."[7]

Melancholy and depression were counted among fancy's lesser reckonings and, left unchecked, were thought to lead to insanity. After all, it was a short journey from illusion to delusion and finally to lunacy. "Madness, Thou Chaos of ye Brain . . . Tyranny of Fancy's Reign," the painter and aesthetic critic William Hogarth (1697–1764) had called it. Even Samuel Johnson, who was disposed to view imagination as a positive and necessary counterweight to reason, voiced his apprehension on this score through a character in his *History of Rasselas*: "By degrees the reign of fancy is confirmed; she grows first imperious, and in time despotic. Then fictions begin to operate as realities, false opinions hasten upon the mind, and life passes in dreams of rapture or of anguish."[8]

In short, the eighteenth-century British view of the mind described a polarized entity with clearly separated functions and preferences. On one side stood reason, its pursuit of steadfast truth and stability unclouded by desire, its reputation burnished and refined from the time of the ancients. For most observers the attributes of reason were embodied in restrained classicism, or the "antique" taste. On the other side stood the tempting attributes of imagination or fancy, which enlivened experience but seemed a diversionary and potentially corrupting influence. Fancy was expressed through the momentary pleasures of "modern" sensibilities and "modern" style—of passing tastes that struck a chord with the senses but had little proven merit.

These distinctions were not solely confined to philosophical discussions or elite circles. They provided a common means of identifying the character of everyday experience. Numerous texts from the day, from coffeehouse literature to Sunday sermons, suggest widespread familiarity with the life-defining attributes of reason and fancy. Understanding the distinction between the two was essential to anyone concerned with matters of manners and deportment, education and learning, and the realms of art and taste. Only by acknowledging the competing influences of reason and imagination, and weighing them carefully against one another, was it possible to attain one's maximum potential. Therefore, though secular in nature, these ideals embodied powerful and often contrasting moral precepts. Discussion of the relationship between reason and imagination implicitly colored every exploration of the intellect and the senses, the art and philosophy of the ancients, and the debate concerning the merits of the "antique" versus those of the "modern" (figs. 27 and 28). Just as fancy was contrasted to reason, so objects inspired by fancy were contrasted to classical design (fig. 29). "In sculpture, did ever anybody call the Apollo a fancy piece?" Ralph Waldo Emerson would ask a century later; certainly not—either in his time or before.[9] Classical art and architecture were thought to raise one's thoughts above sensual pleasure to respect

FIGURE 28   *The Auction, or Modern Connoisseurs,* probably London, November 1771. Copperplate engraving on paper. H. 6", W. 3¹³⁄₁₆". (Courtesy, Lewis Walpole Library.) "Modern" has always been applied to up-to-the-minute fashions. However, in the eighteenth century, the word often carried negative connotations and implied a penchant for frivolous and passing styles that lacked lasting cultural merit. Modern fashions were frequently satirized, as in this print.

FIGURE 29   Hendrick Goltzius, *The Apollo Belvedere,* the Netherlands, ca. 1592, dated 1617. Engraving. 15¹³⁄₁₆" x 11½". (Courtesy, Philadelphia Museum of Art. The Muriel and Philip Berman Gift, 1985.)

immutable, time-honored ideals, not dissolve them in the face of momentary pleasures and modern tastes.[10]

Few men contributed more to the awareness and rising status of fancy—and to a fuller understanding of the later American Fancy style—than English essayist and politician Joseph Addison (1672–1719). His "Pleasures of the Imagination" appeared in a series of eleven short essays in *The Spectator,* a London literary periodical that was the most widely read of its time.[11] Like many public figures of his generation, Addison sought not only to inform, but also to persuade. He intended his elegant and uplifting essays to guide his contemporaries toward a more meaningful understanding of the experience of life, and to strengthen the British character. Addison succinctly identified the salient character of imagination and popularized its fundamental vocabulary. He was among the first to address the subject with clarity, and his work became a touchstone for subsequent writers.

"A man should endeavour to make the sphere of his innocent pleasures as wide as possible," Addison wrote.[12] Although admitting that the pleasures of the imagination were "not so refined as those of understanding," he nonetheless encouraged his audience to carefully observe the world around them—from the sublime expanses of nature to the refined beauty of sculpture and painting. Addison emphasized the primary role of the eye in fueling the storehouse of the imagination: "We cannot indeed have a single image in the fancy that did not make its first entry through sight." By the "pleasures of the imagination," then, Addison actually meant only those experiences that "arise from visible objects, either when we have them actually in our view, or when we call up their ideas into our Minds."[13]

Addison specified three distinct types of imaginative pleasure that would elevate the mind and spirit: the *beautiful,* the *great,* and the *uncommon*. Of the first of these, he wrote: "There is nothing that makes its way more directly to the Soul than Beauty, which immediately diffuses a secret Satisfaction and Complacency thro' the Imagination." Addison emphasized the pleasures that arise from the beauty of "Products of Art and Nature," yet he also acknowledged the imaginative pleasures that arose from the attraction to one's "own kind," referring to romantic attraction: "The very discovery of it strikes the mind with an inward joy, and spreads a cheerfulness and delight through all its faculties." For Addison and his contemporaries, mankind's natural instinct to respond to beauty served to validate the broader range of imaginative response to the surrounding world.[14]

Of the second pleasure of the imagination, the *great,* Addison observed: "Our Imagination loves to be filled with an Object, or to grasp at any thing that is too big for its Capacity."[15] The uplifting and humbling emotions one experiences when confronting the vastness or brutality of nature, when contemplating boundless oceans and mountains too large to grasp, encouraged a "Stillness and Amazement in the Soul."[16] These complex and exalted emotions were considered the highest realization of aesthetic experience, for they conferred an intuitive comprehension of the power of the Creator and the vastness of eternity. In choosing the term *great* to identify these pleasures, Addison appears to have been simplifying his language, avoiding the term *sublime,* preferred in educated circles, but he was speaking of the same sentiments.[17]

The third pleasure identified by Addison was the *uncommon,* or novel, which consisted of the delights of encountering new experiences of any kind. This pleasure elicited a "refreshment" within the imagination, and though it served less exalted ends than the beautiful or the great, Addison, along with much of British intellectual society, viewed novelty as the principal encouragement to "the Pursuit of Knowledge" and, therefore, as a foundation for personal betterment.[18]

By identifying the pleasures of the imagination to a wide audience, Addison opened the gateway to an understanding of the fancy as a complement to, rather than a contradiction of, the powers of reason. For Addison and other proponents of the merits of the fancy, aesthetic taste was a perfect medium in which to exercise the imagination, and so refine the senses and elevate the soul. Yet others were not so sanguine. By nature, choices in matters of taste often differ broadly from person to person, and unlike absolute decisions based on reason, have no uniform standard. Edmund Burke stated in 1756, "If Taste has no fixed principles, if the imagination is not affected according to some invariable and certain laws, our labor is like to be employed to very little purpose; as it must be judged as useless, if not an absurd undertaking, to lay down rules for caprice, and to set up for a legislator of whims and fancies."[19] To individuals wary of fancy, the vagaries of taste therefore constituted a threat to the stability of classicism and, by extension, a threat to British society.

The attempt to resolve this dilemma was at the heart of William Hogarth's *Analysis of Beauty* (1753). Written, in Hogarth's words, "With a View to fix the fluctuating Ideas of Taste," the book was an extended attempt to determine objective and eternal aesthetic standards. Hogarth specifically feared that ever-changing whims would inspire meaningless and constant changes in fashion so that any hope of adhering to an enduring style—one that was rationally proportioned and inspired by classicism or the beauties of ideal nature—would be lost (figs. 30 and 31). Hogarth found aesthetic and, by inference, moral excess in many of the fleeting fashions of his day.[20] He particularly chastised the penchant for the Chinese and Gothic tastes. Like Addison, Hogarth ascribed a moral charge to his declarations of aesthetic judgment, citing ancient architecture and art as the ideal standard: "The deities of barbarous and gothic nations never had, have not to this day, any of these elegant forms belonging to them. How absolutely void of these turns are the pagods of China, and what a mean taste runs through most of their attempts in painting and sculpture."[21] The painter Sir Joshua Reynolds (1723–1792) similarly addressed the Royal Academy in 1771 on the subject of taste and expressed his disappointment in the increasing rein given to individual

FIGURE 30 Side chair, Philadelphia, 1730–1735. Walnut and walnut veneer with pine. H. 40⅝", W. 20¼", D. 17". (Courtesy, Philadelphia Museum of Art. Gift of Daniel Blain, Jr., 1997-67-4.) This chair typifies a style popular in Britain and America between 1730 and 1760. The S-shaped elements reflect the understated aesthetic promoted by men such as William Hogarth, who decried the fanciful excesses of more modern tastes.

FIGURE 31 *Taste, or Burlington's Gate,* attributed to William Hogarth, London, ca. 1731. Copperplate engraving on paper. H. 8⅜". (Courtesy, Colonial Williamsburg Foundation.) The British addressed the subject of taste as frequently in art as in essays. In this print, Hogarth depicted a portal inscribed "Taste" to suggest the importance of classical design to his subject and, simultaneously, to discreetly censure those who made great public displays of taste.

fancy. "The natural appetite or taste of the human mind is for truth," he insisted, and professed himself dismayed by "those who consider [taste] as a mere phantom of the imagination, so devoid of substance as to elude all criticism." Reynolds was particularly disheartened by the inability to discriminate between the widely diverging influences upon aesthetic choices:

AMERICAN FANCY

"We apply the term taste to that act of the mind by which we like or dislike, whatever be the subject. Our judgment upon an airy nothing, a fancy which has no foundation, is called by the same name . . . [as] works which are only to be produced by the greatest efforts of the human understanding."[22]

Ultimately, however, Hogarth and Reynolds' advocacy for a reasoned and timeless style was out of step with the era. Leading British tastemakers increasingly tantalized consumers with a great variety of designs meant to delight the imagination, rather than conform to absolute standards. A year after Hogarth's treatise, London cabinetmaker Thomas Chippendale (1718–1779) published *The Gentleman and Cabinet-Maker's Director*. Chippendale's large folio contained page after page of bold designs in the Gothic and Chinese tastes that Hogarth had so soundly criticized as "barbaric" and eye-catching modern designs—many of them Continental and Catholic in origin—with intentionally distorted naturalistic details and classical motifs that dripped from the pages of his book. With the exception of a brief discussion of the classical orders of architecture, intended to provide a lesson in proportion, Chippendale made scarcely a reference to the ancients. Instead he appealed directly to his readers' imaginations, boasting that his designs were suited to "the Fancy and Circumstances of Persons in all Degrees of Life."[23]

Chippendale's fanciful designs were a precursor of things to come. Over the course of the late eighteenth century, the connection between fancy and the decorative arts would become increasingly pronounced. Among the first to point to this correlation was the pragmatic thinker Voltaire. Like Hogarth, Reynolds, and culturally conservative tastemakers, Voltaire agreed that the products "within the circle of the finer arts" of painting and sculpture should be largely shaped by reason. He also concurred that the creation and selection of such grand conceptions should be acknowledged exclusively with the term *taste*. Yet Voltaire viewed the selection of everyday objects, particularly in the area of dress, as legitimately "arbitrary," that is to say, subject to personal choice. The appropriate term to describe this distinct and lesser realm of judgment seemed perfectly obvious to him: "In this low sphere it should be distinguished, methinks, by the name of fancy; for it is fancy rather than taste that produces such an endless variety of new and contradictory modes" (fig. 32).[24] Although this formulation might seem to denigrate the lower arts, it actually provided a means of appreciating them anew. Voltaire's sentiments reinforced the long-standing tendency to employ the words imagination and fancy in slightly differing ways, and now underscored that distinction by identifying fancy with a specific class of objects, and giving it clearer connections to the transient and worldly arena of popular taste. The caution previously advocated by British philosophers and tastemakers would soon be swept aside.

Beginning in the 1760s, then, the British people acquired positive new means to view material goods and link them to the imagination. With increasing frequency, discussions concerned with fancy focused upon the

FIGURE 32 *Ridiculous Taste, or the Ladies' Absurdity,* London, 1768. Copperplate engraving on paper. H. 13¼" (plate). (Courtesy, Colonial Williamsburg Foundation.)

outward appearance of objects and their capacity to encourage the type of dynamic mental activity that Addison had first promoted. Eighteenth-century writers were particularly intrigued with the ability of three visual stimulants to convey the character of the objects directly to the mind: *light, color,* and *motion*. Yet, writers were equally intrigued that the viewer usually perceived an object to possess other qualities that nurtured even further imaginative responses and emphasized *novelty, variety,* and *wit*. Addison and others interested in the imagination had explored these six enticing phenomena, but in the late eighteenth century, they attained greater status than ever before. Inevitably they became the building blocks of Fancy as it evolved into a fashionable and popular style.

FIGURE 33 Lantern, probably New England, 1750–1780. Glass, lead, and painted sheet iron. H. 23⅛". (Courtesy, Colonial Williamsburg Foundation.)

Writers concerned with the fancy were fascinated by the stimulants of light, color, and motion, which delighted the eye and the senses, infused the mind, and thus provided the basis for dynamic mental activity. All shared the common characteristic of impermanence and in this respect were crucial to the emerging understanding of the fancy as a faculty that processed superficial and transient experience. The essential visual stimulus was *light,* the medium of sight itself. As early as the sixteenth century, writers had recognized the direct relationship between light and the imagination. "Light . . . is the cause . . . whereby coloured things are seen, whose shapes and images pass to the Phantasie."[25] The elusive quality of light was one of its greatest appeals to the fancy, and it provided one of the essential features of the Fancy style, whether glistening from a gilt surface, refracted through a kaleidoscope, or projected by sconces or lanterns where candles generated lively, ever-changing patterns on ceilings and walls (fig. 33).

Light was also recognized for its significance as the medium that conveys *color* to the eye and mind. Of all the pleasures of the imagination, none were lauded more frequently, or more enthusiastically, than the emotions elicited by color. "Among the several kinds of beauty, the eye takes most delight in colours,"[26] Addison had noted; "colours paint themselves on the fancy."[27] As with light, color is elusive and difficult to quantify. Color does not exist entirely within objects but principally as light reflected from an object. Individuals often see color quite differently, and the appearance of a color can vary greatly depending upon the circumstances under which it is viewed.[28] Like light, then, color seemed to epitomize the transient nature of the perceptions that stimulated the fancy (fig. 34). "Light and colours, as apprehended by the imagination, are only ideas of the mind, and not qualities that have existence in matter," observed Addison.[29]

FIGURE 34   Plate, Staffordshire, England, ca. 1830. Earthenware and polychrome decoration. Diam. 9½". (Private collection; photo, Gavin Ashworth.)

The transitory and appealing nature of light and color was closely related to the phenomenon of *motion*. Addison observed that movement enlivens uneventful sights and helps to awaken the fancy: "We are quickly tired of looking . . . where every thing continues fixed and settled in the same place and posture, but find our thoughts a little . . . relieved at the sight of such

FIGURE 35 Plate, England, 1750–1780. Slip-decorated earthenware. Diam. 13¼". (Courtesy, Colonial Williamsburg Foundation.)

objects as are ever in motion."[30] A waterfall or a meteor shooting across the sky impresses the fancy if the individuals who behold it are in a receptive frame of mind.[31] Many nineteenth-century material expressions of Fancy embody motion but do not necessarily move; rather, they depict motion as abstract ornament, thereby connecting the internal process of creativity to material expressions in the external world.[32] The motion captured by such surface decoration embodies the imaginative energy of the artisan, who freezes in place a fleeting moment of intense but measured creativity. Objects inspired by fancy thereby serve as a link between the imaginative faculty of the maker and that of the viewer.[33] Brushing paint over a wooden board or swirling liquid clay on the surface of a ceramic vessel communicates a message that is joyous and spontaneous (fig. 35). The experience of viewing light, color, and motion is of the moment; it affords the viewer a quick smile and a rising of the senses, and thus arouses the fancy.

Novelty, variety, and *wit,* by contrast, were not considered to define visual characteristics but rather psychological ones that existed principally in the imagination of the viewer. The eighteenth-century understanding of these attributes was clarified, in part, by the crucial concept of *association.* This word was used to describe the mental process by which the imagination gathers experiences from the surrounding world and then tightly connects them in the memory to the feelings they elicited when they were first encountered. The theory of association held that every individual's distinct first impressions were inevitably shaped by the circumstances of the moment. The theory made it possible to explain how humans develop individual personalities and why imagination and passing experience were so important to mental and emotional development.

Attitudes toward association matured during the eighteenth century and culminated in the Scottish Enlightenment and the writings of the "Common Sense School of Philosophy." A central figure of this movement, Alexander Gerard (1728–1795), explained that association was particularly important to the development of personal taste, for it shaped the initial emotional attachments that subsequently time and time again attract an individual to certain circumstances and objects.[34] Like others before him, Gerard recognized that the viewer's first impressions of an experience or object cause the mind to automatically evoke the same responses upon subsequent encounters or upon recalling the event from memory. Unpleasant first impressions dissuade individuals from pursuit of an object or experience; pleasant ones inevitably refine the viewer's taste for an object or situation. This notion was emphasized again in 1792 by Dugald Stewart (1753–1828), a professor at the University of Edinburgh. Stewart had a new name for the mental power that connected images and emotions in the imagination and thereby refined taste: he called it "fancy."[35]

Stewart presented fancy as a fundamental building block for knowledge and for shaping personality and taste. His dual emphasis upon "natural objects" and the emotions that accompanied their viewing acknowledged the significance of that fleeting moment when the sight of an object first impresses the mind. "The fancy must be warm, to retain the print of those images it hath received from outward objects," Addison had observed in 1712, and in 1740 Scottish philosopher David Hume noted, "The fancy runs from one end of the universe to the other collecting . . . ideas."[36] It made little difference whether the ensuing emotions reflected an admiration of the visual qualities of the object, or existed merely as responses of surprise and delight in the mind of the viewer. The pleasure taken in a painted whirligig with its arms spinning furiously in the wind could now be seen not as pointless and self-indulgent, but rather as a confirmation of an essential truth about the workings of the mind and the validation of individual character and taste (fig. 36). The theory of association or fancy, as it was now sometimes known, therefore helped to legitimize everyday experience in the way that reason had long been used to legitimize scientific discovery.

The workings of fancy played a vital role in the new respect accorded to the imagination and the material goods increasingly associated with it. Certain concepts associated with the faculty, particularly the viewer's

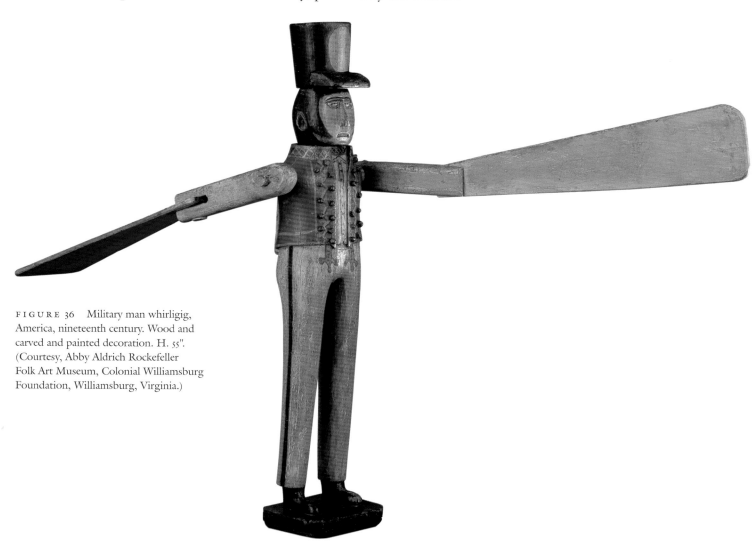

FIGURE 36   Military man whirligig, America, nineteenth century. Wood and carved and painted decoration. H. 55". (Courtesy, Abby Aldrich Rockefeller Folk Art Museum, Colonial Williamsburg Foundation, Williamsburg, Virginia.)

perception of novelty, variety, and wit in an object or situation, were now emphasized and validated because they seemed deeply rooted in the emotional and physiological experience of the beholder. These perceptions usually do not exist in isolation but in conjunction with one another. They exist in the viewer's imagination, help to identify one's response to an object or situation, and embody the principal character of Fancy as a style. Novel experiences were thought to be the most productive to the imagination, for they elicited the strong emotion of surprise and thereby had great impact. "It is the common effect of things unexpected to surprise us into a delight; and that is to be ascribed to the strong appetite, as I may call it, of the fancy," the seventeenth-century poet John Dryden explained.[37] Joseph Addison later concurred: "Everything that is new or uncommon raises a pleasure in the imagination, because it fills the soul with an agreeable surprise, gratifies the curiosity, and gives it an idea of

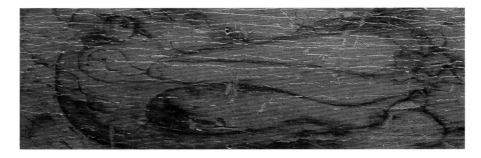

which it was not before possest" (fig. 37).[38] In this regard, *novelty* could be seen not as a trivial attachment to the new, but rather as the wellspring of mental activity and an inspiration to further intellectual discovery.[39]

Every writer who explored imagination considered *variety* essential to stimulate the fancy. Variety could be expressed in glistening surfaces, appealing shapes, ornamental patterns, or motion—whether real or implied. Addison emphasized the appeal of "a variety of colours," for inspiring the pleasures of the imagination (fig. 38). Even William Hogarth, who was not favorably disposed to the fancy, considered variety the essence of beauty and the principal inspiration for human attraction toward aesthetic experience. "All the senses delight in it," he wrote, "and equally are averse to sameness."[40] In the marketplace, variety helped to maintain interest in an ever-changing array of visually stunning Fancy goods by "obviating the objection of too much sameness," to quote Moses Grant, a Boston proponent for Fancy wallpapers.[41]

Variety and novelty were essential to expressions of *wit,* in which artists and artisans combined humor and illusion to great imaginative effect. The English philosopher John Locke wrote at length about men of wit, noting they had "prompt memories" that allowed them to assemble ideas with "quickness and variety" and to elicit "pleasant pictures and agreeable visions in the fancy."[42] To these characteristics, Addison added the necessity of gathering "congruity" out of incongruity in order for humor to qualify as wit. Like fancy, wit has the ability to draw parallels where no real parallels exist. Words are a perfect medium for wit, but it is also easily expressed in material things. An entire class of Fancy objects intended to "fool the eye"—now known by the French translation trompe l'oeil—achieves the goal of surprising and delighting the imagination through double faces and double meanings. Such expressions incorporate the "surprise" that Montesquieu observed to be a product of fertile imagination.[43] Fancy expressions of this type can be understood as a kind of two-sided coin of reality and illusion; they strike one's fancy at precisely the moment their true character becomes evident.

The Fancy style in America experienced its first stirrings in the 1760s and can be seen as the material offspring of the vital philosophical developments of the eighteenth century. Fancy goods invariably possess a character that

FIGURE 38   Dome-top box, New York or New England, ca. 1820. White pine, paper, and painted decoration. H. 4⁵⁄₁₆", W. 7", D. 4⅜". Pantry box, New England, ca. 1840. Maple, white pine, and painted decoration. H. 2", W. 5½", D. 4⅜". Miniature chest with drawer, New York, ca. 1825. Pine and painted decoration. H. 7¾", W. 13⅛", D. 5⅝". (Courtesy, a New York collector; photo, Gavin Ashworth.)

catches the eye and awakens the mind. Some employ a dazzling variety of ornament to elicit a visceral but passing response; some operate principally by surprising the viewer; some allude to other places, ideas, or things; and others leave open-ended possibilities for imaginative interpretation. Their changing appearances and their viewers' shifting perceptions convey the spirit of the objects and their makers. The thoughts they spur and the emotions they elicit are enriching yet transitory in nature. Light and color are elusive and ungraspable; motion, by its definition, is unstable; novelty, variety, and wit exist solely as perceptions of the imagination. By emphasizing these momentary and indulgent characteristics, early nineteenth-century Americans reflected their new outlook on the world and reveled in the pleasures of the mind and of material goods as never before.

By the late eighteenth century, the playing field between reason and imagination had been leveled. The average consumer of Fancy goods probably knew little of the intellectual debate. Yet, even without fully understanding the subtle philosophy from which the style emerged, early Americans intuitively understood how light, color, and motion stimulated the senses. Most would have been conversant with the term "fancy" to designate the mental faculty attuned to such visual enticements. Americans were instinctively drawn to the dynamic perceptions conveyed by the objects and the experience of Fancy, and they willingly responded. The delightful ephemerality of the style bore no less weight than a pointed arch did for the Gothic, or a classical column for the Roman. By gravitating to Fancy and applying the word to the engaging artifacts they selected for their homes, Americans simultaneously conveyed the value they placed on the intangible resources of the mind and their joy in the fleeting pleasures of life.

2 Fancy Takes Form

Fancy, thou the Muse's pride,
In thy painted realms reside
Endless images of things,
Fluttering each on golden wings,
Ideal objects, such a store,
The universe could hold no more:
Fancy to thy power I owe
Half my happiness below.

Philip Freneau, *The Power of Fancy,* 1770

The new relationship between imagination and material goods was soon reinforced in literature, and the virtue of expressing emotion through objects was extolled by poets and writers alike. In his 1770 poem *The Power of Fancy,* American writer Philip Freneau (1752–1832) celebrated fancy as the most creative of all human faculties, that imaginative place whose "painted realms" are filled with "endless images of things." Although his words were primarily rhetorical, they also proved to be prophetic, perfectly describing an essential aspect of the American experience in the decades to come.[1]

This growing fascination with fancy was reflected by a new trend which applied the word directly to material goods. No longer was an object simply inspired by fancy. Rather it became a "Fancy object," owing its very existence to emotional powers that fed the mind and delighted the soul. The shift of emphasis was immensely important, for it stressed the valid expression of imagination and of fanciful response and their realization in the material world (fig. 39).[2]

The use of fancy as an adjective had its own meaning in the eighteenth century. Consider the term "Fancy chair," which first appeared in the 1790s.[3] Fancy here did not necessarily mean a fine chair or a decorated chair, although either "fine" or "decorated" might sometimes define such a chair. Nor did it necessarily mean that the chair struck one's fancy— although Fancy chairs did just that. Rather, if one thinks of fancy as having a domain or realm—albeit within the soul or mind—and imagines a chair designed there, the term takes on its proper meaning. In the way a "Greek" or "Roman" chair came from Greece or Rome, the design for a Fancy chair originated in the fancy. Although this concept may be foreign to our contemporary way of thinking, we, as a modern audience, can nevertheless

FIGURE 39 *Charity,* possibly Hartford, Connecticut, ca. 1810. Watercolor and crystalline decoration on paper. 14¼" x 12¼". (Courtesy, Fenimore Art Museum, Cooperstown, New York.)

understand how the eighteenth century used the adjective fancy and how it was "heard" by the ear and perceived by the mind.[4]

What Fancy things looked like in these early years was not always predictable. Use of the word Fancy suggested the acceptance of a new attitude as much as the attributes of a new style. Yet, without question, Fancy goods possessed the "liveliness" and the "luxuriancy" attributed to imagination by philosopher Dugald Stewart in 1792.[5] One of the earliest recorded artifactual associations for Fancy was the 1761 trade card (fig. 40) of "Martha Wheatland & Sister, Milleners & Haberdashers . . . At Queen Charlotte's Head" in Cheapside, London. Wheatland's shop advertised "all sorts of Haberdashery and Fancy Millenery Goods at the Lowest Prices" and "in the most Elegant Taste." The same year a newspaper advertisement noted that the new and colorful wallpapers available in London shops "are all what they call fancy." Thereafter the concept was used a bit more comfortably when it was employed without further explanation to describe a "fancy dress."[6]

FIGURE 40 "Martha Wheatland & Sister Milleners & Haberdashers," trade card, London, 1761. (Courtesy, Dover Pictorial Archives.) Martha Wheatland was among the earliest to use fancy as an adjective when she advertised "Fancy Millenery Goods" on her 1761 trade card.

In the American colonies the updated use of the word was also assimilated into the language employed in a context where women shopkeepers sought to attract women customers. In 1769 milliner Sarah Pitt of Williamsburg, Virginia, announced for sale "A very fancy assortment of paper boxes." Between 1770 and 1773 milliners in America advertised a variety of costume accessories that ranged from "True Italian Fancy Caps" and "Fancy Stomachers" to "fancy pins" and "French fancy collars."[7] Into the 1780s, the adjective fancy was further associated with costume and costume accessories by its broad application to colorfully decorated textiles. By the end of the decade, it was common to find a variety of Fancy millinery goods and Fancy textiles for sale in any respectable store. In 1790,

for example, Denton, Little and Company of New York advertised the arrival of ships bearing from England "A very handsome assortment of Fall Goods," including "fancy calicoes, in the newest fashions . . . plain, fancy, colored, and tamboured muslins . . . fancy and black ginghams . . . Fancy, sattin, and lutestring ribbons," and "a variety of fancy swansdown vest patterns."[8] These early references to textiles are especially significant for the formative history of Fancy.[9]

Great Britain's rising position in textile manufacturing played a tremendous role in inspiring Fancy fabrics. The shift away from small-scale handcrafted or loom manufacture of textiles to large-scale production in a factory environment made it possible for British producers to compete on an international level. With increased efficiency came ingenious new methods of ornamentation, including the invention of the rotary printing machine in 1783 by Thomas Bell of Scotland (fig. 41).[10] Through the innovative use of regulated turning cylinders, Bell's invention allowed for the rapid application of continuous stripes, floral strands, and other designs to large bolts of fabric intended for clothing, curtains, and bed hangings. The process provided a profusion of decorative detail in an orderly linear progression, a balance of the sensual with the predictable, and rapidly became a hallmark of Fancy textiles.

Fancy defined other materials besides textiles during the last three decades of the eighteenth century. In 1772 an advertisement for the New York City retail shop of Davis and Minnit, announcing the arrival of "all kinds of earthenwares, with some curious fancy wares," may be the earliest association of fancy with ceramics in America (fig. 42). In 1789

FIGURE 41   Fabric, possibly Bannister Hall, England, ca. 1805. Roller-printed cotton. H. 23", W. 36¾". (Courtesy, Winterthur Museum.)

FIGURE 42   Tea canister, England, 1790–1800. Earthenware. H. 4¾". (Courtesy, Elbert H. Parsons, Jr.; photo, Gavin Ashworth.)

John Frederick Amelung, who established one of the first successful glass manufactories in America, advertised his ability to cut "Devices, Cyphers, Coats of Arms, or any other Fancy Figures on Glass." Even agriculture succumbed to the influence of Fancy; in 1784 George Washington observed the virtues of a new variegated grass as feed: "If the cattle or horses will eat the fancy grass in the green state, or made into hay, it certainly must be very valuable." By the 1790s Fancy had begun to acquire a concrete identity for those who considered themselves aware of the latest trends. The literary and philosophical concepts of fancy were fast giving way to the material phenomenon known as Fancy.[11]

The year 1792 marks the first known American reference to "Fancy Goods" when Jonathan Harris advertised in the *Columbian Centennial* of Boston of the arrival from Europe of a "large and extensive assortment of staple and fancy goods of the latest fashion."[12] Before long, this all-encompassing term was used to refer to a wide range of small personal objects—scented soaps, enameled boxes, tortoiseshell combs, painted fans, fine stationery, handkerchiefs, and perfume, to name but a few (figs. 43–45). In addition to signaling the beginning of Fancy as a commercial phenomenon, many of these objects also maintained the earlier ideological associations that linked imagination and fancy to women—an association traceable as far back as the mythology of ancient Greece, where imagination was visually represented as a seated woman draped with colorful robes and wearing a crown ornamented with winged human figures.[13]

Many of the earliest Fancy goods were associated with women's private life: bathing, dressing, applying makeup, corresponding with friends, or discreetly partaking in the pleasures of tobacco. Some were small in scale and required careful handling: tortoiseshell combs were lovely, but fragile, and tiny glass bottles for perfume were easily chipped. Just as expressions of the imagination were used cautiously during this period so, too, were Fancy goods handled with care. Nowhere was the intimate nature of the new goods more evident than in the wide range of

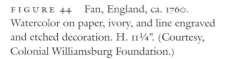

FIGURE 45 Handkerchief, *The Aviary, or Bird Fancyer's Recreation*, England, ca. 1755. Printed linen. 26¾" x 29½". (Courtesy, Colonial Williamsburg Foundation.)

ornamental boxes for holding valued possessions usually stored in ladies' private quarters or dressing rooms. Most were colorfully decorated, such as the elaborately painted dressing boxes made to hold accessories for the chamber table, the Fancy hatboxes covered with colorful wallpaper for storing bonnets, or the Fancy bandboxes that held Fancy collars and detachable Fancy bands or sleeves. Some types of boxes were small enough to be carried in a purse or tucked into a pocket. Among the most popular were the brass-mounted boxes of glistening enamel, which came into fashion during the 1760s. Almost all held products associated with gratifying activities: some were intended for snuff; others served as traveling containers for powder, rouge, or small "patches" for hiding blemishes on ladies' faces.

A large number of these small boxes were adorned with capricious scenes or amusing poetry intended to encourage laughter: "The Hardness of your Heart, causes mine to Ache and Smart." Others were whimsical in form, sometimes emulating frogs or insects. They served as playful trompe l'oeil devices meant to please a gullible bystander when the container was pulled from a pocket or purse. Some Fancy boxes showed domesticated household pets (fig. 46) or creatures from the wild (fig. 47). Still others were sentimental reminders of a place or an acquaintance, as

FIGURE 46 Snuffbox, attributed to Thomas Perry, Bilston, England, ca. 1770. Enameled copper and brass. H. 1½", W. 3", D. 2¼". (Courtesy, Taylor B. Williams L.L.C., Chicago.)

FIGURE 47 Candy box, South Staffordshire, England, 1765–1775. Enameled copper and brass. L. 3½". (Courtesy, Taylor B. Williams L.L.C., Chicago.)

FIGURE 48 Clockwise from left: Patch box, Bilston, England, ca. 1770. H. 1", W. 1¹¹⁄₁₆", Diam. 1½". Enameled copper, brass, and silvered glass. (Courtesy, Studio Antiques and Fine Art, Alexandria, Virginia; photo, Gavin Ashworth.) Patch box, Bilston, England, ca. 1770. H. 1", W. 1⅛", Diam. 1⁷⁄₁₆". Enameled copper, brass, and silvered glass. (Courtesy, Studio Antiques and Fine Art, Alexandria, Virginia; photo, Gavin Ashworth.) Patch box, Bilston, England, ca. 1770. H. ⅞", W. 1⅝", Diam. 1⅜". Enameled copper, brass, and silvered glass. (Courtesy, Paul Johnson; photo, Gavin Ashworth.)

visitors from afar often gave them as gifts to their hosts, and travelers acquired them on journeys to present to intimate friends, such as those inscribed "A gift from Bath" or "A present from Richmond" (fig. 48).

The small size of these boxes helped to inspire the name "trifle." Many small boxes were emblazoned with identifications such as "A Trifle from . . ." or "Remember Her who gives this Trifle." One of the earliest references to such boxes is found in a 1755 letter from Horace Walpole, England's unofficial "Minister of Taste," to his entrepreneurial friend Richard Bentley: "I shall send you a trifling snuff-box," Walpole remarked, then qualified it with, "only as a sample of the new manufacture at Battersea." That men did not present to other men items of inconsequence is clearly implied.[14]

If the *noun* "trifle" identified a favored new type of Fancy goods, the *verb* "trifle" defined the rising emphasis on informality that these Fancy goods encouraged. "To trifle" was the capacity to relish the small things one encountered, or simply to savor doing nothing. For the more progressively minded, the concept of "trifling," like the little boxes so described, was increasingly desirable. In 1779 a casual observer remarked of the new trend, "One of the most important lessons to be learned in life, is that of being able to trifle upon occasion."[15] This informality and lightheartedness bespoke an approach to life that was quite different from the concepts that defined acceptable social behavior in an earlier era. Above all, trifles were intended to please, sometimes on many levels simultaneously. One can imagine a lady reaching into her purse, pulling out a trifle, contemplating its sentimental message, slipping a pinch of snuff between her gum and her cheek, and feeling the rush of tobacco. The ritual may have differed from the profound pleasures of reading philosophy or discussing the classics, but increasingly such activities and sentiments were seen as a vital part of life.

As these early references suggest, Fancy frequently defined objects either worn by, used by, or purchased by women. Observing this, English furniture designer Thomas Sheraton remarked, "Fancifulness seems most peculiar to the taste of females."[16] In general, eighteenth-century social critics saw creations of the fancy as beneficial pursuits for women because they provided acceptable realms for female expression and expanded educational and economic opportunities. Others, however, derided the value of fancy and imagination, in part for their perceived connection to the irrational tendencies of the feminine, which so frightened them.

In the 1780s John Adams, the future president, wrote to his daughter regarding her education, "I don't mean to suggest that Arts and accomplishments which are merely ornamental, should be wholly avoided or neglected, especially by your sex," but that "They ought to be slighted when in comparison or competition with those which are useful and essential."[17] Philadelphia physician Benjamin Rush, also an advocate for women's education, similarly argued that women should make every attempt to be "governed by reason" as opposed to imagination.[18] But a growing number of influential thinkers were more favorably inclined and came to believe, as one writer poetically noted, that women were ill-advised to exchange the "graces of imagination for the severity and preciousness of a scholar."[19]

The domestication of Fancy, particularly the arrival of Fancy goods and their related activities into the home in the latter part of the eighteenth century, stands as a significant moment in American cultural history, precisely because it expresses in material form the same aesthetic responses widely promoted in literature and philosophy. In this way, Fancy provides a clear translation of seemingly abstract philosophy into the realm of tangible cultural expression. That the American home served as the locus for this fruitful transformation and that women were its first practitioners is particularly important.[20]

One of the central aspects of eighteenth-century women's work was the production of needlework adorned with decorative stitches, also widely known as Fancywork. From boldly composed needlework and embroidery to more delicate lace making and tambour, Fancywork provided a significant contrast to mind-numbing "plain" work such as hemming and darning. The term "Fancywork" could also encompass such diverse activities as painting watercolor pictures, ornamenting firescreens and hand screens, or embellishing boxes and household furnishings with designs "which fancy may suggest."[21] These objects had both practical use and ornamental appeal, and Fancywork suggests that they were perceived as essentials even if, in reality, some were not.

The skills associated with Fancywork were intimately tied to evolving attitudes toward female education and literacy. If one of the principal endeavors of eighteenth-century philosophers had been to decipher the workings of the mind, one of the primary goals of nineteenth-century educators was to put those findings to practical use. "The faculty of imagination is the great spring of human activity, and the principal source of human improvement," noted Dugald Stewart, and nowhere was his outlook more clearly articulated than in women's education, particularly in the new emphasis upon Fancywork.[22]

For generations, plain needlework had been among the staple skills learned at home by most American women. By the end of the eighteenth century, a growing number of young women attended schools where, thanks to the affordability of commercial textiles and to the increasing availability of artists' supplies (fig. 49), young ladies could indulge the penchant for creativity that was increasingly central to their education.

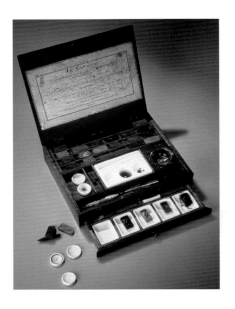

FIGURE 49 Watercolor paint box, London, 1809–1829. Mixed media. W. 10¾". (Courtesy, Abby Aldrich Rockefeller Folk Art Museum, Colonial Williamsburg Foundation, Williamsburg, Virginia.) The box contains a label for "R[udolph] Ackermann," seller of drawing materials.

FIGURE 50 *The Drawing Class: Samuel Folwell's School*, attributed to Samuel Folwell, America, 1810–1813. Watercolor over graphite on cream wove paper laid down on cream board. 14⅔" x 24". (Courtesy, The Art Institute of Chicago. Gift of Mrs. Emily Crane Chadbourne, 1951.202; photo, © The Art Institute of Chicago.)

Needlework, drawing, and other creative work all took place within school walls. Samuel Folwell, a Philadelphia schoolmaster who oversaw one of the most accomplished academies in the early nineteenth century, inspired an entire generation of young women to refine their artistic and imaginative skills. A room in his school, recorded in a watercolor drawing, was furnished with tables and benches where students received instruction and practiced their talents (fig. 50). Folwell, the headmaster, is shown to the right of the composition, overseeing his charges as they draw. A watercolor paint box sits open on the table, and landscape paintings in oil hang on the far wall, perhaps intended to serve as inspiration for the aspiring pupils.[23]

In such an environment, young students would work on ornamental samplers while older ones painted fanciful scenes, sometimes decorated with appliqués of gilded paper or flakes of mica that sparkled when the light struck them. Older students also often completed a large Fancywork picture prior to commencement, perhaps a scene from classical mythology (fig. 51), or a more whimsical creation such as *The Dance,* completed

FIGURE 51 *Aurora*, unidentified artist,
New England, 1818–1822. Watercolor on silk
satin, gold foil, and paper label in original
gilded wood frame. 21⅜" x 24⅝" (sight).
(Collection of the American Folk Art
Museum, New York. Promised gift of Ralph
Esmerian, P1.2001.268; photo, © 2000 John
Bigelow Taylor, New York.)

FIGURE 52   Frances Leverett, *The Dance*,
Danvers, Massachusetts, ca. 1815. Silk satin,
silk and chenille thread, and watercolor. 17" x
23". (Courtesy, Peabody Essex Museum;
photo, Mark Sexton.)

about 1815 by Frances Leverett of Danvers, Massachusetts (fig. 52). These
accomplishments were often quite large in scale, sometimes measuring
twenty by thirty inches or more, and might take half a year or more to
create. Many were intricately stitched with a variety of textured threads.
Worked on a silk ground, details of sky and clouds were carefully painted
in watercolor while painted paper was often used for human faces. When
completed, the needlework picture was framed with an elaborate gilt
molding, and the edges of the glass were painted on the reverse to create
a border. The maker's name was frequently memorialized in gold leaf,
along with the date and location. Parents would hang the picture prominently in their household to highlight a daughter's aesthetic refinement
and the completion of her formal education.

As well as learning needlework and watercolor drawing, New England
schoolgirls received instruction in painting Fancy furniture. This furniture
included dressing tables and dressing boxes, important to a young lady's
grooming ritual, as well as sewing boxes (fig. 53) and a new form known
as a "work stand" or "work table" that served to store the tools and equipment essential to Fancywork. Work tables came with long, pleated bags
suspended below for storing fabric and compartmented drawers for safe-

guarding a host of sewing equipment (fig. 54). In contrast to dressing tables, which were always kept in a bedchamber, these new Fancy work tables were sometimes placed in the parlor, allowing a young lady to socialize with friends and family while refining her imaginative skills and contributing her share to the household.

One woman from Newburyport, Massachusetts, mentioned painting both on paper and wood when she reminisced about her teacher and her schoolgirl experiences in 1812:

> Miss Mary Ann Colman was a good teacher of water color painting; the fruit and flower pieces executed at her school were natural and well done. She also taught painting on wood; several work-boxes and work stands, painted under her instruction, are still to be seen in the residences of some of our older citizens.[24]

FIGURE 53   Sewing box, New England, ca. 1815. Maple and painted, inlaid, and gilt decoration. H. 4¾", W. 12", D. 9⅜". (From the Collections of Henry Ford Museum & Greenfield Village.)

FIGURE 54   Vose and Coates, work table, Boston, 1808–1818. Poplar, aspen, maple, basswood, and painted decoration. H. 28⅞", W. 19⅛", D. 15". (Courtesy, Winterthur Museum.)

FIGURE 55 Rachel Lombard, decorator, dressing table, Bath, Maine, ca. 1816. Birch and maple with white pine and painted decoration. H. 33", W. 32⅛", D. 16¹¹⁄₁₆". (Courtesy, Winterthur Museum.) The ornament is inscribed: "Rachel H. Lombard, Bath, January 1816."

AMERICAN FANCY

A dressing table (figs. 55 and 56) painted by schoolgirl Rachel Lombard of Bath, Maine, shows a sensitivity to the rising power of fancy as a source for artistic inspiration, yet demonstrates the lingering insistence upon balancing gestures of imagination with proper moral and classical awareness. Lombard covered the table from one end to the other with decoration, employing vines that meander up the legs and a pastoral image of Limerich Castle on the top—modes of "ornamental painting" essential to the expression of Fancy and explored in greater detail in a coming chapter. Yet these visual delights were accompanied by detailed written messages, including an admonition that seemed to offset the profusion of detail otherwise found on the table: "Wishing of all employments is the worst. Learn! Know Thyself! All wisdom centers here."[25]

Women of every age participated in the production of Fancywork quilts. Quilting never had been particularly popular in Great Britain. There the industrialization of weaving made woven bedcovers inexpensive, and preferable, to intricate pieced or appliquéd quilts. In America, however, quilting was widely practiced, and designs followed several standards. In some households, quilts consisted of large "patchwork" squares made from leftover or found fabrics. The individual patches varied in size and shape and were cut only when necessary to make them fit into the overall design, which was usually random, yet pleasing.

In fashionable households, early Fancy quilts were significantly more refined. The designs were often classically inspired and always orderly, though their application depended upon the personal taste of the maker.

FIGURE 56   Detail of the top of the dressing table illustrated in fig. 55.

The most common examples consisted of a piece of plain cotton textile ornamented with appliqué designs cut from printed fabrics; the middle usually featured a classical vase, a sumptuous floral spray, or a large tree. A series of running borders surrounded this motif, often with classical architectural details, meandering vines, or repetitive geometric or leaf motifs (fig. 57). The open spaces between the middle and the borders were sometimes filled with smaller vignettes, also cut from printed fabric, such as birds, bouquets, and the like.[26]

Confined within certain moral and aesthetic parameters, Fancywork could express themes that were not at all joyous, themes employed in artifacts of mourning. These artifacts, and mourning itself, evolved as Fancy became respectable. Early in the eighteenth century, mourning jewelry had been the province of educated and wealthy Americans. Starkly adorned with skulls and crossbones that emphasized the finality of death, mourning jewelry often was inscribed with the Latin motto *memento mori* to warn the viewer to "Be Mindful of Death" and therefore live life accordingly.

As imaginative pursuits gained credence later in the century, the subject of death fell more precisely under Fancy's purview, for it represented the ultimate unknown and offered a terrain for a new kind of imaginative, inconclusive play of images. This potential was increasingly exploited by

FIGURE 57 Quilt, America, 1790–1810. Cotton and linen. H. 102½", W. 89¾". (Courtesy, Winterthur Museum.)

FIGURE 58 Lydia Eames, *Indulgent Fancy,* Boston, ca. 1805. Silk satin, silk thread, and watercolor. 14" x 11". (Courtesy, Betty Ring.) The poem reads: "Indulgent Fancy! from the fruitful banks of Avon, / Whence thy rosy fingers cull, fresh flowers and dews / To sprinkle on the turf where Shakespeare lies." The glass mat is inscribed: "Wrought by Lydia Eames at Mrs. Saunders & Miss Beaches' Academy."

FIGURE 59 *Mourning Miniature for Two Children of William Wyche and Elizabeth Reines of Virginia,* attributed to Samuel Folwell, 1803. Watercolor on ivory. 2⅝" x 2⅛". (Private collection; photo, Colonial Williamsburg Foundation.)

girls and women as they augmented their domestic use of mourning jewelry with the fabrication of large-format "memorial pieces" intended to elicit the sentiments of the living, especially those of women, such as one by Lydia Eames (fig. 58). Another memorial is inscribed with a poem, "Sympathy," that begins "Hail, lovely Power, whose Bosom heaves a sigh / When Fancy paints the Scene of deep Distress. . . ."[27]

Fancy mourning jewelry underwent a quick and marked transition in the way it reflected attitudes toward emotional expression. At first, miniature lockets were commonly worn on a necklace. One side held a mourning picture and the other, often, a lock of hair from the deceased (fig. 59). Portraits sometimes show women wearing these lockets facing inward toward the heart to personalize the emotions, not outward to invite inquiry by others. By the early years of the nineteenth century, however, mourning displays were becoming acceptable. The death of George Washington in 1799 provided a forum for public expressions of sympathy, and patriotic

displays to memorialize him occurred on a national level. Mourning lockets now became fashionable in wider circles and were turned outward for all to see (fig. 60).[28]

Large Fancywork pictures with similar, but more elaborate, mourning images were prominently placed in the home, often hung in parlors or bedchambers. Sometimes they depicted Washington garbed in classical robes and ascending to heaven. Period terminology referred to pictures having patriotic motifs, weeping willows, and tombstones as "memorial pieces," whereas images that showed specific renderings of family and friends were called "mourning pieces" or "mourning pictures" (fig. 61). The subtle iconography of the latter often embodied the new receptiveness to more overt expressions of human emotion. Women and children typically were depicted in mourning scenes, sometimes with half-a-dozen or more figures draped over a tomb in heartrending poses. Mark Twain's *Huckleberry Finn* described several mourning pieces he encountered as

FIGURE 61 *Mourning Piece for Mrs. Ebenezer Collins*, attributed to Lovice Collins, South Hadley, Hampshire County, Massachusetts, 1807. Silk satin, silk velvet, watercolor, pencil, ink, silk thread, metallic thread, chenille thread, and printed paper label. Diam. 17" (sight). (Collection of the American Folk Art Museum, New York. Eva and Morris Feld Folk Art Acquisition Fund, 1981.12.8; photo, John Parnell, New York.)

"different from any pictures I ever seen before; blacker, mostly, than is common." The pictures, one of which featured a female figure "leaning pensive on a tombstone on her right elbow, under a weeping willow," had little appeal for Finn: "These was all nice pictures, I reckon, but I didn't somehow seem to take to them."[29]

When male figures were included in mourning pieces, they were often depicted without signs of grief or standing away from the group, underscoring their emotional detachment and representing the way men of the era were expected to deal with issues of death. Many of the male figures appeared stone-faced or puzzled; sometimes they occupied themselves by holding an infant. Men of the era were not expected to mourn publicly, even though overt expressions of grief were appropriate for women and were properly expressed in the Fancy pieces they made.

Whether eliciting sadness or delight, Fancywork was an important new creative outlet for women after 1790. Compared to the dulling, burdensome responsibility of everyday housework and sewing, Fancywork lifted the mind, sparked the imagination, and gave women a substantial sense of self-worth. Fancywork was not an end in itself, however, but a means by which women could measure themselves and develop their tastes while they broadened their horizons. One American woman in the early nineteenth century expressed her glee at having learned these skills: "Fancy work opened up a new world of delight," she exclaimed in her remembrances

FIGURE 62   Frontispiece, Martha Bradley's *British Housewife,* London, 1756. (Courtesy, The Lilly Library, Indiana University, Bloomington, Indiana.)

FIGURE 63   Sweetmeat stand, Plymouth, Gloucestershire, England, 1768–1773. Porcelain and polychrome decoration. H. 4⅛", W. 7⅜". (Courtesy, Winterthur Museum.)

FIGURE 64   Josiah Wedgwood, Etruria Factory, jelly core mold and cover, Hanley, Staffordshire, England, 1802–1818. Earthenware and polychrome decoration. H. 10½", Diam. 7⅜" (cover); H. 8", Diam. 10" (mold). (Courtesy, Winterthur Museum. Museum purchase with funds provided by Special Funds for Collection Objects.)

nearly three-quarters of a century later.[30] Fancywork contributed substance to the formation of Fancy by creating a body of domestic artifacts that were not only embedded with the emotions associated with Fancy, but also empowered through their associations with the most important values in the American home. One of these was Fancy cookery.

In the eighteenth century, female imagination was thought to be an essential component of creative cooking (fig. 62). As early as 1730, Charles Carter observed in his *Complete Practical Cook*—written principally for ladies—that "A curious cook, that has a good Fancy, shall find out many Novelties, hitherto unknown, and Add much to COOKERY." The recipes frequently provided suggestions for garnishes and dressings that gave the dishes significant visual interest (fig. 63).[31] Hannah Glasse, who published the practical *Art of Cookery Made Plain and Easy* in 1747, advised her audience to add ingredients to their recipes "according to your Fancy." Glasse subscribed to the increasing tendency to use "fancy" to describe the process of making sweets and desserts, and she gave recipes for deliberately eyecatching desserts such as "Fashion Cakes."[32] In his 1807 *London Art of Cookery,* John Farley listed many such recipes, including a molded dessert in the form of King Solomon's Temple (fig. 64). Farley noted that when the "flummery" was taken out of the mold, one should "stick a small sprig of flowers, down from the top of every point, which will not only strengthen it, but also give it a pretty appearance. Lay round it with rock candy sweetmeats."[33] In her widely popular publication *The Experienced English Housekeeper, for the Use and Ease of Ladies, Housekeepers, Cooks, & c.,* Elizabeth Raffald similarly noted the imaginative creation of "pretty corner dishes" such as a "pink-coloured PANCAKE" that could be garnished with dyed nuts and fruits or real-life flowers—all of which served to enrich the eater's gastronomic experience by augmenting his or her visual experience.[34]

Although the earliest references to "fancy" as an adjective applied to a specific food appeared about 1800, the preparation of food that required any degree of imagination—whether in the selection of ingredients, shape, or decoration—could be similarly described. The attention given to these culinary creations reflected the relatively high cost of imported sugar and other specialized ingredients, and an assortment of desserts, tempting to both the palate and the eye, placed on the dining table or sideboard bespoke the elevated status and refined tastes of those who served them.[35] Fancy foods pleased the eye and stimulated the imagination. For example, "glazing" or "strewing" Fancy desserts with a coat of sugar, rather than mixing all of the sweetener into the recipe, caused the creation—served for a midday meal, afternoon tea, or a candlelight supper—to sparkle. Just as engaging were dishes such as Elizabeth Raffald's "Artificial Eggs and Bacon," a whimsical trompe l'oeil dessert or conceit that, to use the period definition of Samuel Johnson, served as a "pleasant fancy" (fig. 65).[36] Fancy foods reflected the importance of imagination and good taste in the creative realms of both cooking and dining-room presentation.

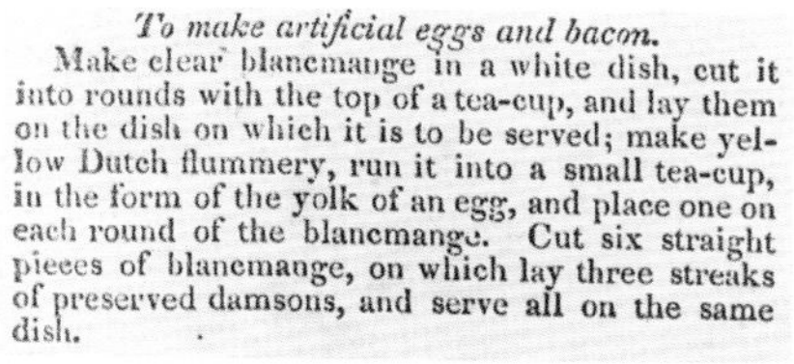

Fancy foods also provided women with an engaging alternative to the more mundane task of preparing everyday, plain foods, a task that dominated much of their existence. Even wealthy women who had servants and cooks began to directly participate in the preparation of Fancy foods, which often took place in a setting away from the heat of the kitchen. This had particular appeal in summer when fruit-flavored ices or ice creams were in vogue. However, the tedious work of making ice cream, or of baking pastry near a hot, smoky fire, was left to the servants in the households of these fashionable ladies.

All of these early manifestations of Fancy needlework and Fancy cooking are perhaps best understood as occupying a place partway between plain work, which was common and expected, and more intellectually rigorous pursuits, such as the study of mathematics or philosophy, which were seen as beyond a woman's sphere. Fancy skills were innocent pleasures that not only safely refined a lady's tastes and talents, they also effectively reinforced her self-esteem without raising expectations to levels that could not be fulfilled within the inevitable responsibilities of motherhood or the limited opportunities offered by eighteenth-century society. It was neither an intentional ploy by men nor blind acceptance by women that caused Fancy to assume such significance. Rather, the increased currency and approval of this human faculty, the relatively progressive social mores of the post-Revolutionary period, and a new sense of economic security that afforded the luxury of spare time all converged to encourage and nurture women's involvement with Fancy. By 1810 women on both sides of the Atlantic had experienced material and emotional benefits. That year an English periodical that also was circulated widely in America glowingly proclaimed the merits of Fancy skills:

To make artificial eggs and bacon.
Make clear blancmange in a white dish, cut it into rounds with the top of a tea-cup, and lay them on the dish on which it is to be served; make yellow Dutch flummery, run it into a small tea-cup, in the form of the yolk of an egg, and place one on each round of the blancmange. Cut six straight pieces of blancmange, on which lay three streaks of preserved damsons, and serve all on the same dish.

FIGURE 65 Recipe for "Artificial Eggs and Bacon" in Colin Mackenzie's *Five Thousand Receipts in all the Useful and Domestic Arts, Constituting A Complete and Universal Practical Library, and Operative Cyclopedia,* Philadelphia, 1829. (Courtesy, The Winterthur Library: Printed Book and Periodical Collection.) First published in Elizabeth Raffald's *Experienced English Housekeeper* (1769), this recipe was reprinted in cookbooks for decades.

> It is impossible to congratulate our fair Country women too warmly on the revolution which has of late years taken place, when drawing and fancy work of endless variety have been raised on the ruins of that heavy, unhealthy, and stupefying occupation, needlework.[37]

In identifying with Fancy and employing it to define certain aspects of their lives, women had a major impact upon their families and their homes. By the last decade of the eighteenth century, the trend toward Fancy began to assume importance with men as well. Artisans across America began to create greater categories of Fancy goods for household use, and at the same time that they transformed the appearance of their products, they transformed the language that defined them. The salubrious effects of the fancy, enumerated a century earlier by Joseph Addison, were now embraced by a larger audience and expressed in an ever wider array of Fancy furnishings.

3 Early Fancy Furnishings

All kinds of Fancy Furniture . . . Of
various colors and of every description,
painted and gilt in the most fanciful manner.

Advertisement for John and Hugh Finlay
Federal Gazette and Baltimore Daily Advertiser, April 2, 1803

etween 1790 and 1815 Americans embraced Fancy with a new sense of
enthusiasm and expanded its limits beyond the confines of bedchambers,
kitchens, and the universe of small goods primarily made or used by
women. Retailers offered a growing range of Fancy furnishings—colorful
wallpapers, patterned fabrics and plush carpets, brilliantly ornamental
ceramics, and glistening mirrors—promoting them widely in advertisements and encouraging the American public to endorse Fancy and enjoy
its material products. As the concepts of fancy and imagination earned
increasing recognition in literature and philosophy during this era, the
style of Fancy was inspired by a rediscovery of the classical arts of the past
and by the changing face of the marketplace. This awakening extended
from America's major urban centers to regional towns and the countryside, where Fancy presented people with new opportunities to participate
in a complex interplay of emotional and intellectual experiences.

Many of the first products were imported from abroad, but soon American artisans began to fulfill the rising demand for Fancy goods, which, in
turn, filled American homes with light and color, pattern and motion.
This widespread embrace of Fancy enabled artisans to imagine the un-
imagined, to envision potential new uses for their evocative new goods,
and to push the limits of design, materials, and emotion. Fashionable consumers, likewise, were eager to enliven the most prominent social spaces
in their homes—entry passages, parlors, and dining rooms—with the
infectious new style. When wealthy Maryland planter and politician
Charles Carroll of Carrollton ordered a new floorcloth in the 1790s, he
did not request the same rigid black and white checks on the cloth he had
acquired in the 1770s, but insisted upon a stylish new cloth painted "not
in diamonds, but a waving pattern" (fig. 66).[1] Francis Guy (1760–1820), a

FIGURE 66   Simon Fitch, *Ephraim Starr,*
Middletown, Connecticut, 1802. Oil on canvas. 59" x 39¹⁵⁄₁₆". (Courtesy, Wadsworth
Atheneum, Hartford. The Ella Gallup Sumner and Mary Catlin Sumner Collection
Fund, 1961.460.) The lively floorcloth of
green and white with floral medallions
reflects the new Fancy aesthetic.

British artist and inventor who settled in Baltimore, turned to Fancy for his livelihood. He first achieved modest success painting local views for wealthy clients and ornamenting "Fancy furniture" with landscape scenes. Infatuated with the creative process, and the profit to be had from it, in 1806 Guy began to focus his efforts on developing and manufacturing highly ornamental, yet inexpensive, floorcloths made of decorative wall-paper that was glued to a canvas ground and protected with a thick coat of varnish. He took five years to perfect his product, finally offering it in 1811 at Mr. Robert Elliot's Paper Hanging Warehouse, at the corner of Liberty and Lexington streets in Baltimore. His advertisement in the local paper touting his accomplishment was a salute to the whimsy and imagination that characterized the new Fancy style:[2]

> The theory of paper carpets at first seems to give common sense a kind of electric shock, and therefore many suppose it to be a dream; a mere flight of fancy; the off-spring of a wild imagination; a rude ingested whim, that Queen Mab has been driving her carriage through my brain, and left me bewildered in the labyrinth of a fairy tale! . . . I know to a certainty that I can make carpets of common hanging paper that will wear as long as the canvas floorcloths; much more beautiful, and above fifty per cent cheaper.[3]

Guy's conviction of the merits of paper carpets was symptomatic of a trend among artisans who envisioned the endless aesthetic and emotional merits of such Fancy creations and saw themselves as offering unprecedented new luxuries to Americans.

America's rising passion for Fancy, which spurred inventive new furnishings, resonated sympathetically with an emerging national spirit. Victory in the Revolutionary War, a booming postwar economy, and a seemingly endless supply of land helped to fuel a sense of American optimism that was well suited to, and reflected by, Fancy. Visitors such as the British traveler who gazed upon dwellings in the Hudson River valley and pronounced them "uncommonly gay and [luxu]riant" were quick to note the unusually bright exteriors of early nineteenth-century American homes.[4] What they saw did more than dazzle their eyes. James Fenimore Cooper, the first American novelist to receive wide recognition and an astute commentator on Americans and their customs, observed that the neat domestic native landscape reflected "the brilliancy of the climate, the freshness of the paint, and the exterior ornaments of the houses."[5] Ironically, the vibrant spirit and fresh look of post-1790 America was fed by a reconsideration of the arts of the ancient past that came from Europe.

Fancy found an unexpectedly rich source for ideas in ancient Greek, Roman, and Etruscan artistic traditions. Excavations at sites around the Mediterranean and Adriatic seas in the mid-eighteenth century, particularly those at Herculaneum and Pompeii, changed established notions about the character of the classical world and classical imagination. In 1738 and 1740 Italian farmers accidentally rediscovered the neighboring towns

FIGURE 67   Bedchamber (*cubiculum nocturnum*), from the villa of P. Fannius Synistor, Pompeii, Boscoreale, Italy, first century B.C.E. Fresco on lime plaster. H. 8' (average). (Courtesy, The Metropolitan Museum of Art. Rogers Fund, 1903 [03.14.13]; photo, © 1986 The Metropolitan Museum of Art.) This image shows the east wall of the room.

on the Italian coast, which had been engulfed by eruptions of Mount Vesuvius in A.D. 79. The ruins of domestic buildings found on these sites possessed an intimate scale not generally acknowledged by even the most astute students of classical architecture. These were not the monumental, sun-washed temples of scrubbed white marble of Athens and Rome, but small, ancient dwellings that contained colorful ceramics and whimsical furnishings. Furthermore, their walls were adorned with painted decoration from one end to the other, including brilliantly colored frescoes that sported mythological subjects and depicted the ancients savoring the pleasures of life. These excavated interiors and furnishings provided a view of the ancients that was more sensual than anything classicism had previously admitted to eighteenth-century European society (fig. 67).

   One European traveler after another pulled out a spade to take back souvenirs, or recorded findings in his sketchbook or diary, so that even those who had not made the journey to Italy were able to realize the significance of the findings. Ralph and Alice Delancey Izard of South Carolina visited Herculaneum and Pompeii on a grand tour in 1775 and were overwhelmed by the discoveries. He wrote from Naples to tell his

Charleston friends of the experience: "I have met with nothing that seems so extraordinary to me as the neighborhood of this place. . . . The beautiful pieces of antiquity . . . that have been found in them, surpass all imagination."[6] The revelations had a direct impact on Western philosophy and design. By the third quarter of the century, a new perception of

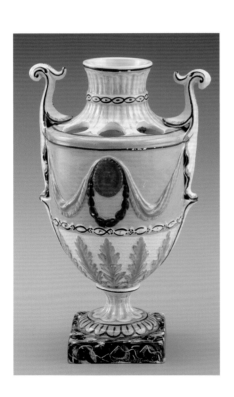

FIGURE 68   Vase, England, 1790–1800. Earthenware and enameled decoration. H. 8¼". (Courtesy, Elbert H. Parsons, Jr.; photo, Gavin Ashworth.)

FIGURE 69   John Davey, Sr., secretary and bookcase, Philadelphia, 1800–1810. Mahogany and satinwood veneers, mahogany, and looking-glass plate with white pine and yellow poplar. H. 94¹¹⁄₁₆", W. 45", D. 22⅜". (Courtesy, The Metropolitan Museum of Art. Purchase, Fletcher Fund and Rogers Fund, Gift of Mrs. Russell Sage, and The Sylmaris Collection, Gift of George Coe Graves, by exchange, 1962 [62.9]; photo, ©1999 The Metropolitan Museum of Art.)

classicism—or neoclassicism—made it possible, within the limits of eighteenth-century cultural norms, to better understand classical attitudes toward emotion and style.

To the great joy of enlightened eighteenth-century artists and thinkers, who still looked to the ancients for inspiration, this stunning evidence provided a legitimate source for emulation. As intellectuals assumed the task of analyzing and debating the meaning of the ancient discoveries, artisans in Britain and America began crafting imitations of excavated arti- facts, particularly small objects like ceramics, or, more often, liberally rein- terpreting the classical spirit (fig. 68). This was apparent in the renewed emphasis on geometric designs. Circles and ellipses, squares and pyra- mids, which were derived from the equations of ancient mathematicians, particularly Euclid, now served as the inspiration for the shapes of fur- nishings large and small: demilune commodes, elliptical teapots, and oval- or square-back chairs. The rational geometry was frequently accented by ancient motifs—paterae or fans, urns symbolic of mourning, or chains of classical bellflowers. These classical elements were strengthened visually through the use of vividly contrasting materials. Delicate inlays of satin- wood and boxwood, veneers of brilliantly patterned mahogany, and col- orful surfaces of polished paint, all served to further heighten the aesthetic effect and classical allusions on goods both large and small (fig. 69). Yet it was the singular role of color, and its surprising classical precedents, that served as the strongest stimulant and set in motion the aesthetic and emo- tional expectations that soon defined the period's boldest expression of Fancy in material goods (fig. 70).

Painted interiors were scarce in all but the wealthiest of households prior to the middle of the eighteenth century, and brilliantly dyed textiles often provided the only visual relief in a world dominated by earthen

FIGURE 70 *Fortune,* England, ca. 1790. Earthenware and polychrome decoration. H. 11", W. 3½", D. 3½". (Private collection.)

ceramics, gray pewter, and unpainted furniture. But change was at hand. Possessing colorful porcelain or delftware, or brightly painted interiors, came not only to suggest wealth and status, but also to indicate the refinement of maker and owner alike. As early as 1693, when Samuel Sewall of Boston entertained friends in his newly painted house, he recorded in his diary an enthusiastic response to painted interiors. "'Tis the first time Mr. Torrey has been at our house with his new wife; was much ples'd with our painted shutters; in pleasancy said he thought he had been got into paradise."[7]

As the century progressed, colorful architecture and ornamented furnishings gradually became affordable and were expressed in the wider use of interior paints, decorative wallpapers, intricately patterned textiles, and lively delftwares and porcelains. By midcentury Europeans and Americans alike reveled in the brilliant hues and the unprecedented designs that emerged from Herculaneum and Pompeii. In the 1750s and 1760s, inspired by these archaeological discoveries, British architect Robert Adam designed the first painted British furniture to accompany the colorful neoclassical interiors of his aristocratic patrons.[8] The style slowly spread across England, and by the 1780s and 1790s, furniture designers such as George Hepplewhite (d. 1786) and Thomas Sheraton (1751–1806) further disseminated the new taste. In 1788 Hepplewhite's *Cabinet-Maker and Upholsterer's Guide* elaborated upon the public's curiosity about this painted furniture:

> For chairs, a new and very elegant fashion has arisen within these few years, of finishing them with painted . . . work, which gives a rich and splendid appearance to the minuter parts of the ornaments, which are generally thrown in by the painter. Several of these designs are particularly adapted to this style, which allows a framework less massy than is requisite for mahogany; and by assorting the prevailing colour to the furniture and light of the room, affords opportunity, by the variety of grounds which may be introduced, to the whole accord in harmony, with a pleasing and striking effect to the eye.[9]

Despite a dedication to classically derived ornamental finishes, Hepplewhite and Sheraton were cautious in acknowledging the influence of Fancy. Hepplewhite admitted that his products had a "rich and splendid appearance," but he intended to avoid "mere novelty . . . whim at the instance of a caprice." He pointedly eschewed "fancies," and instead advocated only articles "of general use and service." Sheraton was equally circumspect in describing the role of imagination in his creations. Although his *Drawing Book* of 1793 included a design for a carved "fancy leaf," he equated "fancifulness" with the taste of women. Sheraton, too, avoided references to imagination and fancy. Perhaps the caption he chose for the frontispiece of his *Cabinet Dictionary* of 1803 best explains his reservations: "Time alters fashions . . . ; but that which is founded on Geometry & real science will remain unalterable." As conservative Englishmen, both Hepplewhite and Sheraton wanted to believe that their contributions to furniture design would survive far beyond their time, and neither was willing to acknowledge the ephemeral influences of Fancy upon his work.[10]

Americans, on the other hand, seemed to be far more concerned with the immediate benefits and effects of the material world than their British counterparts. The last decade of the eighteenth century witnessed a rapid growth of the classically influenced Fancy style in America, as engravings of Hepplewhite and Sheraton inspired a wider audience, imported furnishings were copied and reinterpreted, and immigrant artisans landed on American shores to pursue their craft and train others in its skills. By the 1790s, Americans enthusiastically referred to an entirely new genre of ornamented goods as "Fancy furniture." Among the earliest such references in the United States is one dating to 1790, when the estate inventory of Joseph Barnard of Deerfield, Massachusetts, included a "fancy looking glass" valued at eight shillings.[11] One can only surmise what this artifact looked like, but it probably had a gilt surface that glistened in the light and, presumably, a lively scene painted on the reverse of the glass (fig. 71). As a "Fancy" looking glass, it would have provided a marked contrast to the plainer mahogany and gilt examples in the marketplace.

Several other features separated the first Fancy furniture from traditional mahogany pieces. First, and most important, was the liberal use of paint. In 1803 Fancy chair makers John and Hugh Finlay of Baltimore advertised their ability to make "all kinds of Fancy Furniture . . . Of various colors and of every description, painted and gilt in the most fanciful manner."[12] Every visible surface of the furniture was covered, usually by red, green, or yellow. Sometimes white or blue was used and, on occasion, black. The second distinguishing characteristic of early Fancy furniture was its delicate, or feminine, scale, made possible by the use of hardwoods that were even more durable than the mahogany usually employed for formal examples.[13]

A number of specific artistic techniques contributed to the look of Fancy furniture. Most of these had existed for centuries, and many were equally applicable to architecture. What differed now were the combinations of skills required to produce a single piece, the layering of the ornamentation, and the complexity of the emotional responses they were intended to elicit. Much of the aesthetic and emotional impact of these Fancy pieces can be ascribed to their "Japan Colors" or "japanning"—terms inherited from the seventeenth century, when painted ornament first suggested a connection to the exotic arts of Asia. By the 1790s the words referred, quite simply, to the finely ground paint that could be polished to a high gloss, and then varnished to further heighten its brilliancy. The best shops often advertised "Fancy Japanned Furniture" during this era, and sometimes added further descriptions such as "elegant" or "fashionable." If "polished" sometimes referred to the brilliant sheen of the varnished surfaces, it also defined America's perceptions of those who owned such furniture, and the manners they were felt to possess.

FIGURE 71 Looking glass, America, 1800–1815. Wood, glass, mirror plate, and painted, gessoed, and gilt decoration. H. 48", W. 29". (Courtesy, Winterthur Museum.)

Inviting surfaces and delicate scale are evident in two complementary sets of chairs produced for Oak Hill, a home constructed for Elias Hasket Derby in Peabody, Massachusetts, in 1798. Derby, the wealthiest shipowner and merchant in Massachusetts, filled the house to capacity with up-to-date fashions, among them Fancy chairs having oval backs ornamented with plumage (figs. 72 and 73). In some respects, Derby's chairs differed little from the formal mahogany examples of the period, constructed with

FIGURE 72   Chair, Philadelphia, 1795–1800. Maple and painted decoration with oak and cherry. H. 38½", W. 21⅞", D. 22⅞". (Chipstone Foundation.)

AMERICAN FANCY

tapered legs, mortise-and-tenon joints, and upholstered seats. Nonetheless, their black and white japanned grounds were novel during the 1790s, and the brilliant plumage was largely unfamiliar to American eyes. When the Reverend William Bentley visited Oak Hill's lavish interior in 1801, these chairs were among the furnishings that impressed his acute New England sensibilities: "The furniture was rich but never violated the chastity of correct taste," he respectfully observed of his wealthy parishioner.[14]

FIGURE 73 Chair, Massachusetts, 1795–1800. Soft maple and painted decoration. H. 38½", W. 21⅞", D. 22⅞". (Collection of Mrs. George M. Kaufman.) Derby acquired a second set of chairs produced locally to emulate the Philadelphia set (fig. 72).

FIGURE 74 Side chair, Boston, 1800–1805. Birch, painted decoration, and cane. H. 35⅛", W. 19", D. 20⅛". (Courtesy, Winterthur Museum.)

A contemporary Massachusetts chair, derived from plate 36 of Sheraton's *Drawing Book* (1793), reflects an equally novel aesthetic (fig. 74). One of a large set of chairs, its understated black japanning is highlighted by floral vignettes, a classical urn flanked by columns Fancy painted in imitation of marble, and broad stripes of brilliant blue. Certain elements are accented with gilt, and the seat is stretched taut with expensive caning. In some households, owners of such chairs enhanced the seats with colorful pillows, lending additional comfort and heightening their visual impact.[15]

In the 1790s Fancy furniture was produced in New York as well as in Philadelphia and Boston. The immigrant artisan William Challen, a self-described "Fancy Chairmaker" who left London and arrived on the banks of the Hudson River in 1797, was among the first to manufacture "every article in the Fancy Chair line, executed in the neatest manner and after the newest and most approved London patterns." Challen offered chairs and settees having dyed, japanned, and bamboo finishes, and may have been the first to advertise Fancy chairs in America.[16]

Although products from Challen's shop have yet to be identified, a card table (figs. 75 and 76) and armchair (fig. 77) made between 1795 and 1810 offer insights into representative New York interpretations of the Fancy style and clarify the city's strong indebtedness to London prototypes. Like British furnishings, these New York pieces rely heavily upon painted drapery or festoons of flowers, and upon medallions strategically placed on legs and stiles. The decoration on the top of the card table is particularly notable, for in addition to its abundant swag of roses, it possesses a detailed border consisting of meandering vines and flowers. In front, the skirt is adorned with a highly detailed "trophy of music" (see figs. 79 and 80).

FIGURE 75   Card table, probably New York City, 1795–1810. Maple, white pine, and painted decoration. H. 29", W. 38", D. 18½". (Courtesy, Winterthur Museum.)

FIGURE 76   Detail showing the top of the card table illustrated in fig. 75.

FIGURE 77   Armchair, possibly New York or Massachusetts, 1795–1810. Maple, birch, painted decoration, and cane. H. 34⅜", W. 19¼", D. 19¾". (Courtesy, Maryland Historical Society, Baltimore, Maryland.)

The painted decorations on all of these Fancy furniture forms reflect the emerging art of "ornamental painting," a specialized trade that included a wide range of craft skills: ciphering and lettering, japanning and gilding; the decoration of signs, carriages, and banners; heraldry and painting on glass; and the painting of flowers and other decorative details on furniture and architectural woodwork alike. The skill could be as simple as applying thin lines or "stripes" on the back of a chair or as demanding as decorating entire suites of furniture or rooms with eye-catching details. One exotic

Fancy interior in Alexandria, Virginia, featured a room adorned with vertical stripes of red, white, and blue that converged in the ceiling overhead to suggest a Venetian tent in false perspective.[17]

An 1811 drawing book, compiled by eighteen-year-old apprentice Christian Nestell of New York City, provides valuable insights into the practice of ornamental painting and illustrates designs popular on New York Fancy furniture soon after the turn of the century. Little is known of Nestell's training, or of his work before he moved to Rhode Island in 1820 and became the proprietor of a Fancy furniture warehouse (fig. 78). None-

FIGURE 78 "C. M. Nestell, Fancy, Windsor and Common Chairs," advertisement in *Providence Patriot*, Providence, Rhode Island, August 28, 1822. (Courtesy, American Antiquarian Society.)

theless, he probably spent the early part of his career ornamenting Fancy furniture for one of the larger New York firms. A "trophy of music" from his drawing book relates closely to the skirt detail of the New York Fancy card table in figure 75, and though not close enough to make an attribution possible on the table, the two have much in common. When the ornament on the table and in Nestell's drawing book is considered in its entirety—including elaborate bowknots, honeysuckle designs, and floral meanders—it illustrates the tantalizing range of Fancy ornament popular among New York painters and patrons in the earliest years of the nineteenth century (figs. 79 and 80).[18]

Few manufacturers of Fancy furniture utilized ornamental painting more advantageously than brothers John and Hugh Finlay of Baltimore. Among the most successful in their trade in America, the brothers enjoyed a career that spanned from 1799 to 1837. John (1777–1851), the elder, had established himself as a carriage painter by 1799, and Hugh (1781–1831) joined him in 1803. Although carriage work remained essential to their business, the brothers soon adapted their skills to ornamenting Fancy

AMERICAN FANCY

FIGURE 79   *A Trophy of Music,* illustrated in fig. 74 of Christian M. Nestell's drawing book, New York City, 1811. Watercolor on paper. 33" x 35". (Courtesy, The Winterthur Library: Joseph Downs Collection of Manuscripts and Printed Ephemera.)

FIGURE 80   Detail showing the apron of the card table illustrated in fig. 75. This apron ornament is closely related in design to the *Trophy of Music* pictured in fig. 79.

furniture and helping to meet the rising demand for the alluring new style. Initially working from a manufactory on South Frederick Street, the brothers ran a series of retail establishments, each filled to capacity with inventory. An 1805 advertisement illustrates the wide variety of furniture they offered to the public:

> Chairs and Settees—Card, Tea, Pier, Writing and Dressing Tables, with Mahogany, Satin Wood, Painted, Japanned and real Marble Top Sideboards; Ladies' Work Wash-hand and Candle Stands; Horse, Pole, Candle and Fire Screens; Bedstead, Bed and Window Cornices, the centers enriched with Gold and Painted Fruit, Scroll and Flower Borders of entire new patterns . . . &c.[19]

Baltimore served as an ideal location for the Finlays' flourishing business. In the half century before 1800, the city had expanded from a small village into a vibrant and rapidly growing metropolis situated in the center of the Chesapeake region. Tremendous wealth and the rapid pace of construction provided a healthy market for the Finlay products. When the English writer Frances Trollope later visited Baltimore, she compared the town's flamboyant tastes with those of conservative Quaker Philadelphia: "Both are costly, but the former is distinguished by gaudy splendor, the latter by elegant simplicity."[20]

FIGURE 81   Card table, attributed to
John and Hugh Finlay, Baltimore, 1805–1815.
Mahogany, poplar, and painted decoration.
H. 28½", W. 30", D. 17½". (Collection of
Mrs. George M. Kaufman.)

If Baltimore's taste appeared "gaudy" to some outside observers, it afforded the Finlays opportunities to explore all sorts of classically inspired
Fancy designs, including a sabre-leg card table made for John W. Stump
of Oakington, in Harford County, Maryland (fig. 81). Equally expressive
was a brilliant yellow and red chair with an eagle ornamented crest (figs. 82
and 83). The delicate chair was one of a dozen made in 1815 for merchant
Richard Ragan of Hagerstown, Maryland, for a total cost of ninety-six
dollars, and is an example of the many designs and diverse ornamentation
that were indicative of the tremendous efforts the Finlay brothers must
have made to offer their clients distinctive products.[21]

Among the other offerings coming out of the Finlay shop was "FANCY
and JAPANNED FURNITURE . . . with or without views adjacent to the
city." A simple wood-block print advertisement (fig. 84) illustrated a side
chair that is closely related to an elaborate armchair, part of a large set of
furnishings commissioned about 1804 consisting of armchairs, side chairs,
game tables, and pier tables (figs. 85 and 86). The crest of each chair and
the skirt of each table contained a decorative panel depicting a different
home in the region, each painted by Francis Guy, who also manufactured

FIGURE 82 John and Hugh Finlay, side chair, Baltimore, 1815. Poplar, maple, walnut, and painted decoration. H. 32", W. 18¼", D. 16¼". (Courtesy, Milly McGehee; photo, Erik Kvalsvik.)

imaginative paper floorcloths. The set, in its entirety, represents one of the largest and most ambitious groups of Fancy furniture recorded from early Baltimore.[22]

Between 1804 and 1806 Francis Guy worked closely with the Finlays, specializing in painting decorative vignettes for their furniture. His skills must have helped to transform the Finlay business by providing a personalized and highly stylish product superior to that offered by other local producers of Fancy furniture. That did not stop others from imitating and emulating the furniture made in the Finlay shop. By late summer of 1804, the threat from competitors was sufficiently real that the brothers took out a newspaper advertisement warning potential challengers: "Any Person or Persons infringing [the Finlays'] exclusive right, will be prosecuted agree-

FIGURE 83 Detail of the crest rail of the Baltimore side chair illustrated in fig. 82.

FIGURE 84 "John and Hugh Finley [sic], Fancy and Japanned Furniture," advertisement in *Federal Gazette*, Baltimore, October 24, 1803. (Courtesy, Maryland Historical Society, Baltimore, Maryland.)

John and Hugh Finley

HAVE opened a shop at No. 190¾, Market-street, opposite Mr Peter Wyant's inn, where they have for sale, and make to any pattern, all kinds of FANCY and JAPANNED FURNITURE, viz.

Japanned and gilt card, pier, tea, dressing, writing and shaving TABLES, with or without views adjacent to the city.

Ditto cane seats, rush and windsor CHAIRS, with or without views.

Ditto cane seats, rush and windsor SETTEES, with or without views.

Ditto Window and Recess Seats.

Ditto Wash and Candle Stands.

Ditto Fire and Candle Screens.

Ditto   Ditto.   with views.

Ditto Bedsteads, and Bed and Window Cornices, &c.

Which they warrant equal to any imported.

They as usual execute Coach, Sign and Ornamental Painting.

Military standards, drums, masonic aprons, all kinds of silk transparencies, &c. in the neatest manner, and on the shortest notice.

☞ Old chairs repainted.

N. B. Apply as above or at their manufactory No. 3, South Frederick-street.

October 24.   d

able to law." By the time Guy left the business in 1806 to pursue his own artistic endeavors, the Finlays had attracted the attention of Baltimore's wealthiest and most stylish patrons, and their place in the market was secured for years to come.[23]

Having exhausted the demand for made-to-order furniture with portraits of houses, the Finlays, along with other cabinetmakers, also offered "fancy landscapes" on their furniture (figs. 87 and 88). The concept of Fancy landscapes or Fancy pictures first appeared in fashionable circles during the 1780s, and specifically identified scenes derived from the imagination. Thomas Reid, writing in the early 1780s, helped to clarify the

meaning of these scenes in an essay regarding the powers of the mind.
Reid used the analogy of an artist in describing what he called "the different kinds of our conceptions, and the different works of the painter." A
painter "either makes fancy pictures, or he copies from the painting of
others, or he paints from life," wrote Reid, "and I think our conceptions
admit of a division very similar." He went on to explain what he meant by
"fancy pictures":

AMERICAN FANCY

FIGURE 87 Card table, attributed to John and Hugh Finlay, Baltimore, 1800–1810. Mahogany, maple, painted and gilt decoration, and cane with oak and tulip poplar. H. 28⅞", W. 36", D. 17½". (Courtesy, The Metropolitan Museum of Art. Purchase, Mrs. Russell Sage Gift, 1970 [1970.189]; photo, Paul Warchol, ©1984 The Metropolitan Museum of Art.)

FIGURE 88 Detail showing the apron of the card table illustrated in fig. 87.

They are commonly called creatures of fancy, or of imagination. They are not copies of any original that exists, but are originals themselves. Such was the conception which Swift formed of the island of Laputa and of the country of the Lilliputians; Cervantes of Don Quixote and his Squire; Harrington of the government of Oceana; and Sir Thomas More of that of Utopia. We can give names to such creatures of imagination, conceive them distinctly and reason consequentially concerning them, though they never had an existence.[24]

Imaginary landscapes often adorned fashionable households, whether hung in frames on the wall, depicted on Fancy landscape wallpapers, or applied to furniture. The 1787 estate inventory of John Hancock, president of the Second Continental Congress, included several "fancy pictures," and in 1792 James L. Walker, an artist who advertised from Baltimore, advised the public that he painted "Landscapes, either from Nature or fancy." Imaginary views were also incorporated into wallpapers, and by 1813 Moses Grant, Jr., advertised "Fancy Landscape Paper Hangings" among the "fashionable" goods that he offered for sale in his Boston store.[25]

Charles Codman, a landscape artist and ornamental painter from Portland, Maine, composed an imaginative scene that was exceptional not only for its quality but also for the fact that the artist signed it on the reverse "Fancy Piece" (fig. 89). The cool blues and misty atmosphere give the picture an ethereal quality and suggest an idealized conception rather than a depiction of reality. In America, Fancy landscapes on furniture seem to have first emanated from the Finlay shop—and from the brush of the aforementioned Francis Guy. Artist Rembrandt Peale hailed the "ingenious manner" in which Guy worked, observing that he was often seen in the countryside, "wherever a scene of interest offered itself to his

FIGURE 89   Charles Codman, *Fancy Piece,* America, ca. 1829. Oil on panel. 19³⁄₁₆″ x 26⁵⁄₈″. (Courtesy, Portland Museum of Art, Maine. Museum purchase, 1961.16; photo, Williamstown Art Conservation Center.)

AMERICAN FANCY

fancy."[26] An early critic reviewed one of Guy's Fancy paintings in New York and called it a "cheerful, animated view of pleasing rural scenery." Other painters who worked in the Finlay shop are also presumed to have painted these landscapes, including the Dutch artist Cornelius deBeet.[27] Independent artists, such as the local ornamental painter John Barnhart, may have been called upon to help on occasion.

In New York Fancy landscapes were highly favored for furniture and appear frequently on expensive New York Fancy chairs. One set, owned by the Van Rensselaer family of Albany, illustrates the prominence given these scenes (fig. 90). The painted surfaces imitate highly figured "curl maple" and have accents of red striping and gold leaf. The cane seats—possibly intended for colorful cushions—and the imaginary landscapes

FIGURE 90 Side chair, New York, 1815–1825. Maple, cherry, poplar, hickory, and painted decoration. H. 33⅛", W. 19", D. 16½". (Courtesy, Winterthur Museum.)

FIGURE 91   Pair of side chairs, New York,
ca. 1815–1825. Poplar, maple, painted decoration, and cane. H. 32½", W. 19", D. 15¾".
(Private collection.)

AMERICAN FANCY

differ on each chair. A pair of New York Fancy chairs with related details demonstrates a colorful alternative, but one in which the importance of the landscape is less pronounced (fig. 91). A similar set of Fancy chairs was commissioned in 1816 for *Cleopatra's Barge,* a lavish yacht owned by the successful shipping merchant George Crowninshield of Salem, Massachusetts.[28]

An exceptional painted window cornice with unusually vibrant colors was made in the Finlay shop in Baltimore for Wye plantation on Maryland's Eastern Shore (fig. 92). The home descended in the powerful Lloyd family, who made no less than seven separate purchases of Fancy furniture from the Finlay brothers between 1808 and 1833. Although Governor Edward Lloyd V acquired cornices from the Finlays in 1828, the style of

the cornice suggests it probably dates from an earlier period. The daring palette, and the variety of its ornamental details, typify the period around 1810. At Wye, such cornices must have provided a colorful contrast to the stately mahogany furnishings that otherwise dominated the home. Certainly, this was no timid family in matters of taste.[29]

The Finlays' creative products soon attracted wider attention. Of those artisans and designers who came to work closely with the brothers, few had greater stature than English-born architect and engineer Benjamin Henry Latrobe (1764–1820), who arrived in America in 1796. Like many talented men in his day, Latrobe moved from city to city in order to oversee his principal commissions, residing in Richmond, Washington, Baltimore, Philadelphia, and New Orleans, and designing buildings for clients in both the private and public sectors. From Pennsylvania to Louisiana and inland to Kentucky and Ohio, his architectural designs set new standards in taste. He introduced up-to-the-minute European styles and broke new ground by designing the earliest Greek Revival structure in America, as well as one of the first in the Gothic Revival taste.[30]

Latrobe's 1809 Fancy furniture designs for the President's House in Washington provided the Finlays one of their most important commissions. Latrobe's original drawings (figs. 93 and 94) reveal Fancy's strong indebtedness to ancient prototypes: chairs possessed delicately shaped sabre legs and sweeping backs; sofas, boldly scrolled arms and tapered legs; and settees, dainty bellflower ornament and brass mounted bolsters. Latrobe sent the furniture frames constructed in Philadelphia to

FIGURE 92 Window cornice, attributed to John and Hugh Finlay, Baltimore, ca. 1810. Tulip poplar and painted decoration. H. 8", W. 59", D. 9". (Courtesy, Mrs. R. Carmichael Tilghman; photo, Gavin Ashworth.)

Baltimore for the Finlays to decorate. Consisting of thirty-six chairs, two
sofas, and four settees, the set amassed a final bill of $1,111. Regrettably,
the suite was destroyed when the British stormed Washington in August
of 1814. First Lady Dolley Madison, who escaped one step ahead of troops
determined to destroy the President's House, was unable to rescue more
than several trunks of papers and Gilbert Stuart's invaluable portrait of
General Washington.[31]

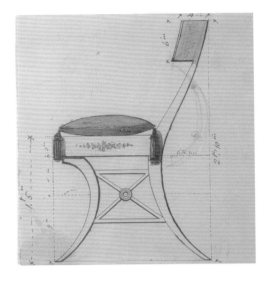  

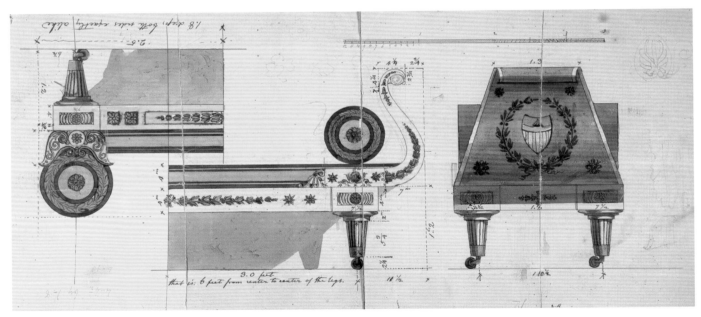

A second suite of Fancy furniture designed by Latrobe in 1808 demonstrates the complexities of attributing such distinctive pieces to a specific
shop and illustrates the interdependence of artisans involved in producing such pieces. Latrobe designed the furnishings en suite with his architectural plans for Philadelphia merchant William Waln (figs. 95 and 96).
Here the architect's taste for classicism merges with the playful dynamics

FIGURE 95   B. Henry Latrobe, designer,
side chair, attributed to Thomas Wetherill,
decoration possibly by Hugh Bridport in
association with John and Hugh Finlay,
Philadelphia, 1808–1810. Tulip poplar, maple,
painted, gessoed, and gilt decoration, and
cane. H. 32", W. 28", D. 27". (Chipstone Foundation.)

FIGURE 96   Detail of the crest rail of the
side chair illustrated in fig. 95.

of Fancy. Latrobe often explained his designs by emphasizing their archaeological correctness—although his ideas of correctness were quite indulgent toward imagination, particularly in the richness of combining Grecian forms with Egyptian and Roman ornament.[32] Latrobe looked to engravings by English designers such as Thomas Hope and George Smith for the former, but he was careful to vary the structural details between chair and bench, card table and pier table. He turned to other sources for the imaginative decoration, including Thomas Sheraton's *Drawing-Book* of 1791 (fig. 97). Latrobe indulged his fancy in the ornament for the chairs, choosing distinct designs for the crest rail of each.[33]

As he did with President Madison's furniture, Latrobe commissioned a Philadelphia cabinetmaker—in this case Thomas Wetherill—to make the frames. The suite included a dozen chairs, a long sofa, three window benches (fig. 98), two innovative card tables (fig. 99), and a pier table with exotic palm columns. Latrobe had commissioned Philadelphia artist Hugh Bridport to paint the interiors of the home and, though documentation is lacking, may have engaged him to ornament the furniture as well.[34] However, the similarity of the chairs to Baltimore work raises the possibility that artisans from that city were also involved in the ornamentation, particularly when one considers the tremendous manpower needed to complete the Waln project.[35] The affinity between Baltimore and Philadelphia work likewise hinders specific attribution of another set of Fancy chairs (figs. 100 and 101).

FIGURE 98 B. Henry Latrobe, designer, window bench, attributed to Thomas Wetherill, decoration possibly by Hugh Bridport in association with John and Hugh Finlay, Philadelphia, ca. 1808. W. 52⁷⁄₁₆". Yellow poplar, oak, white pine, maple, and painted, gessoed, and gilt decoration. (Collection of Mrs. George M. Kaufman.)

FIGURE 100   Side chair, Baltimore or Philadelphia, 1815–1825. Cherry, maple, tulip poplar, and painted decoration. H. 31⅜", W. 20⅛", D. 21½". (Courtesy, Winterthur Museum.)

FIGURE 99   B. Henry Latrobe, designer, card table, attributed to Thomas Wetherill, decoration possibly by Hugh Bridport in association with John and Hugh Finlay, Philadelphia, ca. 1808. Mahogany, yellow poplar, oak, maple, white pine, and painted, gessoed, and gilt decoration. H. 29½", W. 36", D. 17⅞". (Collection of Mrs. George M. Kaufman.)

FIGURE 101   Detail of the crest rail of the side chair illustrated in fig. 100.

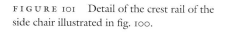

FIGURE 102 Card table, probably
Baltimore, ca. 1810. Mahogany, maple, and
painted decoration with pine. H. 29⅝",
W. 36", D. 18¼" (Courtesy, Winterthur
Museum. Museum Purchase with partial
funds provided by an anonymous donor and
Mr. and Mrs. John R. Donnell.)

The philosophical belief that variety was essential for feeding the imagination was concretely realized by Fancy artisans who produced unexpected new forms with distinct decorations. A table (fig. 102) made about 1810 merges lively shaping, brilliant coloring, and a skillfully executed central Fancy landscape panel. While the underlying serpentine form and turret corners are usually associated with urban New England, some of the ornament suggests the Finlays' work in Baltimore, and the gilt border of delicate leaves relates to the Waln set from Philadelphia.[36]

Many Fancy artisans found themselves in a feverish hunt for new designs to feed the public demand for variety, including Hugh Finlay, who in 1810 visited England and possibly France. There he acquired a significant parcel of designs for the shop, advertising in December 1810 the availability of a "HANDSOME COLLECTION OF ENGRAVINGS, Many of them in colours," as well as "a number of drawings, from furniture in the first houses in Paris and London, which enable them to make the most approved articles in their line."[37] The diversity of furniture produced by the Finlays in the 1810s suggests they had comfortably incorporated these patterns derived from Europe into their ever-expanding repertory of Fancy furniture.

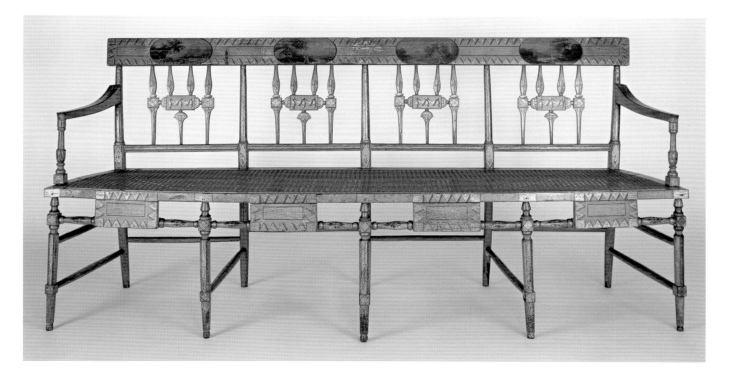

Smaller shops run by men like Thomas Renshaw and John Barnhart also produced highly fashionable Fancy furniture (fig. 103). Thomas S. Renshaw and Co. originally opened its doors in Washington, D.C. during the summer of 1801, when it advertised for sale "FANCY AND COMMON CHAIRS of the neatest workmanship and at the most reduced prices." In October Renshaw dropped "& Company" from his ad and apprised the public that he would continue the business on his own.[38] Apparently disappointed with his reception in Washington, he soon resettled in Baltimore,

FIGURE 104   Settee, attributed to Thomas Renshaw and John Barnhart or John and Hugh Finlay, Baltimore, 1805–1820. Maple, walnut, poplar, and painted decoration. H. 35½", W. 73½", D. 22". (Courtesy, Maryland Historical Society, Baltimore, Maryland.)

where he advertised his skills as a Fancy chair maker. Barnhart, in contrast, by 1799 had begun his Baltimore career as a sign and herald painter, occasionally advertising his services. Whether the two formally went into business is unclear, but their collaboration is further documented by a Fancy settee signed boldly on the rear rail, "Thos. Renshaw No. 32 S. Gay St. Balto." and "John Barnhart Ornamenter," and is suggested by another

FIGURE 105   Samuel Gragg, side chair, Boston, ca. 1808. Oak, beech, and painted decoration. H. 35½", W. 18", D. 19". (Courtesy, Fine Arts Museums of San Francisco. Museum purchase, gift of Martha and William Steen, 1986.56.4.) This example has carved goat feet.

AMERICAN FANCY

brilliant red example (fig. 104). Presumably, the imaginary scenes painted on the crest represent Barnhart's work. Although charming, they lack the sophistication of the work by Francis Guy.[39]

Simultaneously in New England remarkable things were taking place in the development of Fancy furniture. The novel bentwood furniture designs of Samuel Gragg (1772–ca. 1855) of Boston reflect the influence of Fancy both in form and decoration (fig. 105). Gragg patented the design for an "Elastic Chair" in 1808 (fig. 106). His innovation expanded the technology of steam-bending wood to create forms that in the eyes of most early nineteenth-century viewers probably seemed technologically impossible.

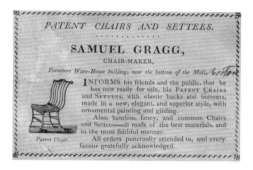

FIGURE 106 "Patent Chairs and Settees, Samuel Gragg, Chair-Maker," trade card, Boston, ca. 1808. (Courtesy, Madison Memorabilia Collection, James Madison University Library, Harrisonburg, Virginia; photo, Winterthur Museum.)

The shape and decoration of Gragg's chairs resonated with the spirit of Fancy. In the days before flexible materials, "elastic" was a term used principally in scientific circles to describe the resiliency of coils or springs, long before they were used for upholstery in seating furniture. Nobody before Gragg had described a piece of furniture in quite that way, and though Gragg was directly referring to the flexibility of the steam-bent wood when he used "elastic," he also echoed the period understanding that the word could suggest a "buoyant" human temperament. In other words, Gragg's choice of the term might have described the response of the user while sitting in the elastic chair, no less than the character of the chair itself. In his own words, the chair was "very comfortable and agreeable to the person sitting on it."[40]

Gragg's Fancy Elastic chairs and settees were adorned with high quality ornamental painting, including delicately painted peacock feathers

FIGURE 107 Detail of peacock feather on the side chair illustrated in fig. 109.

FIGURE 108 Samuel Gragg, armchair, Boston, 1808–1812. Ash, hickory, and painted decoration. H. 34", W. 21", D. 25". (Collection of Mrs. George M. Kaufman.) This chair is branded "S. GRAGG / BOSTON" beneath the front seat rail and "PATENT" beneath the rear seat rail.

FIGURE 109 Samuel Gragg, side chair, Boston, 1808–1812. Birch, white oak, beech, and painted decoration. H. 34⅜", W. 18⅛", D. 25⅜". (Courtesy, Winterthur Museum.) This chair is branded "S. GRAGG / BOSTON. / PATENT" beneath the seat.

(fig. 107) on a ground of polished japanning—usually colored white or cream. His first Elastic chairs employed a row of bentwood elements that formed the back and continued downward to fashion the seat. His choice of goat legs to support the chair was no less imaginative than his bentwood techniques (fig. 108). For literate buyers, Gragg's allusion to the goat functioned as a potent symbol from classical mythology, often associated with the indulgent behavior of the ancients. Dionysus, god of wine, would travel undetected in the guise of a goat, and his lusty companions, the mythical Satyrs, jaunted about on goat legs. Caprice, one of the emotions most often associated with fancy and imagination, derived its name from the Italian word *capriccio*—translated as "the skip or frisk of a goat"—but also signifying "a prank, a trick, or a caper."

In his fully developed Elastic chairs, Gragg abandoned the goat legs for bentwood stiles that continued all the way to the floor, a remarkable craft accomplishment that only increased their visual and functional elasticity (fig. 109). His inspired accomplishment set in motion the development of later chair-making techniques well suited to mass production. Shaped seats would be articulated in the contoured rocking chairs of the 1820s and 1830s, in the popular bentwood chairs of the Victorian period, and, eventually, in the molded plywood and plastic seating of the twentieth century.[41] For early nineteenth-century Americans, however, Gragg's chairs

AMERICAN FANCY

provided an imaginative new approach to furniture production and a pleasing experience for body and mind.

Fashionable Fancy furniture was enlivened in many other ways as well. Transparent painting on glass—today sometimes called "églomisé"—was extremely popular for ornamenting Fancy furniture and played a significant role in heightening emotional responses, particularly on looking glasses and shelf or wall clocks. Artists first drew the design directly on the glass, sometimes with pen and ink, and then highlighted the details with gold leaf or paint. The glistening scene was viewed from the front, through the glass.[42] Sometimes the artist turned to published sources for inspiration, particularly for classical designs, but frequently makers called upon their own imaginations to create original whimsical scenes.

Starting in the 1780s, the popularity of mahogany looking glasses gave way to more dramatic Fancy examples with transparent painting and gilt

FIGURE 110   Pier glass, New York, 1790–1815. White pine, looking-glass plate, glass, and painted, gessoed, and gilt decoration. H. 62", W. 28⅝", D. 9". (Collection of Mrs. George M. Kaufman.)

moldings (fig. 110). Often crafted in pairs, Fancy looking glasses had their greatest impact when placed between windows in grand architectural spaces. They were particularly stunning when illuminated for an evening entertainment, as they were in a Charleston, South Carolina, ballroom in 1785. The room, ornamented with "festoons of myrtle and gold leaf" and a host of candles "luxuriantly reflecting the gay scene in rich mirrors, gave an air of enchantment to the whole, and carried imagination to the paradise of Mahomet."[43]

Aaron Willard, Jr., and his brother-in-law, Spencer Nolen, were partners in an ornamental painting business in Boston between 1805 and 1809. Their shop undoubtedly benefited from the fact that Willard's namesake father

FIGURE 111   Simon Willard, wall clock, New England, 1813–1815. Mahogany, cedar, metal, glass, and painted and gilt decoration. H. 37½", W. 10", D. 4⅛". (Courtesy, Winterthur Museum.) Painted on the glass is: "Willard's Patent."

FIGURE 112   Aaron Willard, shelf clock, Massachusetts, ca. 1815. Wood, glass, painted and gilt decoration, brass, and metal works. H. 35", W. 13½", D. 6½". (Courtesy, Milwaukee Art Museum. Gift of the estate of Louis Uihlein Snell, M1994.239.)

and his brother, Simon, ran the most prolific clockmaking manufactory in America. The Willards designed and produced distinctively shaped and decorated clocks that were shipped all over America. Many of the clocks relied heavily upon gilding and transparent painting (figs. 111 and 112). A "Patent Timepiece" manufactured by Simon in Roxbury had transparent painting depicting an eagle and bore the clear signature of the decorators "Willard and Nolen," in which Simon's nephew was a partner (fig. 113).[44]

The Willard brothers hired other artisans to do ornamental work, among them John Rito Penniman. Penniman learned his trade in Massachusetts, apprenticed in his teens to a British immigrant artist. In 1803, at age twenty-one, he established a studio on Towne Street, Roxbury, conveniently located near Simon Willard's shop. The carver and gilder John Doggett, who specialized in ornamenting picture frames and looking glasses, lived nearby. Penniman maintained an ongoing relationship with both artisans—painting clock faces and ornamental panels for Willard's clocks, as well as painting shop signs and looking-glass panels for Dog-

FIGURE 113 Simon Willard, wall clock, Roxbury, Massachusetts, 1805–1810. White pine, mahogany, brass, glass, and painted and gilt decoration. H. 41½", W. 10⅜", D. 3¾". (Courtesy, Winterthur Museum.) Painted on the glass is: "Willard's Patent." The transparent painting on glass is signed: "Willard and Nolen, Boston." Aaron Willard, Jr., and Spencer Nolen were ornamental painters in Boston from 1805 to 1809.

FIGURE 114 "J. R. Penniman, Painter," trade card, Boston, ca. 1822. (Courtesy, Winterthur Library: Joseph Downs Collection of Manuscripts and Printed Ephemera.)

gett. Although aspiring to earn a livelihood in portraiture and the fine arts, Penniman relied principally upon ornamental work, and as late as 1822 his trade card (fig. 114) documented that he was still engaged in activities such as painting signs and Masonic regalia, or drawing and designing diplomas, only a few of the skills he called the "ten thousand other etceteras of Ornamental Painting" in his biography.[45]

FIGURE 115 William Frederick Pinchbeck, painted looking-glass panel, Boston or New York City, 1803. Glass and painted and gilt decoration. H. 7½", W. 18⅜". (Courtesy, Elbert H. Parsons, Jr.) The panel illustrates a pastoral landscape flanked by figures of Hope and Plenty.

Of the ornamental painters who contributed to the production of Fancy furniture in this early period, few appear more talented than the enigmatic William Frederick Pinchbeck. This painter's appearance in city directories for New York between 1795 and 1809 and Boston between 1806 and 1809 suggested that he supported workshops in both locations. Known to have been a carver and sign painter, Pinchbeck revealed his skills as an artist in an 1803 looking-glass panel ornamented with a pastoral scene and figures of Hope and Plenty (fig. 115). Whereas the panel offers a tantalizing glimpse of an artist otherwise unknown to students of the decorative arts, it provides only a hint of Pinchbeck's other talents in the realm of imagination, including his 1805 Boston publication, *The Expositor: or Many Mysteries Unravelled,* the first book on magic printed in America.[46]

A growing number of furnishings and architectural interiors began to be decorated with "Fancy painting" as well as ornamental painting. Fancy painting was commonly understood to be "the art of imitating the grain of various fancy woods and marbles."[47] Such decoration was not new to households in the late eighteenth century, and though early examples had sometimes been rather wild, as on the chimney breast from the Pitkin

FIGURE 116 Chimney breast, from Pitkin House, East Hartford, Connecticut, ca. 1760. Pine and painted decoration. H. 90", W. 110". (Courtesy, Wadsworth Atheneum, Hartford. Gift of Mrs. William B. Goodwin, 1958.396–.397.)

House (fig. 116), they were also the exception rather than the rule. When this type of decoration began its ascent again in the 1780s, after half a century in eclipse, it assumed a more specific character and, by the 1790s, the name "Fancy painting." An early reference to Fancy painting appeared in an advertisement for William Boyle and Company of Baltimore, placed on May 12, 1792, when Boyle advised the public of his ability to carry out

"House, Ship, Sign, Carpet and Fancy painting."[48] House painters who imitated wood and marble began to be known as Fancy painters. Their products were so commonplace that their occupation was sometimes described specifically as "marblers" or "grainers" who worked at "marbling" and "graining."[49]

Fancy painting was inspired by "scarce woods" and marbles that possessed vibrant grain and brilliant colors and, in synch with the earlier aesthetic theorizing of Addison, provided the variety and the novelty that pleased the eye.[50] In America, finely grained mahogany from the West Indies, South America, or Africa was the most popular wood among fashionable furniture makers and their patrons. Its allure enticed painters to copy the rich grain and reflective surfaces. Mahogany was the mainstay of Fancy painting between 1790 and 1810, but other woods were occasionally emulated, including satinwood and flame birch, which added to the richness of surface decor. Marble, white or gray with veining in black, was also immensely popular, particularly for baseboards in houses and on the tops of sideboard tables in dining rooms. An extremely bold "marbled-topped" pier table (fig. 117) made by the Finlay shop for the wealthy Baltimore merchant Alexander Brown is a notable example.

FIGURE 117   Pier table, attributed to John and Hugh Finlay, Baltimore, ca. 1815. Poplar, other woods, and painted decoration. H. 34¼", W. 38", D. 18⅝". (Courtesy, Maryland Historical Society, Baltimore, Maryland.) The top of this table emulates marble.

Real woods and marbles were available to affluent consumers, but to explain Fancy painting in mere economic terms tells only part of the story. The inaccessibility of beautifully grained wood and marble—with strong reflective qualities, contrasting textures, and rich color—created a dilemma even for the wealthy who wished to show their awareness of taste and their appreciation of the concepts of Fancy. In the absence of the real thing, Fancy painting was a solution and even an improvement. A writer of the mid-nineteenth century, when Fancy painting still was popular, declared, "It is . . . doubtful whether it would be desirable to select many of the fancy woods for house decoration, in preference to the imitations which are produced by modern artists . . . even if they could be obtained at the same cost."[51] Real woods simply could not provide the same variety or visual impact as painted woods.

At first Fancy painting was largely confined to architectural woodwork, especially in public areas of the home: the central passage, the parlor, and the dining room. As one moved into secondary areas—downstairs bed-chambers, for example, or into the upper levels—Fancy painting was less evident, usually confined to doors or to baseboards. As a rule, service areas—kitchens, cellars, and closets—were simply painted or left unfinished. Fancy painting initially was used sparingly on furniture, principally on tabletops to suggest marble, and on doors to suggest mahogany. After 1810 it began to appear on case furniture and, like the interior woodwork to which it was applied, was usually relatively realistic in appearance. Fancy painters created deceptive yet witty allusions to real stone or wood, which in turn elicited delight. Even today, a Fancy chest of drawers made in Liv-

FIGURE 118   E. Morse, chest of drawers, Livermore, Maine, 1814. Pine, brass, and painted decoration. H. 34¾", W. 36⅝", D. 17⅝". (From the Collections of Henry Ford Museum & Greenfield Village.) The chest is signed in pencil: "Made by E. Morse / Livermore / June 7th 1814."

ermore, Maine, in 1814, is effective in its ability to fool the eye (fig. 118). Simulated inlays and veneers combine to suggest a more expensive piece. Seen from across the room, the surface looks like mahogany; even at three or four paces, it appears woodlike. Only upon touching the surface can one relish the intentions of the maker. The game sometimes went one step further when, on chests such as this, the top drawers are false, as are the keyholes. A tug on the drawer pulls elicits no response; the interior space is accessible only by lifting the top, which is hinged on the reverse.

Fancy painting presented a challenge to the talents of painters, and ingenious artisans would go to great lengths to achieve the proper effect. Every intricacy of real wood—color, figure, rays, burls, and "flames"—was executed to add to the overall appearance. As in the Maine chest, some artisans simulated the details of inlay and veneer, carefully reproducing the seams and the mitred corners where real veneer would have been joined.

Such deliberate attempts to deceive the viewer were considered highly admirable. One early nineteenth-century handbook lauded painters who made the painstaking effort to "deceive us into a belief that we look upon marble, mahogany, stone, etc."[52] A midcentury publication, hailing the advancements made in painting techniques, noted that it was "no longer necessary to incur an enormous cost in obtaining substances which may be so well imitated as to evade the detection of an experienced eye."[53]

Imitative Fancy painting reflected the fashionable insistence upon a balance of reason and fancy. Its effect depended as much on understanding as emotion, and to fully appreciate it required both. One first had to decide whether the wood was real or painted. Only after discovering the imitation, could the viewer delight in the character of the material and the skill of the ingenious artisan who had manipulated it—who had pushed the limits of fancy to achieve its effects.

The goal of Fancy painters increasingly was to create surfaces that were novel and whimsical. D. R. Hay, a well-known Scottish painter who wrote a series of manuals on Fancy painting in the second quarter of the nineteenth century, cautioned that the craft should be executed "not with a view of having the imitation mistaken for the original, but rather to create an allusion to it."[54] This may have been the goal that Thomas Jefferson had in mind when he hired Richard Barry, an artisan from Hagerstown, Maryland, to paint the interior of Monticello, his mountaintop home in central Virginia (fig. 119). Jefferson noted in his memorandum book of expenses on March 28, 1805, that "Richd. Barry, painter arrives & begins work @ 30D. pr. month." The artisan visited many times over the next three years, and Jefferson paid him nearly 600 dollars for his services.[55]

Barry's understated doors express a guarded admiration of imagination—and would appear to reflect Jefferson's outlook in the matter. Jefferson generally reserved imagination for practical household inventions—such as the double doors that opened simultaneously to his parlor when only one was pushed, or his so-called whirligig chair, with a seat that swiveled for maximum convenience.[56] He was always cautiously aware of, and respected, the distinctions between imagination and reason and organized his life accordingly. Each book in his library was cataloged according to the mental faculty needed to comprehend the contents: books of philosophy, law, and science he grouped under "Reason"; history, under "Memory"; and works on the arts, under "Imagination."[57] Like so many in his generation, Jefferson thought it acceptable to express imagination in one's personal environment, but he was wary of doing so publicly, admitting of his architectural designs that "fancy I can indulge in my own case," but insisting that "in a public work I feel bound to follow [classical] authority strictly."[58] Painted doors were one way to emphasize the cautious acceptance of emotion in a domestic context, and the entry at Monticello had seven doors. Even if Jefferson often kept them discreetly closed, their lively surfaces teased all who encountered them, suggesting that ingenious things transpired behind them.[59]

FIGURE 119 Door, decoration attributed to Richard Barry, entrance hall at Monticello, Albemarle County, Virginia, 1805– 1807. Wood and painted decoration. H. 77", W. 43". (Courtesy, Thomas Jefferson Foundation, Charlottesville, Virginia; photo, courtesy Frank S. Welsh, ©1977 Thomas Crane.)

FIGURE 120   Mouse, baseboard detail,
from Trower House, Northampton County,
Virginia, now installed in Sylvan Scene,
Northampton County, Virginia, ca. 1808.
Pine and painted decoration. H. 4". (Cour-
tesy, Charles W. Dickinson and Claiborne
M. Dickinson; photo, Gavin Ashworth.)

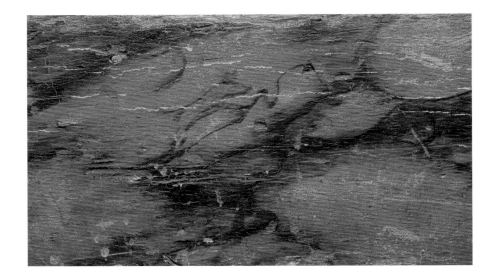

FIGURE 121   Face, baseboard detail,
from Trower House, Northampton County,
Virginia, now installed in Sylvan Scene,
Northampton County, Virginia, ca. 1808.
Pine and painted decoration. H. 4". (Cour-
tesy, Charles W. Dickinson and Claiborne
M. Dickinson; photo, Gavin Ashworth.)

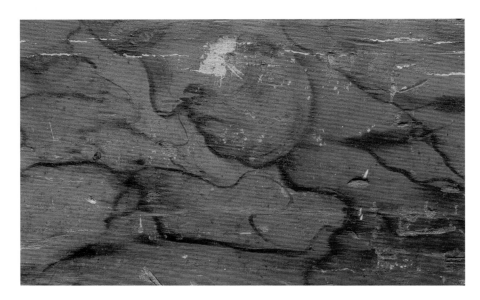

FIGURE 122   Bird, baseboard detail,
from Trower House, Northampton County,
Virginia, now installed in Sylvan Scene,
Northampton County, Virginia, ca. 1808.
Pine and painted decoration. H. 4". (Cour-
tesy, Charles W. Dickinson and Claiborne
M. Dickinson; photo, Gavin Ashworth.)

Among the most intriguing expressions of American Fancy painting are the architectural baseboards from the Trower House, built on Virginia's Eastern Shore in the early nineteenth century (figs. 120–124). At first they look like any other marbled surface. Yet, on closer examination, the dark veins unexpectedly twist and turn and converge to create images hidden within a maze of pattern. Here a mouse, there a peafowl, across the room a rabbit and a grotesque face emerge from the imitation marble.[60] Find-

FIGURE 123   Cat, baseboard detail, from Trower House, Northampton County, Virginia, now installed in Sylvan Scene, Northampton County, Virginia, ca. 1808. Pine and painted decoration. H. 4". (Courtesy, Charles W. Dickinson and Claiborne M. Dickinson; photo, Gavin Ashworth.)

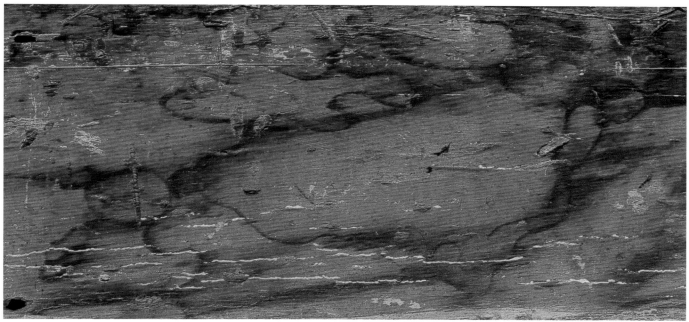

ing images hidden within random veins of marbling was a pleasant surprise and suggested there may be more than met the eye. One recalls Joseph Addison's happy observation of the "accidental landscapes of trees, clouds, and cities that are sometimes found in the veins of marble"[61] and remembers his insight "Things would make but a poor appearance to the eye if we saw them only in their proper figures."[62] American Fancy

FIGURE 124   Rabbit, baseboard detail, from Trower House, Northampton County, Virginia, now installed in Sylvan Scene, Northampton County, Virginia, ca. 1808. Pine and painted decoration. H. 4". (Courtesy, Charles W. Dickinson and Claiborne M. Dickinson; photo, Gavin Ashworth.)

Three EARLY FANCY FURNISHINGS   75

painters breathed new life into conventional subjects, pushing them into imaginative new realms and creating a timeless dialogue between the object, the maker, and the viewer.

Just as Fancy furniture, ornamental painting, and Fancy painting allowed a high degree of creative interaction on the part of makers and patrons alike, other categories of Fancy goods further enriched the imaginative experience. A new category of "Fancy ceramics" described a broad array of ornamented pottery available to complement furniture in the home and to facilitate the process of entertaining and dining. As early as 1772, New York ceramic dealers Davis and Minnit had imported "all kinds of earthenwares, with some curious fancy wares,"[63] but only in the 1790s did advertisements for Fancy ceramics appear with some frequency, such as the ad for the "greatest variety of most useful, elegant and fancy articles" for sale in 1793 at the Staffordshire and Glass warehouse on Bedon's Alley in Charleston, South Carolina,[64] or the "10 casks of elegant fancy articles" subsequently advertised in 1808 by John and Thomas Vowell of Alexandria, Virginia.[65]

Many of these new ceramic pieces were based upon classical prototypes, sometimes profusely decorated and vibrantly colored to reflect current perceptions of the tastes of the ancients. Figures of mythological subjects were a favorite (figs. 125 and 126). While the earliest examples had been modeled in reserved classical poses and dressed in understated colors, later versions depicted their subjects engaged in a flurry of activity,

FIGURE 125 *Jupiter,* England, ca. 1815. Earthenware and polychrome decoration. H. 15⅞", W. 5", D. 5". (Private collection.)

FIGURE 126 *Diana,* England, 1790–1800. Earthenware, polychrome decoration, and copper wire. H. 11⅜", W. 5⁹⁄₁₆", D. 5". (Private collection.)

wearing garish, flowing robes, and surrounded by naturalistic detail. Allegorical figures, often produced in matching pairs or sets, such as "Hope" and "Plenty," or the "Four Seasons," were also popular. Displayed in cupboards or on shelves and tabletops, these colorful ornaments provided consumers unprecedented options to enrich their domestic environment. When tastes permitted a wider range of expression, manufacturers provided further choices such as whimsical figures of animals (figs. 127 and 128).[66]

FIGURE 127   Goat, England, 1780–1820. Earthenware. H. 3". (Courtesy, Leo Kaplan Ltd., New York, New York.)

FIGURE 128   Horse, England, 1780–1820. Earthenware. H. 5". (Courtesy, Leo Kaplan Ltd., New York, New York.)

At first most of these Fancy wares came from England, where potters offered "plain" wares as well as "Fancy" variations.[67] Although the particular ware was rarely specified, advertising terms such as "flowered" indicated that producers and consumers alike found naturalistic ornamentation appealing and sometimes interpreted it rather capriciously. New manufacturing techniques also made it possible to offer the public an increasing variety of eye-catching decoration created through the application of bold, color-contrasted glazes and slip. Josiah Wedgwood in the 1760s and 1770s experimented with "engine-turning" machines that used revolving blades governed by cams to cut away the surface of ceramics in predictable geometric patterns. This process worked so precisely that by the 1780s it was possible to create intricately detailed geometric designs (figs. 129 and 130).

FIGURE 129   Mug, England, ca. 1795. Earthenware. H. 5¹⁵⁄₁₆". (Rickard Collection; photo, Gavin Ashworth.)

FIGURE 130   Mug, England, ca. 1800. Earthenware. H. 3½". (Rickard Collection.)

FIGURE 131 Jug, England, ca. 1780.
Earthenware. H. 5⅝". (Rickard Collection;
photo, Gavin Ashworth.)

FIGURE 132 Bowl, England, ca. 1790.
Earthenware. Diam. 6". (Rickard Collection.)

By periodically changing the cams of the machines and the colors of the clays, it was possible to offer the public an endless array of new designs.

Among the most popular ceramic decorations were those that, as in the realm of Fancy painting, alluded to naturally stunning materials, such as the "marbled" surfaces that appeared on numerous pieces from the 1780s onward. Imported into America by 1781, marbled decoration was frequently "combed" to increase its visual liveliness.[68] By the 1790s some designers abandoned any pretense of copying the original material, sacrificing visual fidelity for ornamental character and, more importantly, magnifying the visual effects and maximizing the potential for an emotional response by the viewer (figs. 131 and 132).

A similar trend toward stylization and vibrant design also was expressed in the designs chosen for wallpaper, a taste that accelerated rapidly during the 1790s. Preferences can be discerned in advertisements for domestic wallpapers, such as those manufactured by the Boston firm of Prentiss and May and marketed in New York under the banner "AMERICAN MANUFACTURED PAPER HANGINGS." "The figures are chosen from the newest European patterns, and are so various, both for rooms and entries, that the tastes and fancies of different purchasers may be easily suited," the vendor boasted. Special orders could be taken for original creations: "Should any one wish for a parcel from original or fancy patterns, by giving notice to Mr. Greenleaf they could be supplied in a short time."[69]

AMERICAN FANCY

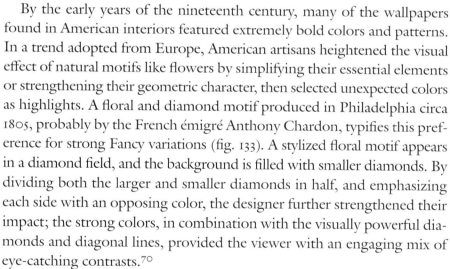

By the early years of the nineteenth century, many of the wallpapers
found in American interiors featured extremely bold colors and patterns.
In a trend adopted from Europe, American artisans heightened the visual
effect of natural motifs like flowers by simplifying their essential elements
or strengthening their geometric character, then selected unexpected colors
as highlights. A floral and diamond motif produced in Philadelphia circa
1805, probably by the French émigré Anthony Chardon, typifies this preference for strong Fancy variations (fig. 133). A stylized floral motif appears
in a diamond field, and the background is filled with smaller diamonds. By
dividing both the larger and smaller diamonds in half, and emphasizing
each side with an opposing color, the designer further strengthened their
impact; the strong colors, in combination with the visually powerful diamonds and diagonal lines, provided the viewer with an engaging mix of
eye-catching contrasts.[70]

The same motif appeared in ceramic pieces as well, such as a pepper pot
and matching mustard pot (fig. 134). These two pieces feature ornament
created by first layering and folding different colored clays to produce a
strip resembling marbled agate; slicing and arranging the strip in a narrow band of diamonds; and then laying the band in a shallow recess
around the waist of each piece.[71] The similarity between these two ceramic pieces and the wallpaper, both in color and motif, illustrates that designs
often crossed back and forth between different media.

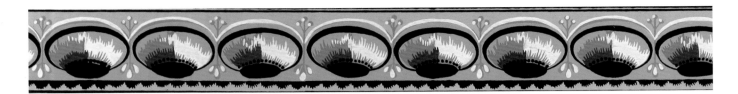

A Fancy wallpaper border made in America around 1810 reflects a novel interpretation of a classical "egg-and-dart" architectural molding (fig. 135). In ancient times, carvers chiseled such elements in durable white marble. In this vibrant American interpretation on paper, the artisan altered the ancient prototype, removed the intricate classical detail, simplified the geometry, and articulated the design with vivid colors. About 1810, when the border was applied to the walls of a fashionable new house in Milton, New York, it not only provided a spirited accent to the recently finished interior, but also suggested some of the animated designs yet in store for the years ahead.

In short, between 1790 and 1815 a growing legion of Americans enthusiastically embraced the Fancy style as a lively alternative to the understated taste of the past. Reserved classical designs may have been well suited for churches and state buildings, yet most Americans preferred to enliven their personal surroundings with goods and modes of decoration that encouraged a different type of emotional involvement—options that better expressed their prospects for the future and their rising station in life.

A balance of classical taste and the more liberating Fancy style remained a desirable model for emulation when Fancy finally moved beyond the confines of the wealthy and well educated, although the latter were a continual force in dictating aesthetic matters. Fancy steadily came to fruition as individuals of moderate means acquired the ability to respond to its pleasures. This started slowly after 1815, gained momentum in the 1820s, and by the mid-1830s culminated in an expression that catapulted Fancy into a realm of total jubilation.

4 The Kaleidoscope

*The kaleidoscope . . . may be ranked among
the most happy inventions that science ever presented.*

Marc Auguste Pictet to Sir David Brewster, 1818

In 1814 Scottish physicist Sir David Brewster (1781–1868) began a series of experiments in the polarization of light.[1] In the course of his investigation, he grouped together several long mirrors in a hollow cylinder and put a light source at one end. When he peered in, he discovered that the device had the amazing capacity to create visual delight. Brewster called his invention the "kaleidoscope"—Greek for "beautiful image viewer."[2] Although he was the first to recognize the scientific, technological, and artistic implications of his invention, which he perfected by 1816, he did not envision its immediate popularity nor its potential to transform popular taste during the next two decades.[3]

The kaleidoscope and Fancy quickly proved to be ideal companions, catalyzing the style after 1816 by directly inspiring novel designs and expanding the boundaries of imaginative expression. The device demonstrated beyond all doubt that objects could be transformed into something they were not while it dramatically extended notions of beauty into unprecedented realms. In the kaleidoscope, the imagination found the perfect tool to "fancy to itself things more great, strange, beautiful than the eye ever saw."[4] Like magic, bits of broken glass were instantly transformed into stars, glittering snowflakes, and shimmering diamonds.

With its ability to turn the ordinary into the extraordinary, the kaleidoscope was an instant success. Before Brewster could patent his invention in 1817, competitors had pirated his design and were producing kaleidoscopes commercially. Two hundred thousand of the new gadgets sold in Paris and London alone during a single three-month period. Within several years they were found "even in the most obscure and retired villages of Switzerland."[5]

Early British kaleidoscopes looked more like telescopes than toys. One of the initial models had a cone-shaped body with adjustable mirrors (figs. 136 and 137), but cylindrical forms proved to be the most popular (figs. 138 and 139).[6] These were constructed of solid brass or of mahogany with brass mounts. Some had stands to facilitate viewing; others were accompanied by a mahogany storage box that also held the interchangeable lenses. Each lens was hollow in the center and filled with materials—bits of visually stun-

FIGURE 136   Sir David Brewster, designer, kaleidoscope, R. B. Bate, London, 1818–1820. Brass, steel, and glass. H. 11¹³⁄₁₆". (Courtesy, Science Museum, Science and Society Picture Library, London.)

FIGURE 137   *90°-90°-90°-90° Kaleidoscope,* illustrated in figs. 18–20 in Sir David Brewster's *A Treatise on the Kaleidoscope,* London, 1819. (Courtesy, The Winterthur Library: Printed Book and Periodical Collection.)

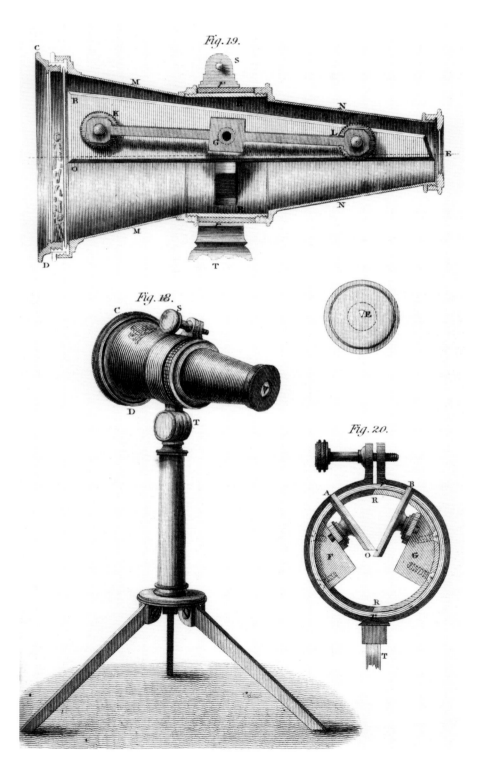

ning colored glass in a variety of shapes, tiny metal stars, buttons, and the like—that moved freely when turned. "The pictures thus presented to the eye are beyond all description splendid and beautiful," observed Brewster.[7]

Americans were quickly caught up in the kaleidoscope craze. In the summer of 1818, instruments shipped from abroad cost two dollars each. *The Idiot,* a Boston periodical devoted to humor and satire, helped to document the introduction of the kaleidoscope. The September 12, 1818, issue contained a tongue-in-cheek article about an immigrant who offered Bostonians passing on the streets a peek into his kaleidoscope, presumably for a fee. As an enticement, he lauded the kaleidoscope's capacity to excite the mind, an experience more wonderful, even, than sighting a sea serpent off the Massachusetts coast (fig. 140), an oblique reference to a recent hoax perpetrated by the paper:

> GENTLEMENS, will you please to take a peep into mine KALEIDO-SCOPE, and tell us what you see there! . . . Will you just take a Kaleidoscupean peep. . . . Gad it will make a Flea look like a Buffaloe! Wont you, sir, take a peep, and tell us what you see there! . . . Ah, the wonderful powers of mine Kaleidoscope! Would you, sir, not like to take a peep, and tell us what you see there! . . . You will acknowledge mine Kaleidoscope a much greater curiosity in transforming and magnifying a HORSE MACKEREL into a Monstrous SEA SERPENT![8]

Apparently the invention was still as scarce as it was novel, for on October 31, barely a month later, *The Idiot* printed a preposterous letter to the editor, in which a "true blue Bostonian, and as brim-full of notions, as any of my neighbors," proposed constructing a huge kaleidoscope made of twelve barrels "sufficiently large, to admit the application of the eyes of a dozen spectators at once . . . [to] view . . . with as much ease, the wonderful powers of the Kaleidoscope, in transforming and throwing its contents into a thousand different shapes." The paper continued, "Let the bulky instrument be placed on a suitable carriage drawn by four lusty horses—permit it to be viewed *gratis* by people of all classes."[9]

This absurd recommendation soon became pointless as American versions of the kaleidoscope in tinware or "pasteboard" appeared in the marketplace and prices plummeted.[10] In 1822, only five years after Brewster had patented his invention, a British traveler in America was surprised to find that the kaleidoscope was fabricated "in quantities so great" that it was given "as a plaything to children." One artist even informed the visitor that his ingenious assistant soon hoped to take out a patent for an improvement on its design.[11]

The kaleidoscope elicited high praise for its ability to inspire "cheerfulness" and "gaiety." "It afforded delight to the poor as well as the rich; to the old as well as the young," rhapsodized one owner in a letter to the inventor. The kaleidoscope awakened the senses in a way that perceptions of the visible world rarely did, leading the mind into a fleeting succession of strange and colorful experiences. When looking into the device with one eye and closing the other, viewers entered a realm of pure fancy—a realm of autonomous and transient optical delight. Even the conservative and sometimes stuffy members of the Royal Society of Edinburgh were "much struck with the beauty of [the kaleidoscope's] effects."[12] One could sit for hours on end gazing into its depths. This popular passion, satirized in a British print of 1818 (fig. 141), was called "Caleidoscope-mania." The craze spread like wildfire.[13]

In 1819 Brewster published *A Treatise on the Kaleidoscope,* which fully described the characteristics of his invention and outlined its useful applica-

FIGURE 141   S. W. Fores, *Caleidoscope-mania or, the Natives Astonished,* London, 1818. Hand-colored engraving. 14⅜" x 9⅝". (Courtesy, Library of Congress.)

AMERICAN FANCY

tions. Brewster's treatise, which was nearly as important to the evolution of Fancy as the kaleidoscope itself, included a chapter with specific instructions for employing the device "in the numerous branches of the useful and ornamental arts."[14] Brewster's approach to design and aesthetics reflected his scientific legacy of observation and experimentation. In its emphasis on a geometric conception of beauty, his work might be viewed as one of the few sustained treatises on Fancy in the nineteenth century. If Brewster stressed the predictable geometric patterns by which any view was replicated, he also acknowledged the emotional responses of the spectators to the arbitrary and engaging images. In a discussion reminiscent of one offered a century earlier by Joseph Addison, Brewster noted that the term "kaleidoscope" was derived from the Greek words for "beautiful," "form," and "to see" and argued that society's ideas of beauty often relied upon predictable form, symmetry, and proportion. By creating abstract patterns that were symmetrical and luminous, the kaleidoscope, though capable of endless variation, reduced beauty to essential components that appealed to the eye and mind alike.[15]

A kaleidoscopic view, significantly enough, was not an end in itself but rather an important source of design and a vehicle to inspire the Fancy. "Heaven knows how often men cudgel their brains for ideas without success—Let them cudgel them no longer, but turn their Kaleidoscope, and ideas will start up like mushrooms," advised a newspaper article in 1819.[16] A twist of the hand or a flick of the wrist changed the image at will, as a mere handful of colored glass was transformed into a spectacular explosion of patterns with infinite variation. Each new configuration served to nurture the imagination, which could draw on an inexhaustible storehouse of images.[17]

The extent to which the kaleidoscopic experience served as a source for inspiration and creativity is revealed by an article that appeared in 1819 in the *Boston Kaleidoscope and Literary Rambler* which suggested that words be added to the kaleidoscope's colored glass to spark the viewer's fancy (fig. 142). The writer of the article advocated a "lovers' kaleidoscope" to encourage the romantic imagination:

> The Lovers' Kaleidoscope must have some words introduced that may easily fall into rhyme, such as "heart and dart, and eyes and sighs . . . and ever and never;" with the addition of these words they may make love without speaking, and in the largest company, by simply peeping into their Kaleidoscopes. If absent, they may make such an arrangement as was done by two lovers of old, who agreed at a particular hour to fix their eyes upon the moon—a mode which the moon herself might, from her known tendency to change, often disappoint, by refusing to shine at the stated hour; but by the use of the Lovers' Kaleidoscope, such a disappointment could not occur. They might resolve each to use it at a certain hour, give it the rotary motion, and peep into it just as they were about to pop into bed—"what dreams might come"![18]

FIGURE 142   Cover, *Boston Kaleidoscope and Literary Rambler,* Boston, January 9, 1819. (Courtesy, American Antiquarian Society.)

Kaleidoscopes were not only significant for their ability "to start up ideas," they also had practical applications, according to proponents. An 1818 Boston newspaper observed, "So great and wonderful are the powers ascribed to the Kaleidoscope, that they are becoming more and more in use," then gave a humorous example:

> A poor man who is so unfortunate as to be the husband of a careless wife, learning that the Kaleidoscope would place every thing in beautiful order, made a purchase of one a few days since in this town, that he might be enabled (as he observed) once to see his household furniture properly arranged![19]

For American artisans at home and in the workshop, the kaleidoscope became a seemingly endless source of designs for furnishings inspired by its array of colors and predictable geometric patterning. With its polished mirrors and a light source at the end—but nothing more to distract the eye—a kaleidoscope gave viewers the sensation of being lowered into the midst of a prism. Brewster did not exaggerate when he claimed, "It will create, in a single hour, what a thousand artists could not invent in the course of a year."[20] He calculated that from twenty-four pieces of glass, the kaleidoscope would produce some 1,391,724,288,887,252,999,425,128,493,402,200 different patterns. Other optical devices, including the camera obscura and the new camera lucida,

FIGURE 143   Plate, probably New England, 1830–1845. Pressed lead glass. Diam. 8¹⁄₁₆". (Collection of the Corning Museum of Glass, Corning, New York. Gift of Louise S. Esterly.)

AMERICAN FANCY

made it possible to project a view from the kaleidoscope onto a sheet of paper to allow the user to trace the pattern and employ it in a design.[21]

Brewster encouraged his readers to use the kaleidoscope for designing stained glass and ornamental painting.[22] A glass plate made in New England between 1830 and 1845 (fig. 143) features a kaleidoscopic pattern, in which the overall design is a replication of any quadrant, repeated four times. A clever artist could create one section and project it into a full circle with the kaleidoscope. Although it was possible to draw out the entire piece by hand, the kaleidoscope allowed the creator to speed up the process and to experience the full impact of many different designs without investing unnecessary time and energy having to visualize them on paper. The kaleidoscope thereby projected minimum effort into maximum design (fig. 144).

Brewster heralded the merits of the kaleidoscope for carpet design in particular. "There is none of the useful arts to which the creations of the kaleidoscope are more directly applicable than the manufacture of carpets," he wrote in his *Treatise*.[23] Indeed, the kaleidoscope was frequently employed for a broad range of textile and wallpaper designs. Yet, if Brewster foresaw the kaleidoscope as having a considerable influence in the production of floor coverings, he did not foresee the astonishing impact of his invention on American quilts, which were revolutionized by the device.[24]

Quilt makers set down in cloth and thread what they saw in Brewster's wonderful new invention. The complexity of the visually evocative patterns was dictated by the particular design of the kaleidoscope, specifically by the number of mirrors and their angles, as well as the number and character of the interior fragments. A simple kaleidoscope having two mirrors and a few bits of broken glass was often used as a design source for the popular "starburst" pattern (fig. 145). The angle of the mirrors determined the number of pie-shaped wedges in the quilt: two mirrors placed at ninety degrees divided the design into four quadrants; placed at forty-five degrees they created eight, and so on.

Some variants of this quilt design featured nervous radial lines that shot outward like the spokes of a wheel, creating a somewhat dizzying effect where segments or wedges adjoined neighbors. The design imitated the way that the image in a kaleidoscope changes direction wherever two mirrored surfaces meet.[25] These quilts also incorporated numerous tiny pieces of patchwork that imitated the bits of glass found inside a kaleidoscope.[26] A quilt by Rebecca Scattergood Savery of Pennsylvania, one of three related examples she made, was constructed of 3,903 pieces cut from larger pieces and then sewn back together again (fig. 146). The radiating designs provided a marked contrast to the large-scale patchwork or naturalistic designs of an earlier period.

As Brewster's influence spread, kaleidoscopic quilts testified to the impact of his invention, yet had implications beyond anything he anticipated. The evanescent quality and radiant patterns of these essential,

FIGURE 144　George Robert Lawton, round box with heart decorations, Scituate, Providence County, Rhode Island, 1840–1850. Pine, maple, and painted decoration. H. 2¼", Diam. 7½". (Collection of the American Folk Art Museum, New York. Promised gift of Ralph Esmerian, P1.2001.82; photo © 2000 John Bigelow Taylor, New York.)

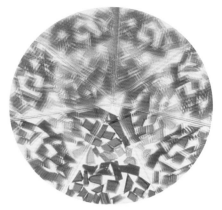

FIGURE 145 View into a simple kaleidoscope with two mirrors. Silvered and colored glass. (Photo, Gavin Ashworth.)

FIGURE 146 Rebecca Scattergood Savery, quilt, Philadelphia, ca. 1827. Cotton chintz. H. 128", W. 132". (Courtesy, Winterthur Museum.)

AMERICAN FANCY

FIGURE 147   Cupboard, probably Pennsylvania, ca. 1825. Wood and painted decoration. H. 82½", W. 52¹³⁄₁₆", D. 23¹³⁄₁₆". (Collection of Robert G. and Mary B. Matthews; photo, Hirschl & Adler.)

everyday goods captured and memorialized a fleeting image produced by the arbitrary intersection of colored glass and light and mirror, and stood in colorful contrast to the severe geometry of Brewster's formal scientific conceptions. The inventor may not have had Fancywork in mind as a by-product of the kaleidoscope's luminous patterns, but when women creatively adapted these patterns for quilts, they transformed Brewster's restrictive idea of beauty into a more permissive, more individualized, interpretation: women quilt makers identified with the kaleidoscope, personalized the experience, and further collapsed the distance between subject and object—between themselves and the image—by fashioning an object for the family bed.[27]

Kaleidoscopic designs inspired numerous other Fancy furnishings. Edgar Allan Poe observed floorcloths with "huge, sprawling, and radiating devices, stripe interspersed, and glorious with all hues" that had been inspired by the kaleidoscope.[28] Similar starbursts also appeared on painted woodwork and furniture, infused with such nervous energy that the surfaces appeared to pulsate (fig. 147). These designs were particularly prevalent on painted chests made during the 1820s and were achieved using a variety of colors and tinted varnish glazes (figs. 148 and 149).

For practitioners of Fancy design, kaleidoscopes with three mirrors proved to be particularly versatile. Two variations stood out: those with

FIGURE 148   Chest over drawers,
New England, 1825–1840. Wood and painted
decoration. H. 40", W. 42¼", D. 18¼". (Col-
lection of the American Folk Art Museum,
New York. Gift of Jean Lipman in honor of
Cyril Irwin Nelson, 1994.5.1; photo, Gavin
Ashworth.)

FIGURE 149   Chest, Pennsylvania,
ca. 1820. White pine and painted decoration.
H. 26", W. 49½", D. 22". (Courtesy, James
and Susan Widder.)

three mirrors placed at sixty degrees to create an equilateral triangle, and those with mirrors set on an uneven triangle of thirty, sixty, and ninety degrees, respectively.

In the equilateral kaleidoscope, any design placed at the juncture of two mirrors was multiplied over and over again in a series of horizontal lines, each offset from its neighbors above and below (fig. 150). This created maximum repetition and, theoretically, maximum impressionability. Carpet design, in particular, benefited from these complex, repetitive designs, as did wallpaper and machine-printed textiles. American bedcovers, too, adopted this new configuration, as illustrated by a stenciled and painted counterpane produced in New England during the 1820s (fig. 151).[29]

FIGURE 150   View into an equilateral kaleidoscope with three mirrors. Silvered and colored glass. (Photo, Gavin Ashworth.) An image viewed with this kaleidoscope is repeated in a series of horizontal lines, each offset from its neighbor above and below.

FIGURE 151   Counterpane, New England, ca. 1825. Cotton and painted and stenciled decoration. H. 92", W. 81". (Courtesy, Abby Aldrich Rockefeller Folk Art Museum, Colonial Williamsburg Foundation, Williamsburg, Virginia.) The design of this counterpane is based on the view into an equilateral kaleidoscope with three mirrors.

In contrast, kaleidoscopes with three mirrors placed specifically at thirty, sixty, and ninety degrees created variations on a hexagon (fig. 152). Quilts with such hexagonal patches, known as "honeycomb patchwork," first appeared in the 1820s and illustrate this perspective (fig. 153). "Perhaps there is not patchwork that is prettier or more ingenious . . . than . . . this," observed an article in *Godey's Lady's Book* in 1835.[30] Honeycomb patterns were especially challenging to make because each piece had four sides where the fabric had to be cut on the bias—diagonally across the grain—which made it difficult to fold the edges under and sew them to the adjoining pieces.

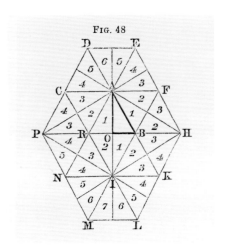

FIGURE 152   *View into a 30°-60°-90° Kaleidoscope,* illustrated in fig. 48 in Sir David Brewster's *A Treatise on the Kaleidoscope,* London, 1819. (Courtesy, The Winterthur Library: Printed Book and Periodical Collection.) Brewster's chart intended to show how an image was replicated. Quilt makers often copied the hexagon design.

FIGURE 153   Quilt, New England, ca. 1830. Chintz, calico, and white cotton. H. 58½", W. 57". (Courtesy, Smithsonian American Art Museum. Gift of Patricia Smith Melton, 1998.149.15.)

A quilt made by Emiline Ellery of Newport, Rhode Island, in 1821 represents an early interpretation of the honeycomb design and suggests the maker's familiarity with both the kaleidoscope and Brewster's *Treatise* (figs. 154 and 155). Just as the inventor had boasted about the kaleidoscope's endless potential for a receptive designer, so this young lady dedicated herself to Brewster's concepts, clearly marking her eye-catching product and observing that it contained 9,750 individual "squares" and approximately 732,000 stitches.[31]

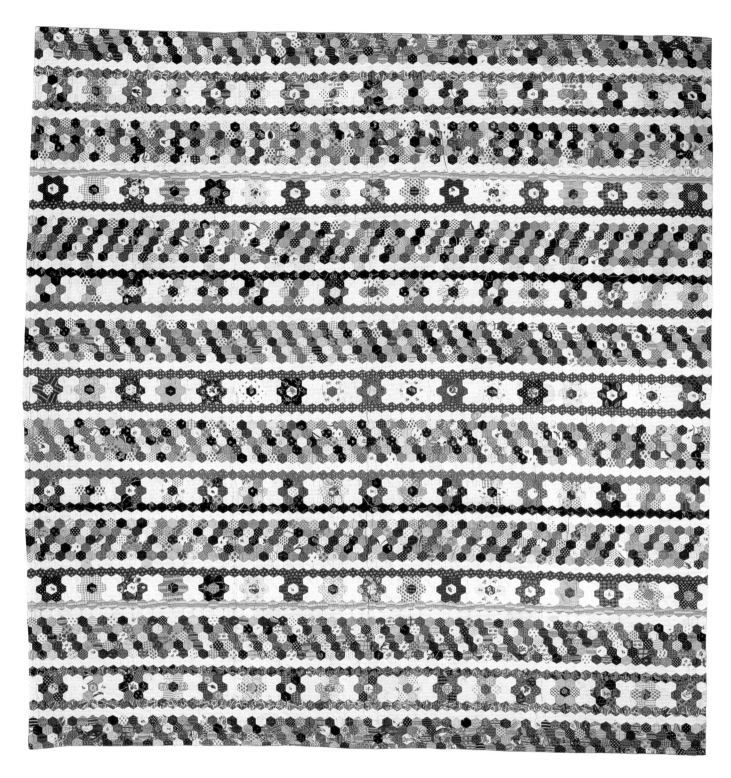

FIGURE 154 Emiline Ellery, quilt, Newport, Rhode Island, 1821. Printed and glazed
cotton. H. 111", W. 101". (Courtesy, Historic
Deerfield.)

FIGURE 155 Detail of the quilt illustrated
in fig. 154.

FIGURE 156   Detail of quilt, America, 1834.
Wool and cotton. H. 79", W. 88". (Courtesy,
Winterthur Museum.)

FIGURE 157   Mary Jane Moore Eastburn,
quilt, Moorestown, New Jersey, 1837–1839.
Cotton. H. 110", W. 107". (Courtesy, Winterthur Museum.)

AMERICAN FANCY

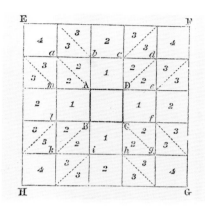

A kaleidoscope with four mirrors positioned at ninety degrees to each other inspired two designs emulated by quilt makers (figs. 156 and 157). Brewster's diagram for the pattern created by such a kaleidoscope shows an eight-pointed star (fig. 158). The details are almost identical, although the inner points of the quilt star converge as they move toward its center. Eight-pointed stars occasionally appeared in eighteenth-century needlework, particularly on samplers and bed rugs, yet were rare during that early period (fig. 159).[32] The star appears frequently after the invention of the kaleidoscope and, most importantly, was often composed of tiny patches that radiate from the center outward. An actual view into a 90°-90°-90°-90° kaleidoscope (fig. 160) shows that the image is repeated in row after row.[33] Quilt makers derived one of the most widely emulated designs from this type of kaleidoscope (fig. 161).

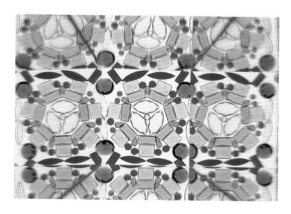

The kaleidoscope opened up completely new and unconventional ways of seeing and creating for the nineteenth-century mind. For Fancy, the ramifications were significant. In the years preceding 1816, perceptions of the beautiful still were shaped largely by classical tastes with emphasis on rational proportions and ornament. Even the discovery of colorful interiors at Herculaneum and Pompeii did not significantly alter the sense of polite reserve that characterized Fancy in an earlier period. The kaleidoscope reinforced the rising popular notion that objects could be transformed into something that they were not (fig. 162). If bits of glass could be reinterpreted for bedroom quilts or stunning designs for painted furniture, then it was perfectly acceptable for wood and paint to suggest marble or for stencils to imitate wallpaper. In the context of the period, this was neither dishonest nor naive. It was simply another way to add dimension to an ordinary object, to make it more visually stunning, more easily impressed upon the mind, and to turn it into something extraordinary.[34]

After 1816, the kaleidoscope dramatically propelled notions of beauty into unprecedented realms, particularly for Americans, who felt less indebted to the ancients than their British counterparts. Unlike much of the ornamentation used during this period, that inspired by the kaleidoscope did not represent the Greeks or the Romans or anyone else from the past. If the discovery of Herculaneum and Pompeii had helped to legitimize Fancy by connecting it directly to the material world of the ancients, the kaleidoscope now made it possible, in certain contexts, to divorce Fancy from classical precedents.

A quilt with a radiating star or a piece of furniture painted with an explosion of color differed from a classically inspired Fancy chair, and it differed significantly from furnishings ornamented with eagles or American flags. Kaleidoscopic ornament represented an affirmation primarily of itself, of the people who happened to experience it, and of the emotional responses generated by the momentary encounters—each of which was uniquely personal and varied depending on the moods or the perspective of the maker or the beholder. Yet even when the new world at the end of the tunnel bordered on the bizarre, the unique and fleeting images had a predictable order that appealed to the rational senses. The kaleidoscope was therefore the ideal vehicle to carry the nineteenth-century mind over the bridge from classical order into a completely new sphere of ornamental abstraction. No other phenomenon of the period more clearly epitomized the character and the identity of the concepts of Fancy, and none had greater impact.

This ephemeral character was reflected increasingly in the surface decoration chosen for an endless array of objects. In tinware, for example, Fancy was expressed in a technique called "crystalline changeable painting" (figs. 163 and 164). "This is the most brilliant branch in the entire art of painting," exclaimed Rufus Porter, who noted that it was usually confined to "fancy boxes, waiters, or tea trays."[35] To produce its effect, an

FIGURE 162   Kaleidoscopic views. Silvered and colored glass. (Courtesy, Colonial Williamsburg Foundation; photo, Hans Lorenz.)

artisan washed an object's iron surface with sulfuric or muriatic acid, which etched the metal and emphasized its crystalline structure. This was then brushed with colorful transparent varnish for added depth, allowing light to pass through a tinted glaze before refracting, and reflecting back to the viewer in totally unpredictable ways. Like a view into the kaleidoscope, the image changed from moment to moment, the crystals alternately receding and then jumping out as the piece moved back and forth before one's eyes—the bright crystals, in a split second, spontaneously turning dark, and the dark ones, light, depending upon their position in relation to the source of illumination. Rufus Porter ingeniously suggested using crystalline changeable painting as a ground for landscapes and seascapes, noting it could be employed to further strengthen their impact: forests would appear to sway in the breeze and oceans to swell and dip.

American Fancy benefited in no small degree from Brewster's "happy invention." The kaleidoscope helped to provide new stylistic options for those who preferred the liveliness of Fancy to the subtleties of understated classical taste or the more restrained expressions that now seemed increasingly to be the province of imagination. It made Fancy more accessible to average Americans, helping to clarify key concepts about the relationship between the mind and the eye that previously had been confined to high literature or scientific treatises. Men, women, and children on every social, economic, and educational level could now grasp the basic concepts of Fancy by merely opening their eyes and surveying their exciting and colorful material possessions—their carpets, their wall coverings, their furniture, and, above all, their quilts. In the two decades that followed the invention of the kaleidoscope, Americans of all kinds found a fresh vision and style that suited them ideally and, inevitably, redefined their interactions with, and in, the world.

FIGURE 163   Bread tray, Pennsylvania, 1815–1835. Tinned sheet iron, asphaltum, and painted and crystallized decoration. H. 2¼", W. 12½", D. 7⅞". (Collection of the American Folk Art Museum, New York. Gift of the Historical Society of Early American Decoration, 64.3.45.)

FIGURE 164   Detail of the center of the bread tray illustrated in fig. 163.

5 Spirited Ornamentation

The practitioner will find in this . . . field . . .
an infinite variety of beautiful fancy work.

Rufus Porter, "The Art of Painting," 1845

Between 1815 and 1840, Fancy blossomed into a more exuberant phase as a broader range of Americans honed their senses and heightened their receptivity to fanciful modes of perception (figs. 165 and 166). Now, in part due to the visual wonders of the kaleidoscope, many Americans abandoned the polite reserve that had characterized Fancy in earlier days. The fashionable, urban-oriented individuals who first embraced the style in the eighteenth century did not fully endorse its changing identity and gradually turned toward more historically grounded interpretations of Grecian classicism, popularly known today as the Empire style. Conversely, America's new advocates for the Fancy style, the burgeoning middle class, soon abandoned all sense of decorative restraint, preferring splashy displays and playful conceits over balanced expressions of reason and emotion.

As Americans pushed Fancy's artistic and emotional boundaries, they inevitably used the word more frequently. Fancy now identified specific

FIGURE 165   Dressing table, probably Portsmouth, New Hampshire, ca. 1825. Maple, white pine, and painted and gilt decoration. H. 32¼", W. 36⅞", D. 17⅜". (Courtesy, Abby Aldrich Rockefeller Folk Art Museum, Colonial Williamsburg Foundation, Williamsburg, Virginia.)

FIGURE 166   Cradle, probably New York, ca. 1825. Pine and painted decoration. H. 20½", W. 21", D. 33¾". (Courtesy, Museum of Art, Rhode Island School of Design. Gift of Mrs. Henry Vaughan; photo, Erik Gould.)

objects with specific characteristics. For example, Fancy carpets came to signify wildly patterned Scotch carpets; Fancy coverlets identified colorful Jacquard bedcovers; and Fancy glass referred to whimsical, free-form glass figures. New categories of Fancy music and Fancy literature also emerged and received growing attention as publishers flooded the market with literary journals and inexpensive sheet music. Creative agriculture even promoted Fancy breeds of plants and animals. By the time Fancy came into full flower in the 1820s and 1830s, little was immune from its influence or its name. A swirling and delightful blend of light, color, motion, and creativity constantly reinforced the new mode of fanciful perception.

The middle class, to whom the style most strongly appealed, concurrently was coming into its own due to a number of developments. England's defeat in the War of 1812 assured American independence and bolstered the national spirit. During the 1820s, voting rights were extended to include all adult white males, thus enfranchising a larger segment of society. The opening of western lands provided opportunities for anyone willing to seek them, and the massive growth of American industry fueled the marketplace and made ornamented goods increasingly affordable, despite the uncertainties of the economy.

Historians have long acknowledged the multifaceted populist "revolution" that reshaped America during the early nineteenth century and have interpreted it through many different lenses—political, social, racial, and economic. Yet one of the greatest transformations occurred in the self-perception of America's middle class. Along with their imaginative vision and changing expectations for themselves, they enjoyed expanding powers as consumers. Admittedly, many of the Fancy goods they bought were less expensive and less refined than those available to wealthier Americans, but everyone—producers, retailers, and buyers alike—recognized the tremendous appeal of these ubiquitous Fancy things.[1]

The trend did not escape notice. Alexis de Tocqueville (1805–1859), the French diplomat who critiqued American culture as he chronicled his travels in the United States, praised American attempts to bring "useful productions within the reach of the whole community." However, he criticized efforts to give those objects "attractive qualities which they do not in reality possess."[2] De Tocqueville bemoaned the American tendency to equate showy things with personal success, and he observed with dismay that the average American associated betterment with novelty: "Besides the good things he possesses, he every instant fancies a thousand others, which death will prevent him from trying if he does not try them soon," he observed in 1835.[3] But de Tocqueville was not an American nor was he able to comprehend the wonderful merits of Fancy.

Of all the improvements that transformed the appearance of the American home and lifted the spirits of its inhabitants, few did so more conspicuously than the Fancy painting that now covered everything in sight. In his 1827 manual *The Decorative Painters' and Glaziers' Guide,* English painter Nathaniel Whittock observed, "Much has certainly been done by modern decorative painters, within the last fifteen years, in producing spirited and natural imitations of fancy wood."[4] An increased emphasis upon efficient techniques, the commercial availability of dazzling new green and yellow pigments, and changing expectations for the appearance and effect of painted surfaces, all had a tremendous impact on America's furnishings and interiors.[5] In 1845 artist Rufus Porter estimated that in his native New England three out of every four doors were imaginatively "grained," as were mantelpieces and wainscoting.[6]

One of the most striking departures from earlier styles of Fancy painting was the unexpected combination of contrasting colors and creative interpretations of highly figured woods and marbles. Mahogany, the principal wood emulated in Fancy painting before 1815, was now only one of many different woods used for the same piece of furniture or on the walls of a room. Fancy painters were partial to other woods with vibrant grain and rich color to add a brilliant contrast. Imitations of flame birch or curled maple, both native to America, were highly popular, as well as wildly grained species from the tropics, particularly shimmering satinwood. Painters also emulated less decorative species, plain surfaces providing a calm contrast to the busy patterns of more exotic woods. Cedar, cherry, and some forms of oak were occasionally used, although one manual advised its readers specifically to avoid yellow oak: "It is a better imitation of molasses candy than the wood of a tree."[7] A variety of marble was also imitated, adding further contrast and increasing the richness of surface decor. The general rule of thumb was to choose materials that would animate the environment, an approach that would influence nineteenth-century tastes for years to come. "Avoid somber hues," cautioned A. J. Downing of paint colors in general. "The general effect should be lively and cheerful."[8]

No combination of woods or colors appeared too adventurous, and artisans often achieved remarkable effects by juxtaposing graining and marbling of different hues and highlighting them with details of contrasting solid colors. The parlor woodwork (fig. 167) from Cedar Level, a house built in Sussex County, Virginia, circa 1835, featured surfaces with an amazing range of different marbled and grained treatments. The moldings were accented in two contrasting shades of green and in black. Beneath the wainscot, the baseboards resembled gray marble with black veins, and beneath the fireplace, gray marble with red. The panels of the mantel were gray and blue, and the cupboard doors were mahoganized. As if this were not enough, the painter went one step further and covered the yellow pine panels and doors with imaginative Fancy painting that, ironically, imitated yellow pine.

In general, colors of interior spaces changed from one room to another. Sometimes the painter subtly inverted his palette, placing red where green had predominated, and green where red had been emphasized. Often the format changed altogether with the introduction of

FIGURE 167   Parlor woodwork, Cedar Level, Sussex County, Virginia, ca. 1835. Pine and painted decoration. (Courtesy, Bobbitt House Interiors; photo, Gavin Ashworth.)

an entirely different range of pigments or the imitation of different woods. Going rapidly from room to room, up the stairs and then back down again, mimicked the experience of viewing a kaleidoscope on a tremendous scale and thus excited the mind with amorphous and ever-changing ideas.

FIGURE 168   Chest with three drawers, North Carolina, 1780–1810 and ca. 1830. Poplar, pine, brass, iron, and later painted decoration. H. 30", W. 49½", D. 22¾". (Courtesy, Robert and Michelle White.)

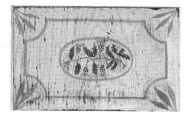

FIGURE 169   Nathan Overton, corner cupboard, Randolph County, North Carolina, 1820–1835. Yellow pine and painted decoration. H. 76", W. 40½", D. 17". (Courtesy, Colonial Williamsburg Foundation.)

FIGURE 170   Detail of the upper right door panel of the corner cupboard illustrated in fig. 169.

Fancy painters of furniture often expressed a similarly energized aesthetic, as seen in the colors chosen for a North Carolina chest (fig. 168) updated about 1830 with a variegated surface of marbled paint and subtle details of green. This taste also is boldly reflected in a North Carolina corner cupboard made between 1820 and 1835 (figs. 169 and 170). Signed by the woodworker Nathan Overton, the piece was decorated by an anonymous painter who consciously selected colors as daring and diverse as those at Cedar Level. The solid green background, marbled moldings in red and gray, and grained panels are startlingly juxtaposed with the panels on the upper doors, where a crisp coat of white silhouettes lively floral sprays.

This preference for visually stimulating Fancy painting is also evident in the work of an anonymous watercolor artist who portrayed his subjects in the midst of interiors with equally imaginative combinations of color and texture (fig. 171). *Andrew Lindsay and His Daughter Mary Eliza,* painted in Guilford County, North Carolina, about 1827, is among the most flamboyant examples of this artist's work. The scene depicts an architectural interior with a blue marbled baseboard, a green molding capping the paneling, and blue window trim. A vibrant carpet covers the floor, and a painted table and chair complete the Fancy scene.

Regional trends in Fancy painting merit further study by students of the decorative arts, but several preliminary observations appear worthy of note. For instance, New England architectural woodwork of the early nineteenth century was seldom as colorful or as varied as that used in

FIGURE 171   *Andrew Lindsay and His Daughter Mary Eliza,* attributed to the Guilford Limner, Guilford County, North Carolina, ca. 1827. Watercolor on paper. 11¼" x 9½". (Courtesy, Mr. and Mrs. Alexander H. Galloway, Jr.; photo, Gavin Ashworth.)

FIGURE 172 Blanket chest, possibly South Shaftsbury, Vermont, ca. 1825. Pine and basswood with painted decoration. H. 24⅜", W. 47⅛", D. 19". (Courtesy, Old Sturbridge Village; photo, Henry E. Peach.)

FIGURE 173 Tall case clock, probably Bennington, Vermont, ca. 1825. White pine and painted decoration. H. 85". (Private collection; photo, James and Nancy Glazer.)

southern homes. Instead, northerners favored other types of surface decoration, including stenciling and mural painting that were practiced less frequently on southern walls. Conversely, the colorful palette often seen in southern interiors is relatively scarce on decorated furniture from the region and also in New England interiors, although such lively surfaces occasionally appear on New England furniture (figs. 172 and 173).

If some artisans preferred kaleidoscopic combinations of contrasting woods and unconventional colors, other practitioners took a different view of Fancy: "Avoid the fault of producing a caricature," warned one training manual that advised practitioners in the techniques of emulating wood.[9] Yet this advice was little heeded by enthusiastic workers whose imaginative flare refused to be encumbered by exacting techniques. A chest from Vermont (fig. 174) and a corner cupboard from Pennsylvania (fig. 175) testify to the fact that nineteenth-century Americans now sought to push the bounds of decoration well beyond the polite imitations so popular less than a decade before.[10]

FIGURE 174 Blanket chest, Matteson type, vicinity of South Shaftsbury, Bennington County, Vermont, ca. 1825. Wood and painted decoration. H. 40", W. 40", D. 17¾". (Collection of the American Folk Art Museum, New York. Gift of Howard and Jean Lipman in honor of Robert Bishop, director [1977–1991], Museum of American Folk Art, 1991.10.1; photo, John Parnell, New York.)

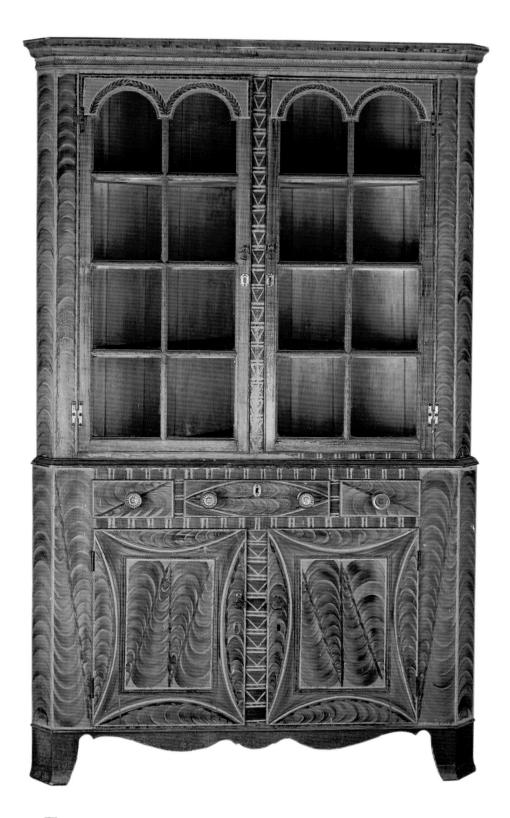

FIGURE 176 Dresser, Vermont, ca. 1835. Pine and painted decoration. H. 86", W. 57", D. 20". (Private collection; photo, © Christie's Images Limited 1995.)

To some artisans, even caricature seemed insufficient to fully satisfy the public's rising taste for Fancy. A kitchen dresser made about 1835 (fig. 176) illustrates the most inventive reaches of Fancy painting. Waldo Tucker, a Vermont craftsman who in 1837 compiled a handbook entitled *The Mechanics Assistant,* advised painters to use whisky as a medium to mix their pigments and urged them to "grain according to fancy."[11] Some painted examples suggest that Tucker's followers used linseed oil anyway and then drank the whisky while they worked.

The most expressive modes of Fancy marbling and graining mirror the rising commitment of American artisans to general aesthetic beliefs first articulated over a century before and a continent away. Scottish philosopher Thomas Reid, theorizing in 1785 about the capacity of the faculty of fancy to combine things that were never combined in the real world, insightfully noted, "[Fancy] may enlarge or diminish, multiply or divide, compound and fashion."[12] Nowhere do his observations seem more appropriate than here. Nineteenth-century Fancy painters shared his commitment, employing the sweeping strokes of an artisan's brush rather than the pen of a philosopher, to express their opinions on Fancy and to magnify reality tenfold for the sake of effect.

From caricatured Fancy painting, it was a simple step for the ingenious painter to leave behind all hints of true wood grain and to move toward highly imaginative and completely original designs. A New England chest (fig. 177) with an intriguing surface of meandering painted trails offers a unique and whimsical example of one artisan's explorations. For Fancy painters committed to such work, the ultimate goal was to fill the eye with dazzling patterns and scenes and to provide the mind with a storehouse of bizarre or unconventional images.

Although they appear complex, most of the surfaces were simply and quickly achieved. Initially, a coat of solid-colored paint—often a bright yellow, red, or orange—was applied and allowed to dry. The surface was then ready for graining. Next, a thin layer of contrasting color—dissolved in water, vinegar, or turpentine—was applied with a brush. The painter immediately manipulated the wet coat using feathers or graining combs or other unusual materials. Painters sometimes rolled a rag or crumpled a piece of paper and dabbed it across the surface from one side to another. Other times they cut small wooden blocks to impress designs through the overcoat of pigment. If the artist was unhappy with the work, he could easily remove the pigment by wiping it off with a damp rag and start over again.

Putty was particularly desirable for manipulating the surface, especially when pressed against a coat of pigment suspended in vinegar. The linseed oil in the putty reacted with the vinegar to create a striking seaweed

FIGURE 177 Chest over drawer, New England, 1825–1840. Wood and painted decoration. H. 35″, W. 40¼″, D. 19″. (Collection of the American Folk Art Museum, New York. Gift of Jean Lipman, 1995.4.7; photo, Gavin Ashworth.)

FIGURE 178 Detail of the document box illustrated in fig. 179.

FIGURE 179 Dome-top document box, New England, 1820–1840, basswood and painted and varnished decoration. H. 11½", W. 27½", D. 13" (rear). Top to bottom: Pantry box, New England, 1820–1840. Pine and painted decoration. H. 2", Diam. 6¾". Pantry box, New England, 1820–1845. White pine, maple, spruce or fir, and painted and varnished decoration. H. 2¾", W. 6¼", D. 4⅝". Document box, New England, 1820–1840. Pine and painted decoration. H. 5⅞", W. 12", D. 7⅜". The piece is inscribed: "Boston, Mass. / Ellridge G. Hall's Trunk." (Courtesy, a New York collector; photo, Gavin Ashworth.)

pattern (fig. 178). Since the putty was pliable, it could be kneaded into any shape. Sometimes it was stretched into a long roll and walked around in a circle like a hand on a clock. This created a starburst effect suggestive of a kaleidoscope design. Other times it was twisted or folded before it was dragged or rolled across the surface. The variety was almost endless, as a group of small boxes from New England shows (fig. 179).

Once a design was dry, a protective coat of transparent varnish or shellac was applied over the surface. Sometimes colorful pigments were mixed directly with the varnish. When this was done, painters frequently em-

AMERICAN FANCY

ployed a thickening agent known as "megilp" to give the lively, tinted varnish extra body. This prevented the glaze from leveling out when it was drawn across the surface, allowing it to remain thick and dark in some areas and thin and light in others. If the glaze was battered with the bristles of a brush or with a rag, it created an intricate surface that afforded even greater variety. The colorful, variegated glaze provided a transparent or semitransparent window to the layer of solid paint below. This was often called a "scumble glaze," and the process of giving it texture was known as "scumbling."[13]

With a little practice, scumble glazes could be used to create a wide variety of effects. Some of the most intriguing of these are found in a sample kit owned by Moses Eaton, a versatile New Hampshire artisan (fig. 180).

FIGURE 180   Moses Eaton, Jr., sample box and ten panels, Dublin, Cheshire County, New Hampshire, 1820–1830. Pine, painted decoration, and brass. H. 8¾", W. 15¹⁄₁₆", D. 2⅝" (box); H. 6⅞", W. 14", D. ⅛" (each panel). (Collection of the American Folk Art Museum, New York. Anonymous gift and gift of the Richard Coyle Lilly Foundation, 1980.28.1A-K; photo, Terry McGinnis.)

Eaton must have tempted numerous potential customers with his kit as he traveled the New England countryside, showing them his work and enticing them to employ him to decorate their interiors or their furniture. The biggest surprise must have come when he opened the drawer and pulled out ten separate boards, each one painted a different color, and having a distinct surface pattern created by his skillful manipulation of the glaze.[14]

Other decorative Fancy techniques offered further visual variety, and artisans began to discover that most of these were significantly easier to produce than exacting imitations. One popular finish, usually applied over a solid coat of paint, is now known as "smoke graining" and relied upon nothing more than a tallow candle for its effect. The rising smoke from the burning candle left a sooty, translucent, cloudlike impression on the partially wet paint, which was then given a protective layer of varnish.

FIGURE 181 Dome-top trunk, America, ca. 1835. Wood and painted, smoked, and stenciled decoration. H. 10¾", W. 23¾", D. 11¾". (Courtesy, Abby Aldrich Rockefeller Folk Art Museum, Colonial Williamsburg Foundation, Williamsburg, Virginia.)

FIGURE 182 Philip H. Saunders, work table, Danvers, Massachusetts, 1820–1840. Pine and painted and smoke-grained decoration. H. 29¾", W. 18", D. 16¾". (From the Collections of Henry Ford Museum & Greenfield Village.) Written on the underside of the top drawer is: "P H Saunders / Mill St Danvers."

Some of the finest smoke graining of the period is found on a dome-top trunk made in New England around 1835 (fig. 181). The painter first "smoked" the piece from one end to the other. Then he or she placed stencils and cutouts on the surface and traced their outlines in the same smoke process to create an exotic peacock and an American Indian whimsically riding a lion. As with the Trower House baseboards (see pages 74 and 75, figs. 120–124) and many other instances of Fancy painting, the artist playfully hid images within the overall decorative pattern.

Smoke graining was sometimes used in combination with other types of Fancy painting for greater variety, as on a work table from Danvers, Massachusetts (fig. 182). Here the artist has used graining combs on the table base to imitate mahogany, raking the combs through a coat of wet black paint over a dry red. Graining combs were often made by artisans out of leather or wood, but by the 1810s commercially produced examples also were widely available (fig. 183). Most graining combs had evenly

FIGURE 183 Graining combs, America or England, 1820–1880. Wood and metal. H. 4", W. 5", D. ⅜" (box). (Private collection; photo, Gavin Ashworth.)

AMERICAN FANCY

spaced teeth which created regularity in the graining, but variety could be achieved by removing selected teeth or, with metal combs, bending them. Further contrast could be obtained by using different colors in successive paint layers.

Other processes included the "dry brush" technique, in which the artist worked most of the wet paint out of the brush before it touched the surface and then created delicate trails of color. Sometimes bristles were selectively thinned from the brush to heighten the visual effect and add further variety. This was among the quickest and most efficient of decorative techniques and had great impact if the artist carefully planned the design and executed it with confidence, as a New England artisan did on a superb cupboard (fig. 184) made around 1825. The evocative surface is covered with wispy trails of paint imparted by a capricious turn of the brush.

FIGURE 184   Chimney or wall cupboard, probably Connecticut, ca. 1825. Poplar and painted decoration. H. 66¼", W. 29", D. 14". (Private collection; photo, Gavin Ashworth.)

FIGURE 185 Storage box, New York, ca. 1825. Poplar and painted decoration. H. 10", W. 5", D. 2½". (Private collection; photo, Roddy and Sally Moore.)

FIGURE 186 William Rice, Vernon Hotel sign, Connecticut, ca. 1841. Pine, painted decoration, and wrought iron. H. 75¼", W. 63⅜"; H. 81¼" (with mounts). (Courtesy, The Connecticut Historical Society, Hartford, Connecticut.)

After 1815 the popularity of the Fancy style inspired greater experimentation in the field of ornamental painting as well as Fancy painting. Artisans often heightened the effects of Fancy artifacts by layering decoration on top of decoration in hopes of eliciting even more ebullient responses. Ornamental painters contributed numerous specialized decorative techniques. They augmented the old forms of gilding with bronze painting, complemented fruit and flower painting with stenciling, and supplemented painted landscapes with printed scenes transferred from paper. These techniques made it possible for traditional artisans to boost their output dramatically, providing a great variety of inexpensive products to an enthusiastic public besotted with Fancy (figs. 185–190).

FIGURE 187   Sewing table, New Hampshire, ca. 1830. Maple, pine, and painted decoration. H. 30¼", W. 18½", D. 17⅜". (Courtesy, Elbert H. Parsons, Jr.; photo, Gavin Ashworth.)

FIGURE 188   Detail showing the top of the sewing table illustrated in fig. 187.

FIGURE 189   Dome-top box, New York or New England, ca. 1820. White pine, paper, and painted decoration. H. 4⁵⁄₁₆", W. 7", D. 4⅜". (Courtesy, a New York collector; photo, Gavin Ashworth.)

FIGURE 190   Miniature footstool, New England, 1820–1840. White pine and painted decoration. H. 7½", W. 28¼", D. 6¼". Pantry box, probably New England, 1800–1850. Maple, poplar, and painted decoration. H. 1⅝", W. 4", D. 3". Wall box, Vermont, ca. 1825. Pine and painted decoration. H. 17⅜", W. 15⅛", D. 5¼". Double candle box, New England, 1820–1840. White pine and painted decoration. H. 6½", W. 13½", D. 10". Pantry box, probably Hudson River valley, New York, 1800–1840. Wood and painted decoration. H. 2⅝", Diam. 5". Slide-lid box, attributed to the Compass Artist, Lancaster County, Pennsylvania, 1800–1840. Cedar, poplar, and painted decoration. H. 6⅞", W. 5⅝", D. 2³⁄₁₆". Pantry box, probably New England, 1800–1850. Maple, white pine, and painted decoration. H. 2", W. 5⅜", D. 3¾". Pantry box, New England, 1815–1840. White pine, ash, and painted decoration. H. 2¾", Diam. 6¾". Dome-top document box, probably Massachusetts, ca. 1820. White pine, basswood, and painted decoration. H. 6⅛", W. 12⅛", D. 6⅛". (Courtesy, a New York collector; photo, Gavin Ashworth.)

FIGURE 191 William Capen, Jr., parade banner, Portland, Maine, 1841. Oil on silk. H. 33⅞", W. 40½". (Courtesy, Maine Charitable Mechanics Association.) Text on the obverse reads: "He that will not pay the / Shoe-Maker / is not worthy of a / Sole." Text on the reverse reads: "Sons of Crispin. / Sherman, Pendrill, Lee, Gifford, Bloomfield, / and a host of their Craft / have laboured / with their / [picture of an awl] / to mend the Soles and improve / the Understandings of mankind."

The previous decades had seen a gradual expansion in the goods deemed appropriate for Fancy, including decorative furniture and smaller household goods, practical and otherwise. Some ornamental painters, such as William Capen, Jr., of Portland, Maine, specialized in certain techniques. In the 1830s and 1840s Capen owned a small business focusing principally upon chairs. Although he decorated new chairs, his primary trade was in redecorating old chairs, and he occasionally painted signs and made toys. Among his most unusual work was a series of banners he produced in 1841 for the annual parade of the Maine Charitable Mechanics Association. The Fancy banner he made for the shoemakers' guild (fig. 191) epitomized both the bold character of his work and his light-hearted sense of humor.

The divergent skills offered by ornamental painters in this period are characterized by the rural Pennsylvania painter Edward Hicks (1780–1849), today recognized principally for his canvas paintings of the *Peaceable Kingdom*. Like the Finlay brothers of urban Baltimore, Hicks started his professional life working with a coach and carriage maker, where he learned the artistic skills essential to ornamental painting. An account book that survives from Hicks' early years in business reveals that in addition to decorating vehicles and painting architectural trim, he painted floorcloths, fire buckets, window cornices, and chimney boards, as well as gilding weathervanes.[15] A variety of these ornamental painting skills come together in his 1825 image of the *Falls of Niagara,* which is not unlike the scenes found on the backs of other examples of American Fancy seating furniture or overmantels (fig. 192).

FIGURE 192 Edward Hicks, *Falls of Niagara,* 1825–1826. Oil on panel. 22¾" x 30⅛". (Courtesy, Abby Aldrich Rockefeller Folk Art Museum, Colonial Williamsburg Foundation, Williamsburg, Virginia.)

FIGURE 193 Chimney board from Waters-Phelps House, West Sutton, Massachusetts, 1815–1830. Oil on wood. 34¾" x 50½". (Courtesy, Abby Aldrich Rockefeller Folk Art Museum, Colonial Williamsburg Foundation, Williamsburg, Virginia.)

Chimney boards provide a fine example of the shifting appearance of the Fancy style and the myriad skills employed by American ornamental painters. Placed in front of unused fireplaces to seal them tightly, chimney boards prevented drafts from entering the house in winter and chimney swallows in summer. In the eighteenth century, when ornamented chimney boards were exceedingly scarce and confined to the wealthy, they often were adorned with painted pots of flowers. John Custis of Williamsburg, Virginia, ordered one such board from England in 1723: "It is to put in ye summer before my chimneys to hide ye fireplace," he wrote. "Let them bee some good flowers in potts of various kinds and whatever else you think fitt."[16]

In the early nineteenth century, the new emphasis on imagination encouraged the development of more complex designs for chimney boards, now commonly called fireboards. Ornamental painters employed many of the same conventions on fireboards that they used on Fancy furniture—landscapes, both real and imaginary, as well as historical subjects and still-life vignettes. Painted pots of flowers like those ordered by John Custis a century earlier remained a popular subject, but ornamental painters now updated them to reflect the more playful nature of Fancy (fig. 193). One of the most engaging designs, devised by an unidentified craftsman, imitates an undisturbed fireplace complete with andirons, shovel, and tongs—an image that undoubtedly caused more than one viewer to do a surprised double take (fig. 194). A similar surviving example depicts two cats quietly resting on the hearth.[17]

FIGURE 194 Mantel piece and chimney board from Daniel Whitmore House, North Sunderland, Massachusetts, ca. 1800. Wood and painted decoration. H. 44½", W. 51", D. 5¾" (mantel piece). (Courtesy, Society for the Preservation of New England Antiquities. Museum purchase, 1963.394.)

One of the more important figures in the story of ornamental painting is New Englander Rufus Porter (1792–1884), who in 1825 published a manual called *A Select Collection of Valuable and Curious Arts*. In this and other works, Porter provided detailed instructions for a variety of decorative techniques, often emphasizing scientific principles to accomplish novel effects, and inspired such an enthusiastic following that the book quickly

underwent six editions. Few artisans better understood the need to meld traditional skills with innovative approaches. Porter acquainted himself with almost every profession conceivable to an early nineteenth-century New Englander.

Initially apprenticed as a shoemaker, Porter also played fife and drum for a company of Connecticut militia, wrote religious tracts, and painted signs and watercolor portraits. Shortly after 1810, Porter increasingly worked as a professional ornamental painter. He learned to paint scenic murals on walls in imitation of expensive French wallpapers (fig. 195). He traveled through Maine, New Hampshire, Vermont, Massachusetts, and Rhode Island, adorning dozens of houses with his work. Porter's murals inspired a host of imitations, making him one of the most prolific and successful American artists of the early nineteenth century and a prominent advocate of the Fancy style.[18]

Porter's career as an ornamental painter was eventually eclipsed by other publishing ventures dedicated to integrating science and the arts. His first periodical, *The New York Mechanic,* met with a modicum of success in his two years as editor and was followed, in 1845, by his establishment of *Scientific American,* one of America's longest-lived and most highly respected periodicals. *New York Mechanic* and *Scientific American* helped artisans of all types keep abreast of new developments in their fields. Ornamental painters benefited from Porter's numerous articles that contained recipes explaining new techniques and discussing advanced materials for embellishing otherwise plain surfaces. Some of his writings focused on the painting of wall murals to compete with paper hangings; others detailed the most efficient techniques for stenciling, gilding, painting on glass, and ornamenting tin and window shades. Porter constantly experimented with new ideas, coming up with such unexpected designs as a "steam carriage for common roads"—one of many forward-looking conceptions that included a rotary plough, a car for moving houses, a horse-powered boat, and various systems of aerial navigation. In short, Porter was a seminal figure in disseminating a wide range of ornamental skills to professionals and amateurs alike.[19]

Of the ornamental techniques promoted by Porter and others after 1815, stenciling proved to be the most efficient and assured the greatest measure of success. Stenciling was relatively easy and fast and, like most other forms of Fancy decoration, was inexpensive to execute. It appeared on walls and on furniture, on textiles and tin alike. Despite its simplicity, stenciling provided an astounding range of ornament. "The practitioner will find in this . . . field . . . an infinite variety of beautiful fancy work," wrote Porter.[20]

In American homes, ornamental painters commonly applied stenciling directly to plaster, where it functioned as a surrogate for boldly printed or painted wallpapers. In many cases the edges of the room were trimmed with contrasting designs, just as printed patterns often provided a border for papered rooms. Jacob Maentel, a Pennsylvania-born watercolor artist who migrated to Ohio and Indiana, sometimes portrayed his subjects in colorful, stenciled interiors, as in his 1841 portrait of Mrs. Rebeckah Jacquess of Posey County, Indiana (fig. 196). Maentel depicted a room with stencils layered on bright blue walls and a window ornamented with brilliant red curtains. All over America itinerant artists traveled the countryside

FIGURE 196 *Mrs. Rebeckah Fraser Rankin Jacquess,* attributed to Jacob Maentel, Posey County, Indiana, 1841. Watercolor and ink on wove paper. 17¼" x 11⅜". (Courtesy, Abby Aldrich Rockefeller Folk Art Museum, Colonial Williamsburg Foundation, Williamsburg, Virginia.)

FIGURE 197   Dome-top box, New England, 1815–1825. Pine and painted and stenciled decoration. H. 14", W. 33", D. 15". (Courtesy, Shelburne Museum, Shelburne, Vermont.)

and decorated architectural interiors and furnishings (fig. 197). Some artisans promoted the use of stencils to adorn floorcloths, and Rufus Porter suggested using them to facilitate decoration on window shades and to imitate carpets. A residence in Dorchester, Massachusetts, decorated circa 1825 by an anonymous artist, featured the patterns of a Fancy Scotch carpet, stenciled directly on the floor (fig. 198).[21] The work kit (fig. 199) belonging to Moses Eaton of Dublin, New Hampshire, in the 1820s and 1830s includes a variety of original stencil patterns that help to document his artistic influence on New England interiors and furnishings and makes

FIGURE 198   Stenciled floorboards, Humphreys House, Dorchester, Massachusetts, ca. 1825. Wood and painted decoration. L. 169", W. 23". (Courtesy, Society for the Preservation of New England Antiquities. Museum accession, 1959.256.)

FIGURE 199   Stencil kit, New England, 1825–1845. Wood, painted decoration, and mixed media. H. 4⅞", W. 25", D. 12¾". (Courtesy, Society for the Preservation of New England Antiquities. Gift of Janet Waring, 1941.16.99; photo, Peter Harholdt.) This kit belonged to Moses Eaton.

AMERICAN FANCY

FIGURE 200 Chest, decoration attributed to Moses Eaton, New England, ca. 1820. Pine and painted decoration. H. 26", W. 50", D. 18¾". (Private collection; photo, Olde Hope Antiques, Inc.)

FIGURE 201 Detail of painted decoration on the back of the chest illustrated in fig. 200.

it possible to attribute the ornament of a simple chest with brilliant green paint to his hand. This chest incorporates several of Eaton's hallmark ornaments: leafy vines, floral vases, and borders of rosettes and diamonds. Other motifs, such as a pineapple and a swag border, further identify his work (figs. 200 and 201).

As professional ornamenters gained self-assurance with the process of stenciling, many attempted more elaborate patterns on Fancy furnishings (fig. 202). The better examples depended upon a complex series of overlaid stencils that helped to fill in different sections of the design. Bronze powders in contrasting colors, rather than mere paint, enhanced the ornament by adding depth and subtle gradations of color. Available "at trifling expense" from Fancy hardware stores, the pigments could be purchased by artisans in gold, silver, brass, and copper, and each, in turn, could be acquired in subtle hues.[22]

The most ambitious ornamental painters in this era heightened the impact of their stenciling by applying their designs over Fancy painted

FIGURE 202 Box, New England, ca. 1825. Wood, bronze powder stenciling, and painted decoration. H. 10", W. 18", D. 10½". (Collection of the American Folk Art Museum, New York. Gift of Jean Lipman, 1995.4.5; photo, John Parnell, New York.)

surfaces imitating rosewood or the explosive grain of flame mahogany. Woodworker and sawmill owner Abraham Cole of Broadalbin, Montgomery County, New York, and his son, ornamental painter Rufus Cole, were highly prolific during the 1820s and 1830s. The numerous pieces from their partnership include a dozen or more tall clocks, several signed on the interior by Abraham. Two other clocks are stenciled boldly on front to advertise the ornamenter, "R. Cole Painter." A virtually identical tall case clock is signed by another decorator, "J. D. Green" (fig. 203), who employed a similar style and many of the same stencils and may have worked in the same shop. Each piece in the group boasts a variety of painted and stenciled details, including clusters of fruit and flowers. Some have

FIGURE 203   J. D. Green, decorator, tall case clock, Montgomery (now Fulton) County, New York, ca. 1835. White pine and painted and stenciled decoration. H. 85½", W. 17", D. 10". (Private collection; photo, Gavin Ashworth.) The wooden movement is by Silas Hoadley of Plymouth, Connecticut.

FIGURE 204   Dressing table, probably New England, ca. 1825. Wood, painted decoration, and brass. H. 39¹⁄₁₆", W. 36", D. 18". (Courtesy, Abby Aldrich Rockefeller Folk Art Museum, Colonial Williamsburg Foundation, Williamsburg, Virginia.)

deer stenciled on either side of the door, leaping playfully up and down the front edges of the case.[23]

The quintessentially Fancy concept of layering ornament upon ornament was sometimes taken to extremes, as on a lady's dressing table made in New England circa 1825 (fig. 204). Here the decorator painted a coat of rosewood graining and then stenciled the center of each drawer and the splashboard with fruit. The fruit was flanked on its outer edges with freehand painting of leafage and tendrils. This imagery was then bordered by brilliant yellow striping and framed by panels of vibrant red—in effect it added a third and fourth layer of ornament.

Similarly inventive combinations of ornamental painting appeared on other early nineteenth-century American artifacts. For example, leather buckets (fig. 205) that were kept in the home, parade hats worn by units of American firefighters (fig. 206), and militia accoutrements, including musical instruments (fig. 207), were made Fancy by the addition of decoration. Every able-bodied American male between sixteen and sixty was required to attend a muster of the local militia, held twice yearly on the village green or courthouse lawn or at designated parade grounds nearby. The colorful, eye-catching uniforms chosen by most volunteer units to be

FIGURE 205   Fire bucket, America, ca. 1810. Leather and painted decoration. H. 18". (Courtesy, Samuel Herrup Antiques.)

FIGURE 206   Fireman's parade hat, probably Philadelphia, ca. 1850. Felt and painted and gilt decoration. H. 6½". (Courtesy, Abby Aldrich Rockefeller Folk Art Museum, Colonial Williamsburg Foundation, Williamsburg, Virginia.)

FIGURE 207   Militia drum, North Carolina, 1775–1820. Wood and painted decoration. H. 16½", Diam. 15½". (Courtesy, Guilford Courthouse National Military Park; photo, Gavin Ashworth.)

FIGURE 208 Militia cavalry helmet, Connecticut, 1800–1810. Leather, sheet iron, silk, brass, and painted and gilt decoration. H. 11½" (overall). (Courtesy, The Connecticut Historical Society, Hartford, Connecticut.) This helmet was worn by a member of the Connecticut governor's Horse Guard.

worn at "Fancy Military Dress Balls" and parades were made by specialized businesses that produced "Fancy Military Goods." The proprietors of these businesses worked in close conjunction with local militia units, such as the Shrewsbury (Massachusetts) Rifle Company, which selected a committee to choose a design for their uniforms and empowered it "to obtain, get made, and trimmed according to their fancy."[24] Militia musicians, for instance, often wore brilliant red suits, and their drums were emblazoned with detailed eagles or trophies of war. Artillerymen wore elaborate uniforms with contrasting coats and trousers; cavalry soldiers wore helmets (fig. 208) with fanciful crests; and infantrymen stored their possessions in brilliantly painted knapsacks emblazoned with insignia. Adding to the Fancy look were ornamentally painted banners with the name and crest of the individual unit. In short, even the most formal public rituals were shaped by Fancy and touched by the colors and techniques of ornamental painting.

Artisans also applied the same ornamental painting techniques to an endless array of utilitarian wares, including innovative Fancy tinwares that were highly popular due to their colorful appearance and low cost.[25] Asphaltum, a coal derivative that ranged from subtle browns to black, provided the most common background. Largely impervious to water, and slightly translucent, a thin coat of asphaltum dried hard and shiny and allowed the brilliant metal beneath to glisten through the finish. Japan pigments in a variety of colors—red, blue, yellow, or rusty orange—provided artisans and customers alike with a lively alternative to asphaltum. When the asphaltum or the painted ground had dried, the painter applied the ornament, consisting most often of leaves, flowers, or decorative swags. The decoration was painted in shades of white and green, red, black, and brown (figs. 209–212). Because of the refined pigments used to ornament Fancy tinwares, they were often identified as japanned work.[26]

FIGURE 209 Oval tea canister, Pennsylvania, 1825–1850. Tinned sheet iron and painted decoration. H. 5⅛", W. 3⁹⁄₁₆", D. 2¾". (Collection of the American Folk Art Museum, New York. Gift of the Historical Society of Early American Decoration, 76.1.7.)

In the early part of the century, most painted tinware hailed from small shops or from independently employed decorators. William Matthew Prior, a well-known portraitist who started his professional life as a Fancy and ornamental painter, advertised in the *Maine Enquirer* during 1827 that he rejapanned "Old Tea Trays, Waiters, &c . . . in a very tasty style." It was not long before demand for these wares caused businesses and shops to expand. In turn, the successful production and marketing of decorative tin transformed the nature of the business itself.[27]

Among the more prolific makers of Fancy tin was Oliver Filley of Bloomfield, Connecticut. Filley's success relied upon his ability to sell his wares throughout New England. While his wife tended shop near their home and oversaw several workers producing tinware, Filley spent much of his early career on the road, developing a network of merchants and peddlers to handle the products, and also brokering the work of other

tinsmiths. In 1810 he founded a second store in Elizabethtown, New Jersey, to provide a center for a business network in the mid-Atlantic region, and soon the growing family enterprise included another in Lansingburgh, New York, founded by his brother Augustus. By 1815 the New Jersey operation was replaced by a larger establishment in Philadelphia, now run by his brother Harvey and, after 1826, by his son Dwight, who then moved to St. Louis, Missouri, where he founded a branch in 1832. The family businesses thrived well into the 1870s, producing and marketing a variety of tinwares and eventually offering a diverse range of general merchandise to the public.[28]

As in the first era of Fancy, the depiction of landscape views on architecture and on furnishings remained an important branch of ornamental painting (figs. 213 and 214). After 1815, however, scenes "taken from nature" acquired increasingly imaginary compositions. These allowed sufficient room for personal expression on the part of the artist, making it possible to "richly embellish" the view and thereby to "excel nature itself in picturesque brilliancy."[29] There also were practical reasons to improve upon these painted scenes. The limitations of a square room, or the confines of a chair back, made it difficult if not impossible to copy most landscapes precisely. Here a little fancy on the part of the painter was encouraged, especially at the corners of walls. "The trees . . . should be so arranged . . . as to . . . fill up such space . . . as could not be otherwise conveniently occupied," advised the prolific New England painter Rufus Porter.[30]

In 1845 Porter proposed that no scenery in the world presented a livelier appearance than the American farm, an observation that echoed James Fenimore Cooper's admiration of the brightness of the painted houses that enlivened the native landscape. Porter preferred images that captured the "swell of land" when its "colored fields" were "well arranged" and its fruit trees were in blossom. Yet he also admitted that reality alone seldom served to fully please the eye or mind, advising that the artist enliven the prospect through the addition of evocative motifs such as balloons navi-

FIGURE 214   William Price, *Landscape Mural,* from stair hall, Ezra Carroll House, East Springfield, New York, 1831. Paint on plaster. (Courtesy, Winterthur Museum.)

FIGURE 215   Rufus Porter, *Landscape Mural with the Steamship "Victory,"* Dr. Francis Howe House, Westwood, Massachusetts, 1838. Paint on plaster on chestnut lath. 76" x 127½". (Courtesy, Donald Heller and Kimberly Washam.)

FIGURE 216   Bellows, New York City, ca. 1820. Wood, painted and gilt decoration, leather, and brass. L. 21", W. 9½". (Courtesy, Museum of the City of New York. Gift of Mrs. Lyman Rhoades, 53.94.)

gating the skies, windmills and waterfalls, parades marching down village streets, and steamboats paddling on streams (figs. 213–216). One of Porter's 1822 advertisements pitched his painted landscape views to potential customers: "Those gentlemen who are desirous of spending the gloomy winter months amidst pleasant groves and verdant fields, are respectfully invited to apply . . . where a specimen of the work may be seen."[31]

Porter incorporated many of his conventions into the American landscape he painted in 1838 for the Westwood, Massachusetts, home of Dr. Francis Howe (fig. 217). He augmented his lively scene with a discreetly hidden image that he would use only once—two trees in a field to form the silhouette of a soldier, arms folded across his chest. Whether the allusion is a patriotic one that suggests a soldier keeping watch over the American countryside, or a reference to Napoléon, as hinted by one scholar, remains open to the viewer's interpretation.[32]

Most artists painted murals entirely by hand, yet Porter's later writings encouraged the use of time-saving devices. In an 1845 article in *Scientific*

FIGURE 217 Rufus Porter, *Landscape Mural with Soldier,* Dr. Francis Howe House, Westwood, Massachusetts, 1838. Paint on plaster on chestnut lath. 60" x 30". (Courtesy, Donald Heller and Kimberly Washam.)

American, he advised his fellow artisans to make paper patterns, particularly for "ships and other vessels," and stencils for outlining houses, arbors, and villages. The recommendations were well-founded. Porter boasted that he knew an artist who in less than five hours painted the walls of a parlor "with a variety of fancy scenery" that included palaces, villages, mills, and vessels, and "a beautiful set of shade trees in the foreground."[33]

The labor-saving techniques helped to make landscape views increasingly affordable. Porter advertised "to paint walls of rooms, in elegant full colors, LANDSCAPE SCENERY, at prices less than the ordinary expense of papering." These Fancy scenes must have seemed exceedingly attractive to consumers compared to costly imported landscape wallpapers, which also were called "Fancy Landscape Paper Hangings," as evidenced by an advertisement placed in 1813 by Moses Grant that described the "fashionable" goods in his Boston store.[34] Porter's fee for painting a room with landscapes is unknown, but it must have been a trifle compared to the thirty-five dollars generally paid for scenic papers during the 1820s and 1830s—a fee that usually doubled by the time the papers had been installed. Expense aside, many middle-class homeowners preferred landscapes of American scenes rather than the anonymous and unfamiliar views imported from abroad.[35]

Rufus Porter also introduced in his instructions the novel method of transferring prints to painted surfaces or to glass, noting that "Prints are sometimes used in ornamental painting."[36] Applying prints to other media, a highly efficient and cost-effective mode of decoration, had long been popular, dating to the seventeenth century and possibly earlier. For example, the "transfer" process had been preceded in the eighteenth century by transfer printing on ceramics and by the practice of gluing prints to the reverse of glass, highlighting the details with paint to enliven them, and then framing and hanging them on the wall. The latter process approximated the appearance of an oil painting but was executed at far less cost and far greater speed. The practice continued into the early years of the nineteenth century, when it was employed to ornament many other materials. As products such as looking glasses and inexpensive shelf clocks entered the mass market, designers frequently ornamented cases and frames with transfer prints.

After 1815 Fancy artisans explored new ways of transferring prints to objects, including gluing the images facedown on a painted surface and then removing the paper, leaving the printed image behind. A final coat of varnish provided a protective covering. The process was used in numerous ways. "This work is frequently applied to fancy sleighs, fire engines, and omnibuses," noted Porter. Furniture makers also applied transfer prints, as on a brilliant yellow Fancy chair (figs. 218 and 219) from a large set accompanied by a matching dressing table and rocking chair, each ornamented with a scene of William Tell shooting an apple from his son's head.[37]

A select group of Fancy furnishings improved upon the specialized technique of transparent painting on glass.[38] The images were painted

FIGURE 218 Chair, New York, ca. 1825. Wood and painted and transfer-printed decoration. H. 36", W. 16", D. 16". (Collection of Jolie Kelter and Michael Malcé; photo, Gavin Ashworth.)

FIGURE 219 Detail showing the crest rail of the chair illustrated in fig. 218.

freehand on the reverse side of the glass, and sometimes included stenciled scenes or gilded details. The techniques were difficult to execute because, unlike a painter's canvas, the glass was in front of the image. Therefore, the image had to be built up in reverse order, with the foreground and highlights applied first and the background last. Inexpensive looking glasses and mantel clocks in elaborate cases, turned out by the thousands in New England factories, frequently incorporated reverse paintings on

FIGURE 220   Eli Terry, Jr., shelf clock, Plymouth, Connecticut, ca. 1845. Mahogany, other woods, glass, and painted and stenciled decoration with wood works. H. 24½". (Courtesy, National Watch and Clock Museum, Columbia, Pennsylvania.)

FIGURE 221   Transparent shade, *Liberty and Washington*, New York or Connecticut, 1805–1815. Oil on canvas. 74" x 44". (Courtesy, Fenimore Art Museum, Cooperstown, New York; photo, Richard Walker.)

glass (fig. 220). In earlier days only the rich could afford clocks, but now, Alexis de Tocqueville's lament about watches in the 1830s was just as apt: "Few are now made which are worth much, but everybody has one."[39] Reverse painting helped to reinforce the novelty of owning a Fancy timepiece, even if it was readily affordable to the general public. One of the few descriptions of an ornamented mantel clock appears in Mark Twain's *Huckleberry Finn*:

> There was a clock in the middle of the mantelpiece, with a picture of a town painted on . . . the glass front, and a round place in the middle of it for the sun, and you could see the pendulum swing behind it. It was beautiful to hear that clock tick; and sometimes when one of these peddlars had been along and scoured her up and got her in good shape, she would start in and strike a hundred and fifty before she got tuckered out. They wouldn't took any money for her.[40]

Beginning in the eighteenth century there emerged a new genre of "transparent" goods intended to tantalize the eye by applying ornament to light-conducting fabrics. Among the earliest examples of this engaging technique were stage sets in which an artist painted designs on thin fabric and lit them from behind. Soon after, three-dimensional parade banners composed of fabric stretched taut over wooden frames and illuminated from within by candles became a popular addition to nighttime marches and celebrations. Artist Charles Willson Peale was one of the first Americans to take transparent painting into the realm of fine art when he incorporated it into a magnificent outdoor "triumphal arch" that he built to celebrate the Treaty of Paris early in 1784.[41]

By the start of the nineteenth century, transparent painting emerged as one of the more imaginative modes of ornamental painting, and it found a receptive audience with transparent shades for windows. Although few of these shades survive today, they, of all objects, epitomize the American love affair with Fancy (fig. 221). Perhaps the first clear documentation for painted American shades appeared in 1792, when Hugh Barkley and Patrick O'Meara of Baltimore advertised "transparent Blinds for Windows." Four years later, William Matthews and Company of Philadelphia, "House, Sign, and Ship-Painters," offered to execute "transparencies, silks for windows" in addition to ornamented fire buckets.[42] Painted shades were common in many fashionable households by the 1820s and 1830s.

Unlike modern window shades, Fancy transparent shades of the nineteenth century were not intended to block light from entering a room but, conversely, to permit it to enter in intriguing ways (fig. 222). Made of sheer fabric, the shades were painted on their interiors with scenes clearly visible to the residents of the house. Light shining through them by day highlighted the colorful designs on the delicate fabric and created whimsical shadows and patterns that moved across the room with the sun. The shades were particularly helpful in summer, for they not only tantalized the eye and protected the carpets and furnishings from the damaging effects of excess light, they also allowed for needed room ventilation while retaining some sense of privacy for those indoors. An advertisement by the New York Patent Transparent Window Shade Manufactory in 1844 warranted their products "to be painted in oil colors and washable to allow a free circulation of air, and not to impregnate with a noxious and disagreeable gas." Wrote another: "Shades keep out the sun as completely

FIGURE 222   Transparent shade, probably New York City, 1830–1845. Oil on linen. 52" x 32". (Courtesy, Wayne Fisher's American Design, Alexandria, Virginia; photo, Gavin Ashworth.)

as the Venetians, without keeping out the light, too."[43] One manufacturer assured his customers that "A neat and beautiful Window Shade never fails to exemplify the taste of its owner," and a newspaper review of his products affirmed that they created "considerable excitement among people of good taste."[44] Passersby did not have to go inside to see the designs. At night, strategically placed oil lamps shone through the shades and impressed people on the street.

The late 1820s and 1830s saw a significant rise in the popularity of not only transparent Fancy window shades but also ornamental valances that accompanied them (figs. 223–226). In 1828 Frances Trollope was overwhelmed by the preponderance of heavy, plain, paper shades that "darkened" interiors and prevented air from circulating: "I . . . met with these same uncomfortable blinds in every part of America," she complained. By the 1830s an insistence upon maintaining light interiors with fresh circulating air induced some manufacturers to claim, as did an advertisement in an 1839 edition of the *Rochester Republican,* that significant

FIGURE 223 "Ball & Price, Plain and Fancy Blind-Factory," trade card, New York City, ca. 1830. Lithograph. (Collection of the New-York Historical Society. Bella C. Landauer Collection, 48287.) Fancy window cornices were used for Venetian blinds as well as transparent shades.

FIGURE 224 Window valance, New England, 1820–1835. Poplar and painted, gilded, and bronze-powder-stenciled decoration. H. 9⅝", W. 45¼", D. ⅝". (Courtesy, a New York collector; photo, Gavin Ashworth.)

FIGURE 225 Window valance, New York, 1820–1835. Poplar and painted, gilded, and bronze-powder-stenciled decoration. H. 9", W. 45", D. ⅝". (Courtesy, a New York collector; photo, Gavin Ashworth.)

advances had been made in shade production: "Perhaps in no article of household furniture has there been more important improvements, both on the score of beauty and utility, than in the inner shades or painted muslin curtains which now so universally adorn the best dwellings of the metropolis."[45]

Formulas for making transparent shades were widely available in artisans' guides and periodicals like *Scientific American*. Rufus Porter suggested painting a mixture of white soap, white flour paste, and white glue onto cambric to create a translucent background (the word "transparent" was actually a misnomer). Stencils provided designs for borders, and pictorial scenes were painted in oil colors.[46] For the first half of the nineteenth century, shades were usually hand decorated by talented painters such as Joseph Whiting Stock, a limner who made them to order as late as 1845. However, their widespread popularity encouraged factory production. Samuel F. Bartol's manufactory in New York City, founded in the 1830s, not only accommodated 150 artists under its roof by 1850, but also claimed to offer 50,000 different patterns (fig. 227). Business was so extensive that the factory exported vast quantities of shades to the West and South. Sawyer, Ashton, and Company's Great Western Oil Cloth and Window Shade Manufactory of Cincinnati, in business between 1849 and 1856, was so successful that it purchased a riverboat and peddled its wares up the Ohio and down the Mississippi as far south as New Orleans.

FIGURE 226   Window valance, probably New York, 1820–1840. Poplar and painted, gilded, and bronze-powder-stenciled decoration. H. 42⅝", W. 7⅜", D. ⅝". (Courtesy, a New York collector; photo, Gavin Ashworth.)

FIGURE 227   Transparent shade, probably New York, 1835–1845. Painted linen. H. 65¼". (Courtesy, Abby Aldrich Rockefeller Folk Art Museum, Colonial Williamsburg Foundation, Williamsburg, Virginia.)

Company representatives complained of Philadelphia and New York competitors who had done the same. The independent Fancy artisan, working on his own, must have felt the pinch of competition.[47]

Although large firms usually produced a standard line of designs, the challenge from independent painters like Stock still made it necessary for some companies to produce "on order," particularly when first building their clientele. Custom Fancy shades could be made to meet particular needs and, if necessary, were sent great distances to customers. Pencil sketches for a number of these, including six for a Masonic temple in Cincinnati, others for a steamboat, a jeweler, a druggist, and even one for an undertaker, survive among the papers of Sawyer, Ashton, and Company.[48]

Salesmen from some of these larger companies immediately recognized the marketing possibilities of shades sold to prestigious households. John Ashton, on an expedition down the Mississippi to sell shades, wrote back to the parent company in Cincinnati for a rush order: "These shades are for a lady, one of the biggest Nabobs in the city, and it is very urgent to have them if possible within three weeks . . . painted shades at such a house have great influence . . . more [influence] than three dozen sold to inferior houses."[49] Middling houses became a mainstay of the industry, however. Mass production pushed down the price of shades significantly. "Many of these varieties are sold at a very low price—so low indeed, as to place them within the reach of every family," said Bartol in his treatise entitled *Practical Hints on the Subject of Window Ornaments*. By 1850, inexpensive shades could be bought for as little as a dollar apiece.[50]

Manufacturers were quick to emphasize that their products were more than just shades; they were art. "With regard to Shades manufactured by me, they are all of the first class material—the work of artists, and from the pencils of tourists and travelers of distinction," claimed Bartol. The better examples were made of silk or "the finest cambric" and were adorned with "pure gold leaf." Some were stenciled, though most were quickly painted freehand in oils, a practice that John Ashton referred to unflatteringly, behind the scenes, as "slapdashing." Bartol had the audacity to claim that painted shades fell "but a little way beneath a first class oil painting" and were actually "preferred by many," as they were "much more distinct" than real pictures.[51]

Of all the subjects chosen for shades, landscapes were the best, according to Rufus Porter. Apparently others agreed with him, since landscape shades seem to have survived in greater quantities than any other painted design. Of these, "wild scenes of America" were the taste for a while, but "promiscuous landscapes" with castles or Gothic ruins were in vogue from the 1840s onward. Emily Dickinson procured one of the latter in 1841: "I had a transparent blind put up in my open window. There is a castle . . . and a castle-gateway and two walks, and several peasants and groves of trees which rise in excellent harmony with the fall of my green damask curtain," she wrote to a friend.[52] Huckleberry Finn had seen a similar

FIGURE 228 *Transparent Blinds,* illus- trated on pl. 48 in Nathaniel Whittock's *Decorative Painters' and Glaziers' Guide,* London, 1827. (Courtesy, The Winterthur Library: Printed Book and Periodical Col- lection.) This published design for a trans- parent blind was among those copied by American artisans.

example in a Missouri parlor: "There was beautiful curtains on the win- dows; white, with pictures painted on them, of castles with vines all down the walls, and cattle coming down to drink" (fig. 228).[53]

Among the more amusing subjects were the trompe l'oeil shades sold by Sawyer, Ashton, and Company in 1850. Known as "Green Curtains" and "Blue Curtains," these were ornamented with elaborate painted ver- sions of drapery that included fringe, tassels, and tiebacks—and were intended to suggest a window with attached hangings. To complete the composition, between the curtains a trompe l'oeil romantic landscape appeared in the distance.[54]

Other popular and diverse designs offered by the New York Patent Transparent Window Shade Manufactory were arabesques, classical motifs like the "Corinthian design," and a "roseate center," which may have been inspired by the kaleidoscope. Designs also included vignettes and "fancy sketches," or perhaps the "sprawling bouquets" or the "flower baskets in gaudy colors" that one critic found distasteful and out of style by 1851. Other companies provided historical subjects, including Mount Vernon, Monticello, American Indians, and the battle of Bunker Hill. Biblical sub- jects were available to "pious families."[55]

"You have subjects which promote contemplation, while they delight both the eye and the mind," wrote Bartol of his ornamental shades. "The harmony of the painting invariably attracts the attention and gradually mingles sweet and pleasing thoughts with the objects of the mind, what- ever they may be." Even Emily Dickinson's father, who had criticized his daughter's selection for her room, was "obviously moved" when the sun shone through it. Yet contemplation and delight were only part of the effect. "No one is completely alone in a room where there is a fine pair of Window Shades," added Bartol, suggesting that the objects could be appreciated for their emotional as well as their visual appeal. It is little wonder that so many people liked Fancy window shades.[56]

AMERICAN FANCY

6 Bold Furniture for All Americans

Besides the good things he possesses,
he every instant fancies a thousand others.

Alexis de Tocqueville, *Democracy in America*, 1835

After 1815 the heightened emphasis upon distinctive designs inspired Fancy furniture makers to push the limits of form and decoration. Cabinetmakers, turners, Fancy and ornamental painters worked hand in hand to create furnishings that exhibited an imaginative and visual intensity never before realized. At the same time, artisans were developing efficient new ways to produce their invigorated designs, reduce costs without sacrificing impact, and make Fancy furnishings accessible to a larger clientele.

The trend toward reduced production costs was most obvious in Fancy chairs. Formal, woven seats of imported cane gave way to colorfully painted domestic rush, and mortise-and-tenon joints were replaced by drilled and turned elements in all but the most expensive chairs (figs. 229 and 230). These Fancy chairs may have resembled more costly furniture in their colorful decoration, but they borrowed their rush seats and drilled joints from everyday, inexpensive ladderback examples. The clever melding of stylish ornament with inexpensive construction was a particularly effective method for introducing Fancy chairs to the popular market (fig. 231).

As expensive cane-bottom chairs fell out of fashion, Fancy Windsor chairs also gained in popularity (figs. 232 and 233). Characterized by durable plank seats and popular since the early years of the eighteenth century, Windsors long had been painted in solid colors. The influence of

FIGURE 230   Side chair, New York City, ca. 1816. Hickory, yellow poplar, soft maple, ash, with a rush seat and painted decoration. H. 33⅞", W. 19¾", D. 16⅛". (Courtesy, Strawbery Banke Museum. Gift of Gerrit van der Woude, 1988.230.4; photo, Bruce Alexander Photography.)

FIGURE 229   *Martha Eliza Stevens Edgar Paschall*, St. Louis, Missouri, ca. 1823. Oil on canvas. 52¼" x 40⅜". (Courtesy, National Gallery of Art. Gift of Mary Paschall Young Doty and Katharine Campbell Young Keck, 1983.95.1; photo, © 2003 Board of Trustees, National Gallery of Art, Washington.) After 1815 glistening ornament and inexpensive but brightly painted rush seats such as those on the Fancy chairs in this painting helped popularize Fancy seating furniture.

Fancy brought this traditional seating form to unprecedented decorative heights, and Fancy Windsors served as a medium for spreading the style to a wider audience. Rush-bottom and plank-seated Fancy chairs, formal and informal, appeared everywhere together in an array of brilliant colors. They were grained and marbled and invariably ornamented with gold leaf

FIGURE 231   Side chair, possibly by Thomas Ash, New York City, ca. 1820. Maple with a rush seat and painted and gilt decoration. H. 33¼", W. 18", D. 16". (Courtesy, Wunsch Americana Collections, New York State Museum, Albany, New York.)

FIGURE 232   Armchair, New York, 1814–1820. Yellow poplar and maple. H. 37", W. 19", D. 20⅛". (Courtesy, Winterthur Museum.) Fancy Windsor chairs were characterized by their solid plank seats.

FIGURE 233   Chair, Pennsylvania, ca. 1825. Poplar, maple, and painted and gilt decoration. H. 33", W. 16", D. 15½". (Courtesy, Joyce and William Subjack; photo, Gavin Ashworth.)

or stenciled with colorful bronze powder. Some chairs were adorned with hand-painted landscapes, while other, more affordable examples sported printed scenes transferred from paper.

Fancy Windsors were available individually or in sets of a dozen or more complete with side chairs and matching armchairs. They were used in kitchens, parlors, and legislative halls—anywhere that seating might be needed (fig. 234). Forms for public spaces like schools, courtrooms, or churches often were special ordered. A chair made about 1831 by a local chair maker for the Union Street Methodist Church of Petersburg, Virginia, was tastefully ornamented with Fancy painting, biblical references, and an image of Jacob crossing the Jordan (figs. 235 and 236).[1] Creativity was especially common in smaller shops, where workmen had greater freedom to interpret decorative details or where customers could specifically

FIGURE 234 *John and James Hasson*, attributed to Joshua Johnson, Baltimore, 1813–1816. Oil on canvas. 47" x 39½". (Courtesy, Winterthur Museum. Gift of the Estate of Mrs. John W. Perkins.) The Fancy Windsor chairs in this portrait are painted to suggest that they are constructed of an improbable material—blue marble.

FIGURE 235 Armchair, Virginia, ca. 1831. Maple, hickory, and painted decoration. H. 32", W. 15", D. 18". (Courtesy, Washington Street United Methodist Church, formerly Union Street Methodist Church, Petersburg, Virginia; photo, Colonial Williamsburg Foundation.)

FIGURE 236 Detail showing the crest rail of the armchair illustrated in fig. 235.

request commissioned works. Here patron and artisan alike had latitude to test their skills by designing works with playful conceits and exceptionally brilliant colors, or distorting certain elements to increase the surface area available for ornamentation and to elicit a response from the viewer.

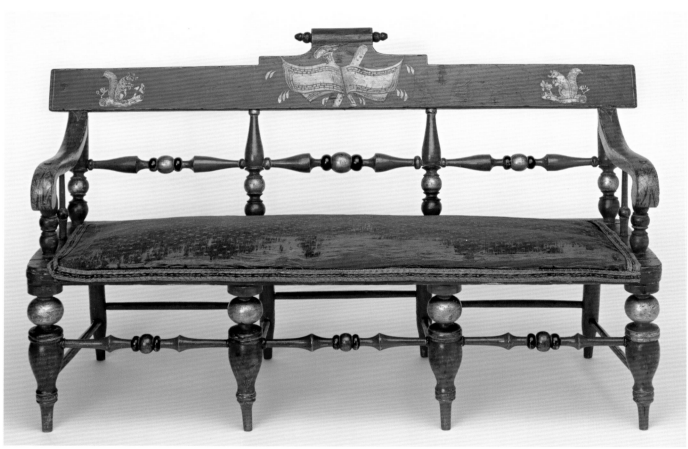

Large, traditional seating furniture like settees were especially well suited to whimsical Fancy adaptations of form and decoration. One example (fig. 237) with exaggerated classical details has tremendous scrolled arms that coil tightly like springs and a massive crest rail painted with three military trophies, each composed of a shield, cannon, sword, and banner. Expanding on the military references, the painter treated the back supports as though they were pikes, with spiky foliate arrows that pierce the crest. A child's brilliant red settee (fig. 238) is similarly decorated with lively turned elements and an exaggerated crest, capped in the center with a scrolled tablet adorned with a trophy of music and, unexpectedly, a squirrel on either end.

A yellow child's chair with improbable proportions epitomizes the enlivened Fancy aesthetic after 1815 (fig. 239). The massively scaled rockers serve no practical function beyond providing an expanded canvas upon which to showcase the gleaming yellow paint and ornamental scenes. Another equally exuberant Fancy footstool (fig. 240) features an elaborately contoured skirt, and painted decoration covers every inch of the piece. The stylized baskets packed with strawberries and the flowers spread on the top of the stool create a dynamic tension, while a bold, black stripe meanders around the skirt and gives the eye a needed diversion from the tightly focused ornament. A Massachusetts dressing table

FIGURE 239   Child's rocking Windsor chair, Virginia, possibly Abingdon, ca. 1825. Yellow pine, poplar, maple, hickory, and painted and transfer-printed decoration. H. 17", W. 10", D. 19". (Courtesy, Roddy and Sally Moore.)

FIGURE 240   Miniature footstool, probably New England or Pennsylvania, 1830–1840. Wood and painted decoration. H. 4⅞", W. 8¹³⁄₁₆", D. 4⅜". (Collection of the American Folk Art Museum, New York. Promised gift of Ralph Esmerian, P1.2001.87; photo © 2000 John Bigelow Taylor, New York.)

FIGURE 241 Dressing table, Salem, Massachusetts, ca. 1820. White pine, birch, and painted decoration. H. 46½", W. 34", D. 17". (Collection of Frank and Barbara Pollack.) The elaborately shaped dressing box, although appearing to be a separate piece, was constructed as a unit with the table.

accompanied by an attached dressing box illustrates one way that design was manipulated (fig. 241). Here the artisan has juxtaposed subtle and extreme elements. The restrained white palette, the modestly scaled urn, and the delicate carving are counterbalanced by a massive, arched splashboard fitted with boldly shaped scrolls that turn severely downward. The piece is taut with visual energy.

Playfully exaggerated elements such as the high backs on chairs from the Ohio River valley epitomize the bold features on many forms of post-1815 Fancy furniture. Although New England artisans produced similar chairs, principally in Vermont and New Hampshire, the midwestern examples are uncommonly narrow and therefore extremely vertical in emphasis. A Masonic chair (fig. 242) made for Union Lodge #2, of Madison, Indiana, and a writing chair (fig. 243) represent two of the most successful pieces in this form and may have been constructed by James Huey of

FIGURE 242   Masonic master's chair, western Pennsylvania or Ohio River valley, ca. 1840. Poplar, maple, and painted and gilt decoration. H. 50½", W. 19⅞", D. 22½". (Courtesy, Elbert H. Parsons, Jr.; photo, Gavin Ashworth.)

FIGURE 243   Writing armchair, western Pennsylvania or Ohio River valley, ca. 1820. Wood and painted decoration. H. 45¼", W. 38", D. 32⅞". (Courtesy, Abby Aldrich Rockefeller Folk Art Museum, Colonial Williamsburg Foundation, Williamsburg, Virginia.)

Zanesville, Ohio. Huey established his shop in 1828 and was ideally located to ship his products east and west via the highway that ran through town, or down the Muskingum River to the Ohio River, giving him access to the extensive hinterland. He enjoyed great success, employed dozens of workmen, and, adapting his products to the times, remained in business until 1851.[2]

A Windsor side chair (fig. 244) made in New York or New England is a lively example of a simple form heightened in unexpected ways. The spindles are blown out of proportion to create arrows wide enough to contain grape clusters, and the lively crest arches upward to highlight the central landscape panel. The painter did not depict an ordinary scene but rather an imaginary jungle in which a lion strides confidently across the terrain, glancing outward toward the viewer. The chair originally came from a larger set that depicted other exotic animals. The set may have alluded to a familiar event; no less than thirty different menageries with exotic animals traveled the country during the 1820s, offering Americans in every walk of life their first live views of these foreign creatures. Promoters often advertised the shows on large, pictorial broadsides, frequently illustrated with wood-block prints of lions, tigers, and elephants just like those that appear on the crests of the chairs (fig. 245).[3]

FIGURE 244   Side chair, New York or New England, ca. 1820. White pine, maple, and painted decoration. H. 35¼", W. 21¾", D. 18". (Courtesy, New York State Historical Association, Cooperstown, New York; photo, Richard Walker.)

FIGURE 245   Detail showing the crest rail of the side chair illustrated in fig. 244.

Occasionally cabinetmakers designed and produced wholly unprecedented forms, such as the bizarre desk-and-bookcase attributed to Joshua Livingston Wells of Long Island, New York (fig. 246). The eye-catching piece with Fancy painted surface and curious pinwheel decorations is every bit as fanciful in form and function as in ornament. Wells seemed determined not only to make this desk as versatile as possible, but also to utilize every possible space within. While the shelves of the upper case presumably are intended to hold books, the interior compartments are configured in unexpected ways. In the space usually concealed within the pediment, Wells created a display cabinet featuring a hinged glazed door; to the lower case he added windows in a space reserved for a drawer. If storage, writing, and display were not enough, the piece also served as an entertainment center. The central slide is painted with an ornamental tray; when it was pulled out and bedecked with a tea set and pot filled with steaming tea, it surely would have been a Fancy sight to behold.[4]

FIGURE 246   Desk-and-bookcase, attributed to Joshua Livingston Wells, Aqueboque,
New York, ca. 1820. White pine and painted
decoration. H. 83", W. 43½", D. 29¼". (Courtesy, Abby Aldrich Rockefeller Folk Art
Museum, Colonial Williamsburg Foundation, Williamsburg, Virginia.)

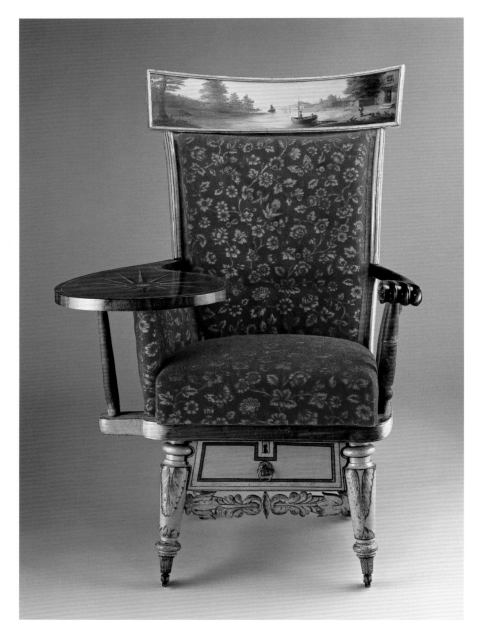

Equally idiosyncratic is a Fancy writing chair (fig. 247) that was designed
to serve numerous functions and probably was a special-order item. The
writing surface is elaborately veneered and inlaid with a compass star
(fig. 248), while the crest is ornamented with an expansive and imaginative landscape scene. Unlike most Fancy furniture, the seat and back were
intended to be upholstered, in this case, with plush, patterned wool, and
beneath the seat is a sliding drawer for storage.

Odd as the all-in-one writing chair may seem, it was joined increasingly
after 1815 by a furniture form that would become commonplace in American households—the rocking chair. Just as kaleidoscopic quilts and floorcloths with undulating patterns had provided visual motion in household
interiors, Fancy rocking chairs offered Americans the opportunity to per-
sonally participate in real-life motion. Rocking while sitting, familiar as it

is today, was a novel experience for early nineteenth-century consumers. Rocking chairs were unknown in America for most of the eighteenth century, when social conventions encouraged people to sit erect in their chairs and place their feet squarely on the floor.[5] The possibility of adding something as frivolous as rocking chairs to parlor seating was not even considered. As in Great Britain, the primary setting for furniture with rockers was in the nursery, on pieces intended for children, specifically, cradles for infants and on chairs for nursing mothers and wet nurses. The 1740s account book of the Philadelphia upholsterer Solomon Fussell notes the production of a rush-seated "Nurse Chair with Rockers."[6] In the nineteenth century, however, Americans in particular began to gravitate toward rocking chairs, an affinity that cut across all social levels.[7]

The earliest American rocking chairs were made by adding rockers to straight-legged chairs, often inexpensive ones with rush bottoms and ladder backs. A few had arms, but most did not. Not until the era of Fancy, however, did the demand for decorated rockers increase, and Fancy artisans seized the opportunity to standardize the form and begin producing decorated rocking chairs by the thousands. The majority were large armchairs painted in bright colors and ornamented with freehand painting or stenciled decoration (fig. 249). Many had loose cushions of colorful fabric that appealed particularly to the elderly or infirm. Variations included chairs with swivel seats, rocking benches, and rocking benches with crib

FIGURE 249 Windsor rocking chair, New England, ca. 1825. Maple and painted decoration. H. 46", W. 21¼", D. 27". (Courtesy, Marshall Goodman; photo, Katherine Wetzel.)

FIGURE 250   Rocking settee, Maine, 1830–1845. Basswood, birch, maple, pine, and painted and stenciled decoration. H. 33", W. 56", D. 27¼". (Courtesy, Maine State Museum, Augusta, Maine.)

attachments (fig. 250). As with later versions of Fancy furniture, most Fancy rocking chairs were relatively inexpensive. Connecticut chair maker Lambert Hitchcock charged a client $1.75 for "1 fancy rocker" in 1828. Evidence strongly suggests they were preferred by women and, when used by men, were employed principally by the elderly.[8] In 1828 William Hancock of Boston offered for sale a "fancy nurse chair," and evidence suggests that these specialized Fancy rocking chairs were less expensive than standard versions.[9]

One popular variant developed in Boston during the 1820s was ergonomically designed to maximize the comfort of the sitter (fig. 251). This rocking chair featured a shaped wooden seat, undulating scrolled arms, contoured spindles to support the back, and a commodious crest that served as a headrest. Highly ornate examples with landscape scenes and elegant upholstery were sometimes produced for wealthy customers, but most versions were affordable for middle-class clients. America's rapidly expanding national transportation network made it possible for merchants and auction houses from afar to capitalize on the great popularity of these rockers. In 1830 Richard Wright, a merchant in Washington, D.C., advertised "those much admired high back Boston-made Rocking

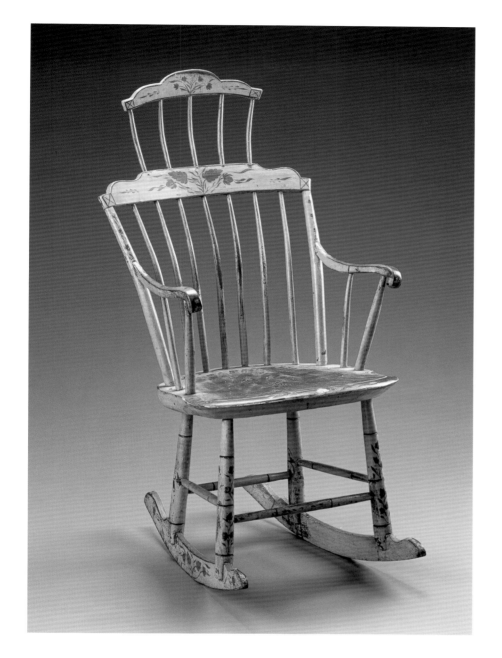

FIGURE 251   Rocking chair, New England, probably Massachusetts, 1830–1840. Pine, maple, and painted and stenciled decoration. H. 45", W. 26¾", D. 28". (From the Collections of Henry Ford Museum & Greenfield Village.)

FIGURE 252   Rocking chair, New England, 1815–1825. Maple, pine, other woods, and painted decoration. H. 42¾", W. 21", D. 25¾". (Courtesy, Milwaukee Art Museum, Layton Art Collection. Gift of Anne H. Vogel, in memory of her mother, Mrs. Faith Henoch Selzer, L2003.1; photo, Larry Sanders.)

Chairs." So many were exported from New England in the late 1820s and 1830s that they were identified generically as "Boston Rocking Chairs" or, when highly decorated, "Fancy Boston Rocking Chairs." Even James C. Helme, an artisan working in rural Plymouth, Pennsylvania, in 1838, made Boston Rocking Chairs costing two dollars each.[10]

British travelers had much to say about Americans' infatuation with Fancy rocking chairs (fig. 252). When James Frewin entered a household in St. Louis in the 1830s, he was amused by the ceremony that attended the use of a rocking chair. "It is considered a compliment to give the stranger the rocking-chair as a seat; and when there is more than one kind in the house, the stranger is always presented with the best," he noted.[11] Likewise, British visitor Harriet Martineau observed, "A beloved pastor has every room in his house furnished with a rocking chair by his grateful and devoted people."[12] Martineau was surprised to see great numbers of rocking chairs in taverns and inns and to find that women used them primarily. She was aghast at the behavior they encouraged:

> In these small inns the disagreeable practice of rocking in the chair is seen in its excess. In the inn parlors are three or four rocking chairs in which sit ladies who are vibrating in different directions and at various velocities, so as to try the head of a stranger. . . . How this lazy and ungraceful indulgence ever became general, I cannot imagine, but the nation seems [so] wedded to it, that I see little chance of its being forsaken.[13]

On a visit to England in 1835, Amherst College president Heman Humphrey was amazed to find that rocking chairs were almost unknown there. When he finally encountered one, he learned that they were considered "Americanisms" and noted that the "staid" and "upright" British were unlikely ever to adopt them. Rocking chairs had become vital to American social life, however, and Harriet Martineau remarked in 1838, "When American ladies come to live in Europe, they sometimes send home for a rocking chair."[14]

If Fancy rocking chairs reflected the American temperament and Americans' emboldened approach to design and form, so too did a growing variety of other Fancy chairs. Among the most successful Fancy furniture makers was William Buttre, whose retail stores flourished for sixteen years—in New York City from 1805 until 1814, and in Albany between 1814 and 1821. In 1814 he offered "A large assortment of elegant well made and highly finished" chairs sold "on the most moderate terms," including "Settees, Conversation, Elbow, Rocking, Sewing and Children's Chairs of every description" (fig. 253).[15] His was no ordinary establishment, for he could accommodate customers with tremendous demands, boasting "A thousand Windsor chairs will be delivered at a few

FIGURE 253   "William Buttre's Fancy Chair Store," advertisement in David Longworth's *Longworth's American Almanac, New York Register, and City Directory,* New York, 1814. (Courtesy, Winterthur Library: Printed Book and Periodical Collection.)

FANCY CHAIR STORE.

William Buttre, No. 17, *Bowery-Lane, near the Watch-House, New-York, has constantly for sale,*

A large assortment of elegant well made and highly finished black, white, brown, coquelico, American Eagle Chairs, Gold and Fancy Chairs, Settees, Conversation, Elbow, Rocking, Sewing and Children's Chairs of every description, and on the most moderate terms.

Orders from any part of the continent will be attended to with punctuality and despatch. A liberal allowance made to shippers, &c.

Old Chairs repaired, varnished and regilt.

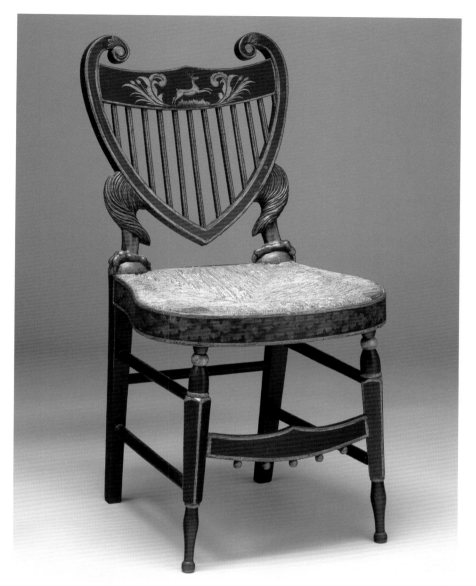

FANCY CHAIR STORE.

WILLIAM BUTTRE,

No.17, Bowery, New York and 124, State-street, ALBANY,

HAS CONSTANTLY FOR SALE,

A LARGE assortment of elegant, well-made, and highly finish'd Black, White, Brown,
Coquelico, Gold, and Eagle Fancy Chairs, Settees, Conversation, Elbow, Rocking, Sewing,
Windsor, and Children's Chairs
of every description, and on the
most reasonable terms.

ORDERS

From any part of the country
will be attended to with punctuality and despatch

☞ *Old Chairs repaired, varnished, and re-gilt.*

Albany, February 16, 1815.   14 1y

hours notice." Buttre's best chairs were highly ornate and expensive. In
1816 he offered "curled maple Fancy Chairs" for $4.25 apiece, about four
times the cost of a plain painted chair. He also attracted important public commissions, charging the New York Supreme Court $135.00 in 1818
for a set of forty-two "Bamboo Fancy Chairs" accompanied by five
"Fancy Arm Chairs."[16]

A distinctive "Eagle Fancy Chair" is among the more engaging forms
produced in Buttre's establishment (fig. 254). His advertisement for the
chair (fig. 255) included an engraved image to attract customers and was
placed in the *Albany Advertiser* on February 16, 1815, the day before President Madison ratified the Treaty of Ghent, which would end the War of
1812. Although it is not clear whether Buttre made many chairs exactly like
those he advertised—with an eagle's head projecting above the crest and
a carved fan attached to the front stretchers—his patriotic allusion and
imaginative form were perfectly in tune with Fancy.[17]

By the 1820s a great variety of relatively inexpensive Fancy chairs, including rockers, was available to individuals of moderate means. Regional tastes can be discerned from the illustrations chosen to advertise these chairs. One particularly popular type of New York Fancy chair had a rush seat, simplified turnings, and a pierced horizontal slat (fig. 256). This model appears on a trade card for John Knox Cowperthwaite's "Fancy and Windsor Chair Store" at 4 Chatham Square (fig. 257), where "on hand [was] an elegant and large assortment of curled maple, bronze and painted Fancy Chairs." His 1816 invoice to Stephen Wheeler charged twelve dollars for a set of eight chairs—a mere dollar and a half apiece.[18] Newspaper advertisements for the firm of Wheaton and Davis, "Fancy Chair Manufacturers" at 153 Fulton Street, New York, employed precisely the same chair design.[19]

FIGURE 256 John Knox Cowperthwaite, armchair, New York City, 1810–1820. Maple, tulip poplar, and painted decoration. H. 34", W. 20", D. 16⅛". (Courtesy, Winterthur Museum.)

FIGURE 257 Trade card of John Knox Cowperthwaite, New York City, printed 1810–1812, inscribed 1816. (Courtesy, Winterthur Library: Joseph Downs Collection of Manuscripts and Printed Ephemera.)

FIGURE 258 Billhead and bill of John Knox Cowperthwaite, New York, printed 1823–1824, inscribed 1825. (Courtesy, Bronson Family Papers, Manuscripts and Archives Division, New York Public Library, Astor, Lennox, and Tilden Foundations.)

Cowperthwaite was among the most successful of New York's Fancy chair manufacturers, and his business grew rapidly during the 1810s and 1820s. By 1818 he had acquired neighboring property and advertised that his establishment now extended from the Chatham Square address through the block to 2 Catherine Street. In 1824, when he ordered a new billhead, the logo bore an engraving of his impressive "Fancy & Windsor Chair Manufactory," its principal entrance leading to the furniture ware-room and other doorways designated for "Hardware" and "Turning" (fig. 258). The business remained in the location only slightly longer, for in 1826 his success necessitated a move to an even larger building in New York City.[20]

One of the city's leading artisans, Cowperthwaite was elected president of the Master Chair-Makers Society by his peers. He was instrumental in planning for the year-long celebrations that attended the completion of

SEYMOUR WATROUS,

INFORMS the public that he has lately commenced the Cabinet and Chair Making business in Central Row, No. 6, directly south of the State-House Square, at the sign of the "Hartford Cabinet and Chair Ware-House," where he is manufacturing from the best materials and by experienced workmen, CABINET FURNITURE and CHAIRS of every description, which he will warrant to be finished in a style equal if not superior to any, and will sell on as reasonable terms as can be purchased at any other Store in this city, or in the city of New-York.

Old Chairs repaired, painted and re-gilt so as to look nearly as well as new.

WANTED IMMEDIATELY,

One Journeyman Chair Maker, and two young lads from the country, fifteen or sixteen years of age, as Apprentices to the Chair making business.

Hartford, March 2, 1824.   1y75

FIGURE 260 "Seymour Watrous, Cabinet Furniture and Chairs," advertisement in *Hartford Times,* Hartford, Connecticut, March 9, 1824. (Courtesy, Connecticut Historical Society, Hartford, Connecticut.)

the Erie Canal in 1824, a task of monumental proportions. The celebration featured a visit by France's Marquis de Lafayette in honor of fifty years of American independence, a grand parade of city officials, and New York hook and ladder companies wearing parade best. Fancy painted fire engines with gilt eagle ornaments were pulled by teams of horses with brass-mounted harnesses and colorful cockades. Each trade organization assembled and marched; John Cowperthwaite led the Chair-Makers Society, its members proudly carrying its banner (fig. 259), recorded for posterity in a memorial booklet published to celebrate the event.[21]

Creating eye-catching advertisements as well as formulating distinctive shapes and decoration was essential for Fancy artisans competing in the American marketplace. Some of the most successful furniture notices sported small but evocative illustrations, such as that by Connecticut chair maker Seymour Watrous published in an 1824 issue of the *Hartford Times* (fig. 260). A Fancy chair made by an unknown artisan reveals the lively painting and animated details characteristic of many such forms (fig. 261). The brilliant green paint and yellow rush seat combine with the mythological sea creatures silhouetted within the pierced splat to heighten the effect. As was the common practice, the Fancy scene in the crest of each chair in this set depicts a different landscape.

In response to the rising demand for Fancy furniture after 1820, American artisans increased their output. Although small shops still made Fancy chairs in villages across the country, large-scale production became the norm. Fancy furnishings from large factories were less individualistic than earlier pieces, as it no longer paid to experiment with daring new forms or unique creations. Producers standardized designs and streamlined production to maximize efficiency, permitting prices to plummet in the 1820s and 1830s. Soon only factories were competitive in an increasingly crowded Fancy market.

The capacity to provide a thousand chairs on short order became a standard for the larger manufactories. Connecticut, a state that lacked large cities but still boasted some of the most highly developed early factories, owed its commercial preeminence in chair making to Lambert Hitchcock (1795–1852). He was a pivotal figure whose mechanical skills transformed the traditional craft of chair making into a factory industry and whose business acumen allowed him to find a national market for his Fancy wares (fig. 262).[22]

In 1818 the energetic and aspiring twenty-three-year-old Hitchcock borrowed money from a group of friends and set up shop in the hamlet of Riverton, tucked away on the Farmington River in northwestern Connecticut. With abundant waterpower to turn lathes, inexhaustible forests to supply wood, and industrious workmen from nearby towns to produce

FIGURE 261   Side chair, probably New York or Connecticut, 1815–1825. Wood, painted decoration, and rush. H. 32¼", W. 18⅞", D. 18⅝". (Courtesy, Abby Aldrich Rockefeller Folk Art Museum, Colonial Williamsburg Foundation, Williamsburg, Virginia.)

FIGURE 262   Lambert Hitchcock, side chair, Hitchcocksville, Litchfield County, Connecticut, 1826–1829. Wood, cane, bronze powder stenciling, and painted and gold-leaf decoration. H. 34¾", W. 18", D. 15". (Collection of the American Folk Art Museum, New York. Gift of the Historical Society of Early American Decoration, 58.29.)

goods, Hitchcock's business epitomized modern efficiency and employed innovative sales strategies. When limited space hampered his capacity to produce chairs and store the finished products, he began to sell chairs unassembled to merchants and artisans up and down the East Coast. The tightly bundled chair parts were inexpensive to ship, and Hitchcock could tap distant markets unimpeded by competition. Local buyers assembled the interchangeable pieces and sometimes decorated them according to regional tastes.[23] Vast numbers of Hitchcock's chairs were sent to southern markets through Charleston, South Carolina, where traders were encouraged by his liberal extension of credit.[24]

Hitchcock's isolation from his expanding markets made it necessary for him to rely upon a well-developed transportation network to connect him with store owners, peddlers, and auction houses. Even today, with paved roads, Riverton is not an easy place to reach. In spite of being hindered by mountainous terrain and bad winter weather, Hitchcock still managed to send completed Fancy chairs halfway across the country. The turnpike ran nearby, and Hartford was some twenty-five miles or a day's ride away.

Hitchcock's best distributors would take on hundreds of chairs at a time, selling them during the 1820s for prices that ranged from forty-five cents to one dollar seventy-five cents retail, and from twenty-five cents to one dollar wholesale—a significant reduction from the prices charged by William Buttre just a decade before. Steamers out of Hartford transported the chairs to the ports of New York and Boston, and southward to Philadelphia, Baltimore, Norfolk, Richmond, and Charleston.[25]

Hitchcock's factory specialized in the production of all sorts of Fancy seating furniture—chairs, armchairs, and rocking chairs; settees, benches, and "settee cradles" (figs. 263 and 264). They were available with rush seats, cane seats, or plank bottoms. Most were stenciled with still lifes in inexpensive bronze powders, rather than painted in oil with artful landscape scenes. The firm's daybooks reveal that it also produced on a lesser scale washstands, tables, and chests of drawers. Documented examples of these forms are rare today.[26]

In 1832 Lambert Hitchcock formed a chair-making partnership with his brother-in-law Arba Alford (fig. 265). This was a means not only of

FIGURE 265 Hitchcock, Alford, and Company, side chair, 1832–1843. Maple, spruce, painted and stenciled decoration, and rush. H. 33", W. 17", D. 16". (Courtesy, Abby Aldrich Rockefeller Folk Art Museum, Colonial Williamsburg Foundation, Williamsburg, Virginia.) The chair is stenciled: "HITCHCOCK, ALFORD, & CO. HITCH-COCKSVILLE, CONN. WARRANTED."

pooling financial resources and craft skills, but also of sharing responsibility for the rapidly expanding business. Alford assumed the task of managing the factory and its workers, while Hitchcock focused on marketing and sales. Two years later Hitchcock brought in Alfred Alford, another of his wife's brothers, and placed him in charge of a new retail outlet in Hartford. With one member of the family now overseeing production, and another sales, the entrepreneurial Hitchcock was free to float back and forth between the two as needed.[27] It soon was evident to him that a vast market in the American Midwest remained untapped. With the Erie Canal completed in 1825, it was now possible to ship chairs inland and to extend sales into the interior of North America. In the fall of 1835 Hitchcock took a four-month journey hoping to find agents to sell his products. He first traveled to New York and Philadelphia, made important contacts, then advanced to Cincinnati and St. Louis, up the Mississippi River toward Chicago, and returned to Connecticut via a northern route, a journey that proved to be lucrative.[28]

FIGURE 266 *The House and Shop of David Alling,* Newark, New Jersey, 1840–1850. Oil on canvas. 21" x 30". (Collection of The Newark Museum. Purchase, 1939, Thomas L. Raymond Bequest Fund.)

The national marketing of Fancy chairs by makers such as Hitchcock resulted in the dispersal of details from region to region, making it difficult today to identify the specific origins for many of the pieces. Consider the products of David Alling, whose prosperous shop in Newark, New Jersey, was painted by a local artist who may also have worked there

FIGURE 267   Side chair, attributed to David Alling, Newark, New Jersey, ca. 1835. Wood and painted decoration. H. 34½", W. 17¾". (Collection of The Newark Museum. Gift of Madison Alling, 1923.)

FIGURE 268   Isaac Wright, washstand, Hartford, Connecticut, ca. 1830. White pine, basswood, and painted decoration. H. 37", W. 18", D. 16⅞". (Courtesy, Connecticut Historical Society, Hartford, Connecticut.) The washstand bears the maker's stencil: "Isaac Wright & Co. / Cabinet / Chair / Upholstery / & Warehouse / Hartford / Con."

(fig. 266). One chair line that Alling made (fig. 267) is similar in style to Hitchcock's chairs, which may well have been his intention. Undaunted by competition from Connecticut, Alling sent chairs to New England for sale, where he apparently met with great success.[29]

While Hitchcock and Alling specialized in Fancy furniture, other manufacturers provided various stylistic options for their customers. Isaac Wright and Company of Hartford, Connecticut, sold austere veneered Grecian furniture, such as the sofas and card tables offered in 1837, as well as colorfully painted Fancy pieces. A Fancy washstand bearing his label (fig. 268) was described in an 1835 invoice as a "painted washstand grape bush pattern," and illumines the character of the Fancy furniture he sold alongside the staid Grecian examples.[30]

FIGURE 269 John and Hugh Finlay, side chair, Baltimore, ca. 1820. Tulip poplar, maple, and painted and gilt decoration. H. 32¾", W. 17⅜", D. 15⅜". (Courtesy, Colonial Williamsburg Foundation.)

FIGURE 270 Center table, attributed to John Finlay, Baltimore, ca. 1825. Poplar, other woods, and painted, gessoed, and gilt decoration. H. 30¼", Diam. 33". (Courtesy, Brooklyn Museum of Art. Purchased with funds given by an anonymous donor, The American Art Council, and Designated Purchase Fund, 88.24.)

Similarly, established firms like John and Hugh Finlay of Baltimore adapted their products to keep pace with mainstream stylistic developments, including America's growing appreciation of the Grecian taste in neoclassical design. There was little doubt that their "Grecian Fancy Chairs" (fig. 269) or "Fancy Grecian center tables" (fig. 270) still teased the imagination. Yet new style features, such as the table's central pedestal and imported top depicting classical ruins, and new forms, such as the Finlays' distinctive chairs, reflected a changing aesthetic. These Fancy chairs found an enthusiastic following throughout the region. As more furniture makers in the East began to copy and produce variations on the Finlay forms, they, like the Boston rocker, became identified with a place and acquired the generic name "Baltimore chairs."[31]

In short, 1815 to 1840 witnessed a feverish era of Fancy furniture making in America. Artisans from a wide array of craft specialties worked together to elevate the style through the creative exploration of form and ornament, and consumers eagerly incorporated these Fancy expressions into their homes. Fancy furniture, once affordable only to the most affluent, emerged as a truly democratic American furniture style in the arts. The concurrent rise of larger-scale manufacturing and the creation of greatly improved national transportation networks hastened the spread of Fancy into all parts of the nation and allowed a number of eastern manufacturers to consolidate large segments of the Fancy furniture market.

7 Wares to Enrich the Home and the Mind

Stepping into a Fancy Store, I was not only gratified but astonished at the richness and brilliancy of the wares.

Anne Royall, *Travels Continued in the United States*, 1829

By the early 1800s the industrialized production of a host of goods helped to free Americans from some of their most time-consuming household responsibilities—and similar changes occurred in almost every sector of the marketplace. Small shops and large manufactories alike began to produce household goods far less expensively than they could be made at home. Concurrently, Americans—especially those in urban areas—went to the store to acquire an ever-expanding range of Fancy goods.[1] The specialization of American retail establishments increased dramatically after 1815, and all types of trendy "Fancy" stores came into vogue: Fancy Dry Goods Stores, Fancy Milliners, Fancy Bakers, and Fancy Grocers, as well as warehouses that specialized in Fancy Furniture or Fancy Glass and Ceramics. Fancy Hardware stores of the era expanded their retail offerings to include a broader range of household furnishings, such as ornamental lighting fixtures, decorative hardware for windows and beds, ornamental tinware, and a variety of other stylish goods, ranging from personal notions to doorknobs and furniture casters. English-woman Anne Royall must have echoed the sentiments of most Americans when she stepped into a Baltimore Fancy Store in the late 1820s. "I was not only gratified but astonished at the richness and brilliancy of the wares," she recalled.[2]

The success of some of these Fancy establishments was legendary. Isaac D'Young's Fancy Store, depicted in an 1831 book that identified the landmarks of Philadelphia, was among the most notable (fig. 271). An 1840 publication entitled *Wealth and Biography of the Wealthy Citizens of Philadelphia* estimated D'Young's net worth as $50,000: "[D'Young] made his money in the fancy business," the book observed, and was worth "at least this sum."[3]

FIGURE 271 *Isaac D'Young's Fancy Store,* in Thomas Porter and James Mease's *Picture of Philadelphia*, Philadelphia, 1831. (Courtesy, The Winterthur Library: Printed Book and Periodical Collection.)

—ISAAC D'YOUNG'S FANCY STORE.—

Advertisements for the numerous Fancy goods now available often were illustrated, unlike eighteenth-century promotions that simply listed available goods. For further emphasis, the word "Fancy" was typically highlighted and set in large, contrasting type. Occasionally, ads referred to Fancy goods as "notions." A notion implied a spontaneous whim, a momentary indulgence, or a superfluous but well-earned luxury and had been one of Samuel Johnson's nine definitions for "fancy."[4] The rising acceptability of "indulging one's notions" inevitably drew commentary—in one case from the satirical editors of *The Boston Kaleidoscope and Literary Rambler*:

> When a man takes a notion to be notional, he should be careful what kind of notions he imbibes. Notions are of three kinds, good, bad and indifferent—but among the endless variety of notional notions, which the most notional person can entertain, if he does not sometimes give up his notions to the notions of others, they will be apt to say that he is a notional fellow, and very absurd in his notions.[5]

Among the Fancy wares offered in period advertisements were a variety of textiles (fig. 272). In 1798 James Alexander, an artisan from Orange County, New York, first advertised what he called "fancy weaving." The

FIGURE 272 "Hiram Bundy, Fancy Weaving," advertisement in *Political Clarion*, Connersville, Indiana, April 30, 1831. (Courtesy, Indiana University Libraries.)

term identified any fabric with threads that formed a decorative pattern. It could be applied to white linens with subtle designs, including twill weaves, as well as to patterns with more engaging names like "bird's eyes," and "M's and O's." Fancy weaving also described more visually stunning work, especially overshot coverlets, which combined white cotton warps with colorful wool wefts into pulsating, geometric designs (fig. 273). Beginning in the last quarter of the eighteenth century, these coverlets were made in quantity by weavers across the country, from itinerant artisans in New England to enslaved African-Americans on southern plantations.[6]

FIGURE 273 Overshot coverlet, probably Pennsylvania, 1825–1850. Wool weft and cotton warp. H. 70", W. 68". (Courtesy, Abby Aldrich Rockefeller Folk Art Museum, Colonial Williamsburg Foundation, Williamsburg, Virginia.) The pattern appears to pulsate when viewed at length.

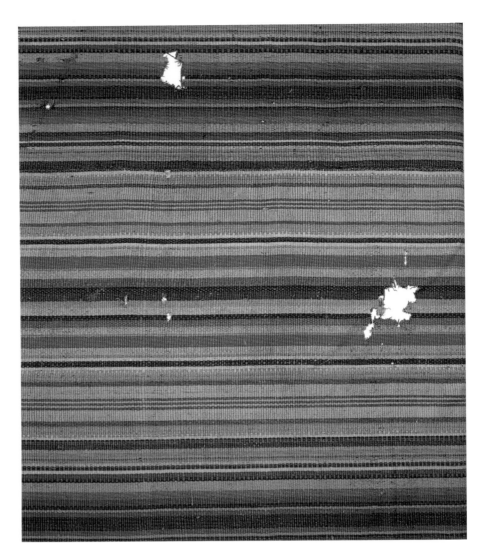

FIGURE 274 Olive Prescott, Venetian carpet, Massachusetts, ca. 1830. Cotton warp and wool weft. W. 39". (Courtesy, Peabody Essex Museum; photo, Jeffrey Dykes.)

FIGURE 275 Deborah Goldsmith, *The Talcott Family,* probably Hamilton, New York, 1832. Watercolor, pencil, and gold paint on wove paper. 14¼" x 17¾". (Courtesy, Abby Aldrich Rockefeller Folk Art Museum, Colonial Williamsburg Foundation, Williamsburg, Virginia.) When Venetian carpets were installed, the colorful stripes sometimes extended from wall to wall, as shown in this family portrait.

Other woven products satisfied the public demand for Fancy weaving, particularly carpets. Some were desirable for their unpredictable combination of vibrant colors and because they made economical use of materials. Thrifty individuals sold discarded woolen rags to the carpet weaver—just as they took cotton rags to the papermaker. The weaver then cut them in narrow strips and used them as the weft threads. If the colorful strips were woven into the design by chance, the product was called a "rag" carpet, a "list" carpet, or, more popularly, a "hit or miss" carpet. The random placement of color provided the pattern its particular charm.

Frequently the weaver dyed the woolens a uniform color and then wove them back and forth through a multicolored warp strung on the loom. As a result, colorful stripes ran the entire length of the finished product (figs. 274 and 275). This was called a "Venetian" carpet, although the origin of the term is unknown. "The names of our carpets do not always denote either the present or the original place of manufacture," stated the *American Family Encyclopedia* in 1858. "It is not known that what we call Venetian carpeting was ever made in Venice." Pieces of Venetian or rag carpet were often sewn together, edge to edge, to form large floor coverings.[7]

Overshot weaving, together with hit or miss and Venetian carpets, only hinted at the decorative patterns yet to come. Just before 1800, a Frenchman named Joseph Marie Jacquard perfected a new loom that made complex pictorial designs, also known as "damask" patterns, with minimal effort. Even an unskilled weaver, working alone, could operate the loom. The pattern was determined by a device that was programmed by punched cards like an early computer, and it governed the raising and lowering of the warp threads in a predetermined sequence that created the design. By the time the invention was introduced to America in the mid-1820s, it had been simplified so it could be attached to any traditional loom. The technology was an immediate success.[8]

Jacquard's machine made damask weaves, previously available only to the wealthy, affordable to the less affluent. These complex, figural patterns could be endlessly varied. The punched cards could be purchased in any large city, and weavers often had a large selection on hand. Clever craftsmen could program their own designs into the cards, and at least one claimed to be able to weave any figure "that can be drawn on paper."

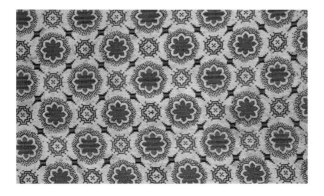

FIGURE 276   Detail of an ingrain carpet, England, 1830–1840. Wool. H. 35½", W. 27¾". (Courtesy, Old Sturbridge Village; photo, Henry E. Peach.) The carpet came from the Dickinson-White House in Amherst, Massachusetts.

"Scotch Fancy," which had "a beautiful Thistle in the border," and "Harrison's Fancy" with a border "composed of a wreath of Tulips and Roses" were available by 1841. Sometimes executed in two, three, and even four or five different hues, Jacquard coverlets made their impact by combining a complex pattern with pleasing color.[9]

The Jacquard loom was often employed for Fancy carpets, which were sometimes called "Scotch" or "ingrain" carpets (figs. 276–278). The woven strips could be sewn together to cover an entire floor from wall to wall. This was hardly new, since British textile mills had been turning out plush rolls of floor coverings since the 1750s. Although the earliest strips of patterned carpets were made in widths of only twenty-seven inches, when joined the coordinated designs made bright additions to households. But not until the advent of Jacquard's invention was patterned carpeting affordable to the middle class (fig. 278). Admittedly, this inexpensive new

FIGURE 279 J. M. Davidson, detail
of a coverlet, Lodi, New York, 1837. Wool.
H. 87¾", W. 82¼". (Courtesy, Denver Art
Museum Collection. Gift of Mary Willsea,
1962.37; photo, ©2003 Denver Art Museum.)

carpet had a flat, woven surface rather than a raised pile, and it looked
more like a heavy coverlet placed on the floor than the plush carpets on
the floors of the wealthy. But it was important in helping working families cover still more surfaces with vibrant color and rich pattern.

Signature blocks on coverlets made after 1820 included every imagina-
ble combination of the word "Fancy": "FANCY WEAVER," "FANCY WEAVER
AND DYER," "FANCY COVERLET," "LADY'S FANCY," "FARMER FANCY,"
"FANCY PATENT," and simply "FANCY" (figs. 279 and 280).[10] Even viewers
who were insensitive to other hints knew what these words meant: "I am

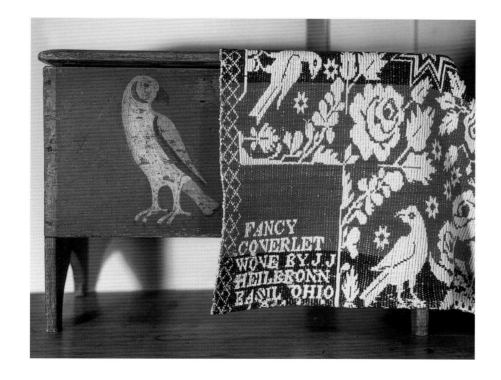

FIGURE 280 J. J. Heilbronn, coverlet,
Basil, Ohio, 1841. Cotton warp and wool
weft. H. 82", W. 62". (Courtesy, Elizabeth
B. Beebe.) Chest, probably Nantucket,
Massachusetts, 1825–1840. White pine and
painted decoration. H. 17¼", W. 24⅜",
D. 11⅞". (Courtesy, Historic Deerfield.)

going to delight your eye." Josiah Cass from Lodi, New York, capitalizing on the appeal of these textiles, advertised in 1841:

> Having purchased looms for fancy and Ingrain carpeting, [Cass] would inform his old customers, and the public generally, that he is now prepared to weave Double and Single Carpets and Coverlets of every Description and Figure . . . many of which cannot fail to suit the taste of the most fanciful, which will be wove to order. He has also made arrangements for Coloring Yarn for fancy Carpets.[11]

In a middle-class household, small Fancy objects might adorn a room whose floors, walls, and furniture were already gaily covered with textiles and other delightful and inexpensive decoration. These objects might be enchanting fixtures for candles and lamps, ceramics and glass, colorful painted tinwares, or ornamented fire buckets. Against a backdrop of Fancy painted walls and ornamental carpets, small objects were the props that encouraged emotional response and interaction among the players of early nineteenth-century America. In the end, they contributed far more than their size would suggest.

Like many other household furnishings, lighting and lighting devices underwent significant improvements in the late eighteenth century. Although most rural families still calculated their workdays from sunup to sundown, fewer men in urban areas worked at home during the day, and evenings provided the principal opportunity for families to spend time together. Traditional methods of lighting improved greatly with the development of devices and materials that were neater, cleaner, and increasingly more efficient. The Argand lamp, invented in 1783 by the Swiss scientist Ami Argand, had a font of whale oil and burned a tubular wick that produced much stronger illumination than a candle. The nineteenth century improved on Argand's design by replacing the large reservoir of oil with a smaller, ringlike font that sat beneath the flame. This did not block the light like its predecessor, and thereby did not create a shadow on one side. Variations of this lamp were generally referred to as an "astral" lamp, meaning "of the stars," or "sinumbra" lamp, a Latin term translated "without a shadow." The resulting light was practical, clean, and bright. Frosted shades with brilliant cutwork designs often graced more expensive lamps and scattered the light in every direction.[12]

Surprisingly, these improved lighting devices did not make the traditional candle obsolete. Candles still were a primary source of light even after the middle of the century, when gas lighting fixtures and inexpensive kerosene lamps were introduced on a commercial scale. Many of the early lamps simply could not compete with the mobility or emotional effect of candles.[13] Candles also remained competitive because of advancements in materials and design. In 1820 manufacturers discovered that a plaited wick, unlike the traditional wick of twisted cotton, curled into the outer edges of the flame and would be fully consumed. This freed the user from frequently interrupting what he or she was doing to trim the twisted wick common to old-fashioned candles. Candles were further improved by new fatty acids with higher melting points, which burned more slowly and dripped less. These candles displaced the greasy, drippy, and smoky candles of earlier times. Candles could now be left alone for some time, making it possible for the user to relax without constantly having to attend to safety measures.[14]

Their greater reliability encouraged people to continue to use candles, especially in lanterns that were quintessentially Fancy in design and expression. Unlike earlier examples that sometimes incorporated sheets of glass, nineteenth-century lanterns often were made entirely of pierced metal. Many lanterns had incised or punched decoration, sometimes consisting of arches, and some were personalized with an owner's initials or a date. Masonic emblems or original designs like human faces appeared on others (figs. 281 and 282). Although these lanterns barely provided enough light to lead the way to the privy on a dark night, this mattered

FIGURE 281 Lantern, New York, Pennsylvania, or New England, 1820–1850. Sheet iron and horn. H. 13¼". (Courtesy, Abby Aldrich Rockefeller Folk Art Museum, Colonial Williamsburg Foundation, Williamsburg, Virginia.)

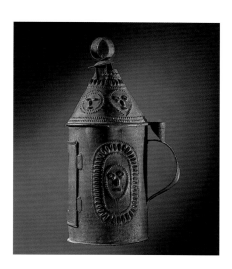

FIGURE 282 Image projected by the lighted lantern illustrated in fig. 281.

FIGURE 283 Sconce, America, 1790–1820. Pewter, glass, and wood. H. 13¼", W. 9³⁄₁₆". (Courtesy, Winterthur Museum.)

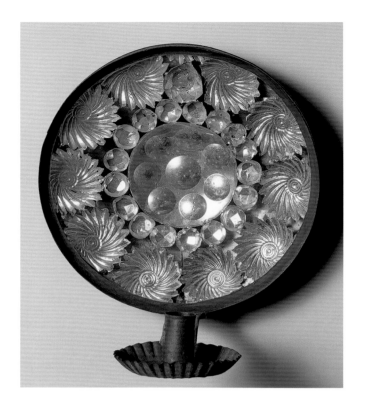

FIGURE 284   Sconce, America, 1810–1840.
Tinned sheet iron and glass. H. 10½", Diam.
9⁵⁄₁₆". (Courtesy, Winterthur Museum.)

FIGURE 285   Sconce, America, 1800–1850.
Tinned sheet iron and looking-glass plate.
Diam. 9⅜". (Courtesy, Winterthur Museum.)

little. Such Fancy lighting devices provided an exciting addition to early nineteenth-century households, and their emotional impact was just as important as their function.[15]

Sconces also were designed in highly imaginative ways that teased the eye. Some had deep "shadow box" frames with ornamental pewter reflectors behind glass (figs. 283 and 284) and projected glittering patterns of light around the room. Others had a multitude of tiny mirrors radiating outward from the center of a concave plate, scattering kaleidoscopic candlelight in a thousand different directions (fig. 285). As with lanterns, Fancy sconces often relied as heavily upon shadows for effect as they did upon light. Artisans constructed sconces of cut sheet iron in a variety of forms, sometimes with punched or painted decoration to make them equally appealing by day. Yet their effect was most dramatic at night, when their decorative crests projected fantastic images upward toward the ceiling, or their cutwork edges threw eerie shadows outward from the source of light (figs. 286 and 287). Few sconces projected enough light for intricate work like sewing or reading—what mattered was that they turned light and shadow into pattern, and the resultant images into Fancy.

One of the most delightful of these devices was a sconce popular among Moravian settlers of the Piedmont region in North Carolina (figs. 288 and 289). By day, the shaped crest had a simple but pleasing profile. At night, when the piece was illuminated, the projected shadow formed a perfectly proportioned butterfly, with wings that fluttered as the candle flickered. Most butterfly sconces are attributed to tinsmith Gottlieb Shober, who

FIGURE 286   Sconce, New England, 1825–1875. Tinned sheet iron. H. 20½", W. 7⅜". (Courtesy, Winterthur Museum.)

FIGURE 287   Charles Baker, sconce, America, modern reproduction of the sconce illustrated in fig. 286. Tinned sheet iron. H. 17½", W. 7". (Private collection; photo, Gavin Ashworth.)

designed some of the earliest about 1800 for the Home Moravian Church in Salem, North Carolina, and subsequently produced numerous others for inhabitants of the community. If the pattern was one of the most appealing Fancy lighting devices, it was also one of the most evocative, as the butterfly was widely recognized in the eighteenth and early nineteenth centuries as a symbol for the Resurrection of Christ.[16]

FIGURE 288   Sconce, attributed to Gottlieb Shober, Salem, North Carolina, ca. 1800. Tinned sheet iron. H. 11⅞", W. 5¼". (Courtesy, Old Salem Inc., Collection of the Wachovia Historical Society.) This sconce was made for the Home Moravian Church in Salem.

FIGURE 289   Charles Baker, sconce, America, modern reproduction of the sconce illustrated in fig. 288. Tinned sheet iron. H. 11⅞", W. 5¼". (Courtesy, Charles Baker; photo, Gavin Ashworth.)

FIGURE 290   Dendritic agate. (Private collection; photo, Gavin Ashworth.)

FIGURE 291   Jug, England, ca. 1830. Earthenware. H. 7". (Rickard Collection.)

FIGURE 292   Bowl, England, 1800–1810. Earthenware. Diam. 7¼". (Rickard Collection.)

Among the most stunning of household wares available from Fancy stores after 1815 were whimsical and brilliantly colored ceramics. The term "Fancy ceramics" is not in use today, although in the 1820s Americans used the term and its variations freely in inventory references and in advertisements. A "Set Fancy tea Cups & Saucers" appeared in Joshua Evans' Pennsylvania inventory in 1834, and dozens of imported "fancy quart bowls" and "fancy pitchers" were sold in 1826 by the Boston merchants Atkins and Homer. These widely divergent Fancy ceramics were covered with vibrant colors and lively designs and, as utilitarian as they might seem, also served as vehicles for imaginative play.[17]

Most of these eye-catching ceramics were relatively inexpensive and featured ornamental techniques similar to those employed for Fancy furniture and related Fancy wares. Fancy painting and decorating Fancy ceramics have obvious parallels in the way the artisan worked wet paint over wood and wet slip over ceramic. Adjectives like "enameled," "painted," and "flowered" were used to describe these pieces, expressions inextricably linked to the heightened emotions they inspired.

Especially popular among the Fancy earthenwares were "dipt" or mocha wares, first introduced in the 1790s. The name "mocha" derived from the lively, treelike design which resembled agate, also known during this period as "mocha stone" (fig. 290). Widely used in fashionable jewelry during the late eighteenth century, agate was exported to Europe from the Yemen port of al-Mukha—from which coffee, or mocha, was also exported—and similarly adopted its name. The agate and the ceramic have in common a certain design, accomplished on the clay by placing a drop of acidic dye, usually a solution of tobacco juice in water, onto the alkaline ground of the slip decoration. The two incompatible agents reacted to each other and puckered to create a treelike pattern (figs. 291 and 292). Mocha ware ceramics emulated patterns from nature, but also were among the first commercially available goods that deliberately stylized naturalistic decoration. The decoration varied significantly from piece to piece, permitting both the maker and the viewer great latitude for interpretation. Whether the viewer saw the image as alluding to mocha stone, imitating "seaweed" (as the ornament was sometimes called in period documents), or suggesting a wooded landscape, mocha ornament tantalized the eye and gave free range to the imagination.[18]

Much of the allure of hand-painted ceramic wares, including mocha ware, lay in the inventive combination of patterned bands and abstract decoration made of slip, or liquid clay. After the body had been cast and dried, the piece was placed on the lathe for ornamentation. Here, the edges of the details were sharpened and a wide band of slip was usually painted around the center. At the next stage, narrow bands of colored slip

FIGURE 293   Bowl, England, ca. 1820. Earthenware. Diam. 9⅜". (Rickard Collection.)

were trailed onto the body as it slowly turned. The earliest examples of mocha ware had thin rings of blue, ochre, and dark brown slip. At the height of its popularity in the 1820s and 1830s, tones of chestnut brown, green, orange, tan, gray, and blue-green were available. Today, such pieces are sometimes known as "annular wares," in reference to their rings.[19]

Mocha ware was sometimes further ornamented with slip applied with a small tin cup. A single spout cup made it possible to trail thin lines of clay to create stylized, naturalistic designs, sometimes known today as "sprig" ornament (fig. 293), or to drizzle meandering lines in playful, haphazard configurations interspersed with dots (fig. 294). Cups with three compartments and three converging spouts that delivered three different colors simultaneously were first documented in 1811. This tool was known as a "worming" cup, and with it a skilled artisan could produce a variety of

FIGURE 294 Mug, England, ca. 1810. H. 4¾". Earthenware. (Rickard Collection.)

FIGURE 295 Mug, England, ca. 1825. Earthenware. H. 4¾". (Rickard Collection; photo, Gavin Ashworth.)

FIGURE 296 Jug, England, ca. 1835. Earthenware. H. 6¾". (Rickard Collection; photo, Gavin Ashworth.)

distinct designs. Although the period terms for these designs are not known, certain names capture their essence, such as "cat's-eye"—a term borrowed from children's marbles of the 1800s (figs. 295–297).[20] Such designs were sometimes emulated in paint on wood, as on a pantry box made almost contemporaneously (fig. 298). Another design looks like the

FIGURE 297   Bowl, Staffordshire, England, ca. 1830. Earthenware. H. 3⅛", Diam. 5½". (Courtesy, Shelburne Museum, Shelburne, Vermont.)

FIGURE 298   Pantry box, America, 1815–1840. Maple, pine, painted decoration, and brass nails. H. 2", Diam. 4". (Courtesy, a New York collector; photo, Gavin Ashworth.)

plume of exhaust from an acrobatic plane, a series of abstract loops formed by overlaying cat's-eyes in a wild, meandering pattern. Merchants who sold such wares sometimes referred to them somewhat inexactly as having "cable" decoration (figs. 299 and 300). It was actually more worm-like, referring to the worming cup used to apply the design. Similar

FIGURE 299   Bowl, England, ca. 1810. Earthenware. Diam. 10¾". (Rickard Collection.)

FIGURE 300 Bowl, England, 1825–1835. Lead-glazed earthenware. Diam. 5". (Courtesy, National Museum of American History, Smithsonian Institution.)

FIGURE 301 Chest, New England, ca. 1780 and ca. 1833. White pine and later painted decoration. H. 23¾", W. 48½", D. 19⅝". (Courtesy, Elbert H. Parsons, Jr.; photo, Gavin Ashworth.)

FIGURE 302 Detail showing the painted surface of the chest illustrated in fig. 301.

designs were employed in the abstract painting of Fancy furniture, such as the wild pattern that appears on a New England chest dated circa 1833 (figs. 301 and 302).

Other methods used to achieve the exuberant look of Fancy ceramics included "peppering" some pieces with tiny specks of iron and "combing" others with parallel trails of slip around the body, frequently in a serpentine pattern. A technique developed during the 1790s is known today as a "dipped fan" but is also called a "tobacco leaf," "balloon," "lollipop," or "palmate" design (fig. 303). On one mug (fig. 304), leafy green tendrils flank the principal ornament, suggesting that the decorations are intended to refer to flowers, although some appear more closely to resemble a feather. Other types of ceramics besides mocha wares had their own highly imaginative embellishments, such as the amorphous design in green, yellow, and black applied to the surface of a dessert plate made by England's Josiah Spode (fig. 305). This pattern is

AMERICAN FANCY

FIGURE 303 Mug, England, ca. 1810. Earthenware. H. 5⅞". (Rickard Collection.)

FIGURE 304 Mug, England, ca. 1810. Earthenware. H. 4¾". (Rickard Collection; photo, Gavin Ashworth.)

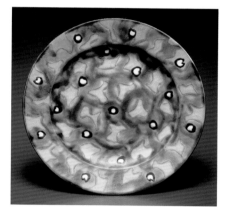

FIGURE 305 Josiah Spode, dessert plate, Stoke-on-Trent, Staffordshire, England, 1800–1810. Earthenware. Diam. 8". (Courtesy, Elbert H. Parsons, Jr.; photo, Gavin Ashworth.)

FIGURE 306 Jug, England, 1820–1840. Earthenware. H. 8". (Courtesy, Old Sturbridge Village; photo, Thomas Neill.)

sometimes thought of as a free interpretation of a Chinese "egg and spinach" design, yet suggests parallels to Fancy finishes that also appear on painted furniture.[21]

Most of these Fancy wares were produced in England (fig. 306), but the largest market for them was in America. By the start of the eighteenth century, Great Britain produced numerous goods for export to foreign markets, and by 1800 its dominance in the world ceramics trade was fueled by its responsiveness to regional tastes and markets thousands of miles away. Representatives of British commercial enterprises, scattered widely across the map of America, kept a careful watch on local preferences for Fancy goods and conveyed these tastes to their manufacturers in Great Britain.[22] Fancy wares abound in American archaeological sites from the first half of the nineteenth century.

FIGURE 307 Bowl, England, 1820–1835. Earthenware and polychrome decoration. Diam. 5¹¹⁄₁₆". (Courtesy, Elbert H. Parsons, Jr.; photo, Gavin Ashworth.)

FIGURE 308 Coffeepot, England, 1815–1840. Earthenware and polychrome decoration. H. 9½", W. 10¼". (Courtesy, Winterthur Museum.)

Of all the painting techniques shared by the makers of Fancy ceramics and furniture, freehand decoration was probably the most common. British potters who made wares for the American market knew the American predilection for flowers, fruit, and other gaudy decoration. Flowers, sometimes large and bright, were wildly popular during the 1820s and 1830s (figs. 307 and 308). A popular fruit design is typified by the "strawberry pattern" (fig. 309), which represented a halfway point between the abstractions found on tavern wares and the dinner sets of white porcelain reserved for more formal occasions. Not surprisingly, the strawberry pattern generally appeared on tea sets and dessert plates used during social occasions—forms that encouraged the expression of Fancy yet still required some degree of decorum.[23] Spatterware designs (figs. 310–312) were also popular. Small,

AMERICAN FANCY

FIGURE 309   Cup and saucer, England, 1820–1840. Earthenware and polychrome decoration. Diam. 5⅞" (saucer). (Courtesy, Paul Johnson; photo, Gavin Ashworth.)

FIGURE 310   Plate, England, ca. 1840. Earthenware and polychrome decoration. Diam. 8⅜". (Private collection; photo, Gavin Ashworth.)

FIGURE 311   Cup and saucer, England, 1830–1840. Earthenware and polychrome decoration. Diam. 4⅝" (saucer); H. 1⅞", Diam. 3" (cup). (Private collection; photo, Gavin Ashworth.)

FIGURE 312   Teapot, England, 1830–1840. Earthenware and polychrome decoration. H. 3⅝", W. 6", D. 3½". (Private collection; photo, Gavin Ashworth.)

FIGURE 313 Dessert plate, England, 1825–1840. Earthenware and polychrome and lustre decoration. Diam. 7⅝". (Courtesy, Elbert H. Parsons, Jr.; photo, Gavin Ashworth.)

FIGURE 314 Jug, probably Thomas Harley's pottery, Lane End, England, 1802–1808. Lead-glazed earthenware and lustre decoration. H. 12". (Courtesy, National Museum of American History, Smithsonian Institution.)

hand-painted vignettes served as focal points on many pieces, but their principal impact was derived from powdered pigments that were blown onto the surface through a straw, providing a lively field of color, often with contrasting hues, and energized, radiating patterns.[24]

Another decorative technique that transformed ordinary pots into extraordinary expressions was the use of lustre, a metallic glaze that gave the piece a highly reflective surface, almost as if it were gilded (fig. 313). Lustre was available in several hues, though copper, silver, and pink were most popular. An entire piece might occasionally be covered with lustre, but normally it was used to highlight details or to form narrow bands that enclosed and set off painted or transfer-printed ornament—much the same as ornamental gilding on furniture. A remarkable Fancy pitcher, probably made by English potter Thomas Harley, has a faceted lustre surface that reflects light and evokes the spirit of the kaleidoscope (fig. 314). Like bronze

powders on furniture, lustre ornament on ceramics was an inexpensive means to achieve the effects of gilding and differed from the more expensive use of real gold on valuable porcelains. Attractive but affordable lustrewares sat somewhere in the middle of the decorative continuum.[25]

Another decorative approach found on Fancy ceramics was the use of transfer-printed scenes. This revolutionary technology originated in the 1750s in Britain and quickly gained popularity on both sides of the Atlantic. Although one critic called the early patterns "coarse and unmeaning," the invention of a fine, pliable paper around 1800 made it possible to transfer the delicacy of stipple engravings. Henry Fourdriner, the innovative Frenchman who perfected the new paper, set up a mill in Staffordshire to supply his product to the British ceramic industry.[26]

The new transfer-printing techniques allowed potters to completely cover their wares with beautifully detailed engravings. Rich cobalt blue was the color most favored by consumers. At first the wares relied heavily upon British landscape views or exotic scenes from the Orient. English producers soon realized the market potential of the United States. In response to enthusiastic buyers, ships loaded with brightly colored transfer-printed tablewares left British docks destined for every port city from Montreal to New Orleans.[27]

Many Fancy transfer-printed wares were more aesthetically restrained than wildly painted furniture or abstract ceramic designs. Nonetheless, they elicited the same broad range of responses, including delight in their rich colors and a sense of pride in their patriotic scenes. They were not pure Fancy by any means, yet Fancy was an integral component in their design and, balanced with more imaginative elements, contributed significantly to their appeal. While the British were partial to serene European landscapes, by 1820 they were manufacturing North American scenes as well. Americans preferred transfer-printed Fancy ceramics that portrayed the natural wonders of their new land, from views in New England to Niagara Falls in New York to Natural Bridge in Virginia. Just as desirable were images linked to American popular culture and history, such as views of side-wheel steamboats or the homes of American heroes. The landing of General Lafayette at Castle Garden, New York, in 1824 was one of the most popular scenes (fig. 315). Occasionally plates were purely

FIGURE 315 James and Ralph Clews, Cobridge Works, dessert plate, *Landing of Gen. Lafayette,* Cobridge, Staffordshire, England, ca. 1825. Earthenware and transfer-printed decoration. Diam. 9". (Courtesy, Colonial Williamsburg Foundation.)

FIGURE 316   Dixon and Company, frog mug, England, ca. 1825. Earthenware and polychrome, lustre, and transfer-printed decoration. H. 5⅛". (Courtesy, Julie Elizabeth Hunter.)

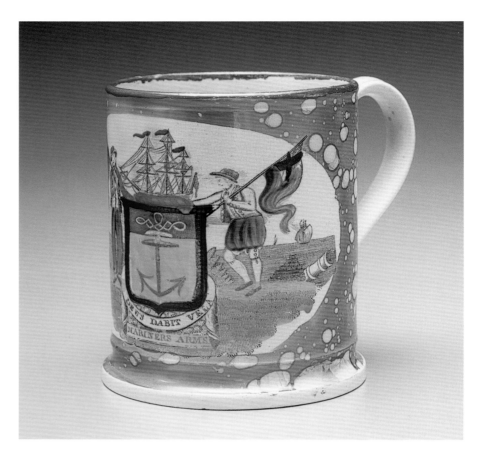

FIGURE 317   Puzzle jug, Sunderland or Newcastle, England, ca. 1820. Earthenware and polychrome, lustre, and transfer-printed decoration. H. 8¼". (Courtesy, Milwaukee Art Museum, Wehr Fund, M1964.122; photo, Gavin Ashworth.)

commemorative—like those celebrating the "civil improvement" of Utica, New York, "thirty years since a wilderness" and now, in 1824, "inferior to none in the Western Section of the State."

If the subject matter of these printed Fancy ceramics had a certain appeal, so too did their price. Records of a firm in Louisville, Kentucky, show that plates sold wholesale for ten cents apiece in 1833, a cost that included not only shipping and insurance, but also a profit for the English manufacturers. Presumably a few cents, added for the retail market, provided the American shopkeeper his due.[28]

In the nineteenth century, ceramic whimseys continued to delight the eye and expand the realm of Fancy. However, the style's emphasis had changed. Puzzle jugs, popular in the eighteenth century, were now joined by jocular "frog mugs" (fig. 316). This was not accidental. With a puzzle jug (fig. 317) the goal was to drink the liquid in the bottom without spilling it through the piercings in the side, an impossible task until the user figured out that the handle was hollow like a straw and that it wrapped around the lip of the jug and ended with three spouts. By blocking two of these, and sucking through the third, one could empty the jug with no effort at all. To solve the mystery of a puzzle jug required a rational approach, and made it a perfect source of amusement for a period when reason was highly valued. A frog mug, in contrast, required nothing more than a capacity for surprise and delight—ideal responses for the fanciful mentality.[29]

AMERICAN FANCY

At first glance, the exterior of most frog mugs appeared perfectly ordinary. Some were adorned with painted or transfer-printed scenes—including ships, landscapes, and memorials—or lauded architectural wonders. Others were inscribed with notable quotes or sentimental bits of poetry, words that gave the drinker a serious message to contemplate and distracted him from the surprise awaiting within—a frog (fig. 318). Identical mugs—one with a frog and the other without—added another dimension to the game, especially when a bartender switched the vessels of an unsuspecting tippler.[30]

After 1830 frogs were sometimes cast hollow, with a hole in the mouth. They not only shocked the drinker but insulted him by spewing a stream of liquid toward his nose. Frogs were usually placed at the juncture of the base and side, sometimes perched to leap, but more often staring upward or climbing toward the drinker. Sometimes two frogs ascended opposite sides. Larger quart mugs occasionally contained three frogs—one lounging in the depths and two more hopping upward. One design contained five of the little creatures.[31]

Some of the most entertaining adaptations of the frog mug are found in English Staffordshire chamber pots created in a number of variations that were intended as humorous wedding gifts (fig. 319). Like many of the mugs, the outside of the chamber pots were often inscribed with serious verses to draw the new couple's attention, or to catch them off guard:

This pot it is a present sent.
Some mirth to make is only meant.
We hope the same you'll not refuse.
But keep it safe and oft it use.[32]

Inside, a frog climbing up the side of the pot unexpectedly greeted the viewers (fig. 320). A surprised human figure and a second poem were printed on the bottom for the amusement of the betrothed. "Oh dear me,

FIGURE 318 Detail showing the interior of the frog mug illustrated in fig. 316.

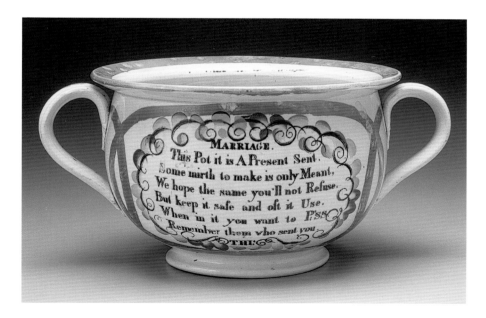

FIGURE 319 Chamber pot, England, probably Sunderland, 1825–1835. Earthenware and polychrome and transfer-printed decoration. H. 5⅝", Diam. 8¾". (Courtesy, Thomas A. Gray.)

FIGURE 320 Detail showing the interior of the chamber pot illustrated in fig. 319.

FIGURE 321 Cow creamer, England, 1765–1810. Creamware and polychrome decoration. H. 4". (Courtesy, Leo Kaplan, Ltd., New York, New York.)

what do I see," the poem begins. It was a novel way for a couple to get acquainted.[33]

Consumers on both sides of the Atlantic had other, less bawdy, options that similarly appealed to their sense of fancy and imagination. Cow creamers (fig. 321), which functioned to pour milk or cream into one's tea or coffee, soon came to adorn American breakfast tables and kitchen dressers, and a myriad of humorous inkwells (fig. 322) now enlivened desks and writing tables. Pipe whimseys were another favorite, if the many extant examples provide any indication of their popularity. Some of the most elaborate had stems that twisted like pretzels, and some ended in multiple bowls, only one of which connected to the smoker (fig. 323). They were extremely fragile, and therefore impractical to use, yet offered an engaging alternative to more conventional forms of pipes.[34]

FIGURE 322 Inkwell, Staffordshire, England, ca. 1835. H. 6½". Earthenware and polychrome decoration. (Courtesy, Strong Museum, Rochester, New York.)

FIGURE 323 Pipe whimsey, Staffordshire, England, 1815–1820. Earthenware and polychrome decoration. W. 11⅞". (Courtesy, Paul Vandekar.)

AMERICAN FANCY

Although goods from England filled much of the demand for Fancy ceramics, American potters were not idle. During the years after the War of 1812, American producers of earthenware and stoneware began to enliven their goods by making playful new forms (fig. 324) or by adding decorative elements to their standard line of production. In Vermont, the Bennington Stone Ware Pottery produced "fancy flowerpots" as an alternative to their unadorned pieces. Costing seven dollars and fifty cents a dozen, they were three dollars more per dozen than their plainer counterparts. Bennington offered them to the public as a standard product.[35]

FIGURE 324 Bottle, attributed to Bethabara or Salem, North Carolina, 1786–1821. Lead-glazed earthenware. H. 5", W. 2½". (Collection of the Museum of Early Southern Decorative Arts.)

The decoration on even the simplest of utilitarian goods made an important statement about changing tastes. Everyday ceramics used by most eighteenth-century Americans had been relatively plain. Now even pots and jugs used for the storage of beverages or food warranted the addition of ornament (fig. 325). Whether produced in small shops or in factories, decorative ceramic wares became staples in the middle-class American home.

FIGURE 325 Jug, New York, ca. 1825. Salt-glazed stoneware and incised cobalt decoration. H. 17". (Courtesy, Allan Katz Americana, Woodbridge, Connecticut.)

FIGURE 326 Joseph Lowndes, watercooler, Petersburg, Virginia, 1820–1835. Salt-glazed stoneware and cobalt and applied decoration. H. 13½". (Courtesy, Marshall Goodman.)

FIGURE 327 Henry Remmey, Jr., jug, Philadelphia, ca. 1838. Salt-glazed stoneware and cobalt decoration. H. 8½". (Courtesy, National Museum of American History, Smithsonian Institution.)

FIGURE 328   Jug, New York, ca. 1825. Salt-glazed stoneware and incised and cobalt decoration. H. 17¾". (Courtesy, National Museum of American History, Smithsonian Institution.)

Some Fancy ceramics were customized to meet the needs of the consumer. The retail firm of Clark and Fox of Athens, New York, advertised "Fancy Ware . . . made to order" in 1837.[36] For a price, almost any potter would ornament his products—whether they were meant to entertain or to instruct—to satisfy one's whim. Joseph Lowndes of Petersburg, Virginia, adorned his gray stoneware vessels with patriotic symbols of eagles and stars in cobalt blue relief and painted vines and leaves, all of which were intended to raise the passions (fig. 326). Other potters crafted whimsical, out of the mainstream forms. An expressive face jug made about 1838 by the Philadelphian Henry Remmey advises the user to "Keep me full" (fig. 327). Often artisans incised and colored the ornaments on their wares, as did the anonymous artisan who chose as his subject a "catfish" (fig. 328). Here the maker depicted the subject with a cat's head superimposed on a fish's body. Just as the viewer figured out the pun, he or she was thrown off balance upon noticing that the bizarre creature was supported by the legs of a bird.

FIGURE 329 Animal figures, America, 1820–1900. Chalkware. H. 7⅛" (cat). (Courtesy, Winterthur Museum.)

Decorative figures, used primarily on mantelpieces, were also immensely popular and further added to the colorful and lighthearted character of Fancy interiors. Some American producers copied Staffordshire examples but made them of local clays. Also available were inexpensive plaster figures made in England in the mid-eighteenth century as an alternative to more expensive Staffordshire pieces. As early as 1770, Henry Christian Geyer, a Boston stonecutter who may have cut his own molds, advertised earthenware pieces of "this country product," including images of the king and queen of Prussia; busts of Homer, Milton, and Prior; and a menagerie of animals: parrots, cats, dogs, lions, and sheep.[37]

The plaster or chalk figures of the nineteenth century were brightly painted and then varnished so they glistened (fig. 329). Evidence suggests that they were sometimes made by Italian immigrants, probably plaster

AMERICAN FANCY

craftsmen from Tuscany, and were often sold on the streets. An 1812 children's book described a New York "image vendor" and acknowledged the emotional appeal of his products by saying, "This man strives to please by presenting a variety of images, or representations of animals. They are made of plaster of Paris—by Italian lads carrying boards on their heads." An anonymous Philadelphian likewise wrote in 1851 of "expatriated" Italians who roamed the streets selling plaster busts "of the glorious heroes of America." The writer continued, "The itinerant seller of plaster casts is a regular street figure in all of our great cities."[38]

These plaster figures were primarily Fancy in color or theme. Others were Fancy in function, particularly casts of animals with a tiny bellows and whistle attached beneath the base. When the figure was pushed downward, or its bellows was compressed, it whined. While primarily intended as playthings for children, it is probable that the figures also were used as household decoration by adults. Huckleberry Finn noted of the chalk figures on the mantel of a Missouri parlor:

> Well, there was a big, outlandish parrot on each side of the clock, made out of something like chalk, and painted up gaudy. By one of the parrots was a cat made of crockery, and a crockery dog by the other; and when you pressed down on them they squeaked, but didn't open their mouths nor look different nor interested. They squeaked through underneath. . . . On the table in the middle of the room was a kind of lovely crockery basket that had apples and oranges and peaches and grapes piled up in it, which was much redder and yellower and prettier than real ones is, but they warn't real because you could see where pieces had got chipped off and showed the white chalk, or whatever it was, underneath.[39]

Outlandish decoration found on Fancy ceramics was generally considered inappropriate for formal wares, most notably, large dinner plates. Fancy decoration was not necessarily less expensive than that used on expensive porcelain; in many cases, just the opposite was true. Applying slip decoration, meticulously painting floral ornaments, or even transferring prints were labor-intensive processes when compared to making the more austere ornament often seen on the white porcelains preferred for the dining room. Fancy ornamentation was fine for the porch or kitchen, fine for a tavern, fine even for tea but not for Sunday, when the preacher came for dinner.

American consumers after 1815 also delighted in the new range of imaginative glasswares that was available in the marketplace. Specific use of the term "Fancy glass" seemingly was reserved for whimsical figures. Many of these items were constructed by itinerant glassblowers who earned a living exhibiting both their skills and their wares to the public. Using small burners and glass rods, which they heated and then bent into daring forms, they astonished crowds with their displays. Those in their audience who stood up close might walk away with a complimentary "glass pen" or a "specimen of fancy work." Also available at higher cost were more elaborate pieces. Abigail Quincy of Massachusetts, who attended a glass-making exhibition, purchased a glass ship complete with masts and rigging and took it home to show her friends and neighbors what words alone could not describe. To properly safeguard the delicate sculptures, the Fancy glassblower sometimes provided the purchaser a specially fitted pasteboard box, such as that supplied by "Mr. L. Finn," an artisan who plied his trade during the early 1830s in cities across America (fig. 330).[40]

Mr. Finn's self-proclaimed renown as a Fancy glassblower can be deduced from his advertisements in the New Orleans newspapers during January of 1832 (fig. 331). This "ingenious artist" arrived from the North, where his work of modeling figures from "red hot glass" had been greatly admired. Within days Finn set up his demonstration over a jewelry store downtown, where he intended to practice his "curious and interesting art" only a short time before moving on. He charged fifty cents for adults, twenty-five for children, and promised a performance well worth the investment. His art was "so wonderfully curious" that it struck every beholder with "astonishment." Soon the local paper carried its own appraisal of Finn in a column entitled "Sights in New Orleans." "No painter or sculptor can delineate objects with more faithfulness or interest, than he," the paper marveled. After four months in the city, Finn extended the inhabitants a sincere thanks and offered them one final sale of miniature ornaments "made of different colored glass and enamel." Only then did he pull up stakes and move on, although apparently his reception in New Orleans enticed him to return again in 1833.[41]

FIGURE 330   Storage box for Fancy glass, America, 1830–1835. Printed paper and pasteboard. H. 3", Diam. 1¼". (Courtesy, Richmond History Center, the Valentine Museum.) The box reads: "Fancy Glass Work from L. Finn's Exhibition."

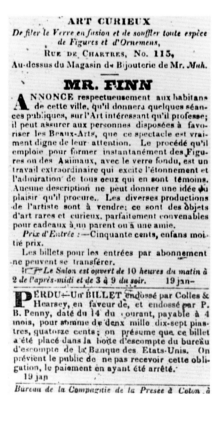

FIGURE 331   "Art Curieux," advertisement in *Le Courrier de la Louisiane,* New Orleans, January 19, 1832. (Courtesy, Library of Congress.) Attempting to draw a large crowd while in New Orleans, Mr. Finn simultaneously advertised "Fancy Glass Blowing" in the English-language newspapers and "Art Curieux" (Curious Art) in the French papers.

FIGURE 332 Pig bottle, America, 1820–1850. Glass. H. 5¼", W. 3", D. 8¼". (From the Collections of Henry Ford Museum & Greenfield Village.)

Factory workers also provided a wide range of fanciful glass forms. Sometimes they made them on their own time rather than on the job, often at the end of a long day using the leftover glass from the furnaces. Unlike itinerant glassworkers, who usually depended upon heated and twisted glass rods in order to produce their delicate work, these men had larger quantities of molten glass at their disposal. Their products, as a result, were considerably more substantial. Glass walking canes were particularly popular. Other workmen made containers in a myriad of playful forms, including bottles (fig. 332), powder and hunting horns (fig. 333), and banks (fig. 334).[42]

FIGURE 333 Hunting horn, attributed to the American Flint Glass Manufactory of Henry William Steigel, Manheim, Pennsylvania, 1770–1775. Blown and pattern-molded lead glass. H. 8¹⁄₁₆". (Collection of the Corning Museum of Glass, Corning, New York.)

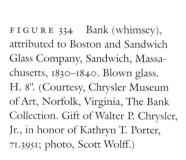

FIGURE 334 Bank (whimsey), attributed to Boston and Sandwich Glass Company, Sandwich, Massachusetts, 1830–1840. Blown glass. H. 8". (Courtesy, Chrysler Museum of Art, Norfolk, Virginia, The Bank Collection. Gift of Walter P. Chrysler, Jr., in honor of Kathryn T. Porter, 71.3951; photo, Scott Wolff.)

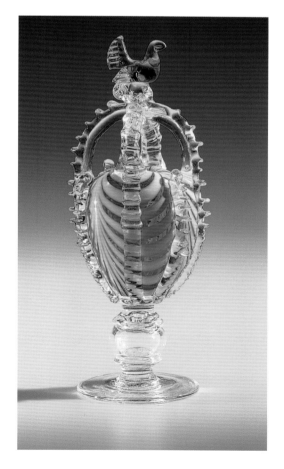

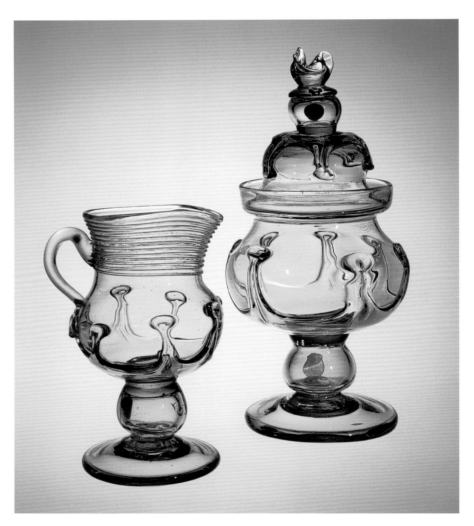

Although whimseys were specifically known as Fancy glass, the term generally applied to a broad range of decorative glassware, such as the parcel of "fancy glass" that appeared in a Pennsylvania inventory in 1832. An unmistakably Fancy aesthetic is found in countless other forms, including a blown-glass bowl (fig. 335) and a sugar bowl with matching creamer (fig. 336) typical of work from Redwood and Redford, New York. The Fancy interest in color and ornamentation in the early nineteenth century spurred the creation of decorative glasswares for people of moderate means. Brilliant blue, emerald green, and amethyst-colored glass began to compete with practical wares that were previously plain or dark green. Ornamental techniques like stringing, which layered one color of glass over another in rich patterns, added greater variety.[43]

Changes in the look of glassware were due, in part, to advances in technology. Beginning late in the eighteenth century, there was a gradual shift away from free-blown glass with smooth surfaces to patterned surfaces achieved with wooden molds. By the early years of the nineteenth century, the use of metal molds made it possible to produce more refined detail. Many of the brilliantly colored products that came from these molds resembled costly, cut-glass tablewares and reflected light around the room in delightful ways (fig. 337).[44] Other metal molds were used for bottles, particularly whiskey or medicine bottles (fig. 338). There were hundreds

FIGURE 337 Boston and Sandwich Glass Company, jug, Sandwich, Massachusetts, 1825–1840. Lead glass. H. 6⅝". (Collection of the Corning Museum of Glass, Corning, New York.)

FIGURE 338 Left to right: John Robinson and Son, Stourbridge Flint Glass Works, scroll flask, Pittsburgh, Pennsylvania, 1830–1834. Glass. H. 7¹¹⁄₁₆". Union Glass Works, Columbia-eagle flask, Kensington, Philadelphia, Pennsylvania, 1826–1830. Glass. H. 7½". Thomas Stebbins, Lafayette-Masonic flask, Coventry, Connecticut, 1824–1825. Glass. H. 7½". Eagle flask, possibly South Boston Flint Glass Company or Thomas Cain Phoenix Glass Works, Boston, 1813–1830. Glass. H. 7¼". (Collection of the Corning Museum of Glass, Corning, New York.)

of patterns, some with Masonic subjects, others with patriotic motifs, yet others with political messages or commemorative themes. Such ornamental flasks bolstered the sale of their contents and were more appealing to buyers than the old-fashioned bottles of plain green glass.[45]

Perhaps the greatest boon to American glass production in the nineteenth century was the industrial development of pressed glass. Perfected by Deming Jarvis of the New England Glass Company, the process relied on a press—which looked much like a large lemon squeezer—and a mass of molten glass. The technique of pressing glass in itself was not new. The ancients had practiced it in crude form three thousand years ago, and by 1740 in Europe, Bohemian artisans had rediscovered the process. They used it primarily to make faceted glass pendants for chandeliers. In the first two decades of the nineteenth century, both English and American producers used wooden molds to make pressed bottle stoppers and stems, objects which were otherwise blown, for goblets and bowls.[46]

Jarvis developed a metal press in the 1820s and almost immediately transformed the industry. Workers who pressed glass into molds did not require the sophisticated skills of the glassblower and could be hired for lower wages. Furthermore, the process allowed them to work at a much faster pace. Five men could turn out a piece every forty seconds. That meant ninety pieces could be made every hour; as many as nine hundred by a team in the course of a ten-hour workday.[47]

As the cost of glassware plummeted, it challenged inexpensive American earthenwares and imported Staffordshire and undercut the market for pewter as well. Certain glass forms, primarily for serving or to facilitate

FIGURE 339   Plate, New England, 1830–1845. Pressed lead glass. Diam. 5¼". Sugar bowl with cover, New England, 1840–1860. Glass. H. 5¼". Salt dish, New England or Bohemia, 1830–1840. Stained lead glass. W. 2¹⁵⁄₁₆". Cup plate, probably Boston and Sandwich Glass Company, Sandwich, Massachusetts, 1841–1850. Glass. Diam. 3¹¹⁄₁₆". (Collection of the Corning Museum of Glass, Corning, New York.)

tea drinking, appeared on tables all across the country. They included pitchers and compotes, saltcellars, sugar dishes, bowls, dessert plates, and cup plates (fig. 339). By 1839 the Boston and Sandwich Glass Company employed 225 workers at its manufactory on Cape Cod to produce these items by the tens of thousands.[48]

At first, the new products attempted somewhat feebly to emulate more expensive English and Irish cut glass. However, pressed glass lacked the crystal clarity of cut pieces and by the late 1820s manufacturers began to acknowledge its unique characteristics. There emerged a new style, one that took advantage of the decorative capacities of the process and also hid imperfections. Unlike cut glass, every inch of pressed glass could be filled with elaborate ornament—diamonds and hearts, scrolls and stars, arches and interlaced leaves. The background, almost never left plain, was stippled with minuscule dots that caught the light and caused the surface to sparkle (fig. 340).[49]

FIGURE 340 John and Craig Ritchie, windowpane, Wheeling, West Virginia, 1829–1839. Pressed glass. H. 7". (Collection of the Corning Museum of Glass, Corning, New York.)

By the 1820s and 1830s the increasingly efficient manner in which Fancy wares were produced and sold was transforming the American marketplace and shifting the centers of production away from the home. This effected a significant change as Americans were freed of some traditional responsibilities as producers, permitting them to acquire a wide range of goods from local stores. As handmade goods were supplanted by store-bought ones, women took on different responsibilities both in the domestic environment where these goods were used and displayed and in the marketplace where they were acquired. Women's new role made it necessary for them to refine their fanciful sensibilities and taste essential to meet their families' material needs. Young women were trained not only in the traditional academic subjects but also in the art of establishing a well-ordered, well-furnished, and well-adorned household. The shift was evident in the activities pursued by women and their daughters at home and at school and by new types of homemade Fancy goods that refined the senses and augmented goods from the commercial sphere.

A dollhouse with a "Fancy Store" (figs. 341 and 342) on the first floor and the residence of the merchant and his family on the second is representative of the changing role of women in the American marketplace. The accurately rendered floor plan of this dollhouse mirrored the real-life circumstances of many merchant families all across America and may even

FIGURE 341   Dollhouse, America, 1815–1830. Wood and painted decoration. H. 33½", W. 23½", D. 20¾". (Property of Anne B. Timpson; photo, Gavin Ashworth.)

FIGURE 342   Detail showing the front of the dollhouse illustrated in fig. 341.

have replicated the living situation of the children for whom it was made. Young girls who played within would have learned how retail stores were organized and what they sold. More importantly, this dollhouse reveals how American parents of the era extended education from the schoolroom to the playroom by teaching their daughters important skills as homemakers and consumers.[50]

The creativity and taste emphasized in schoolgirl education since the closing years of the eighteenth century and refined through the skills of needlework, watercolor drawing, and ornamenting Fancy furniture, prepared young women for their growing responsibilities. Yet now, females on every social level turned their attention to increasingly efficient, and increasingly varied, artistic skills to refine their fancy. The aesthetic training of young women during this era downplayed the meticulous aspects of needlework and painting and encouraged less time-consuming endeavors to elevate their taste. Drawing books—like *A Series of Progressive*

FIGURE 343   *Vase of Flowers,* unidentified artist, America, ca. 1860. Reverse painting on glass with foil. 14⅞" x 12⅞". (Collection of the American Folk Art Museum, New York. Gift of Mr. and Mrs. Day Krolik, Jr., 1979.3.4.)

FIGURE 344   *Mount Vernon, Va.,* probably New Hampshire, ca. 1845. Sand and chalk on wove paper. 14½" x 19½". (The Plotkin Family Collection, Nyack, New York; photo, Gavin Ashworth.)

Lessons, Intended to Elucidate the Art of Flower Painting in Water Colors and *The Progressive Drawing Book*—methodized techniques and helped students attain some level of proficiency in the shortest possible time.[51]

The ornamental convention of reverse painting on glass inspired the new art of "tinsel painting" (fig. 343). Here a scene or vignette was painted on the reverse of glass in transparent colors and then backed with crinkled metal foil to provide a sparkling effect—revealing yet again an interest in light and color, as well as the essential Fancy interaction between artifact, eye, and emotion. "Grecian paintings" were equally popular in the 1830s and 1840s (fig. 344). Against a twinkling background composed of marble dust embedded in paint, students used "sauce crayons" similar to modern pastels to create the image and then softened or blurred portions of the composition using padded wads of leather called "stomps." Executed in black and white, accented with shades of gray, these paintings often featured gentle landscapes rather than fanciful vignettes.[52]

Of all the new Fancy techniques practiced at home or school, theorems were the most popular and assured the greatest measure of success (fig. 345). Theorems were stencils, and even though the process of making pictures with them was called "painting," it was actually more mechanical than creative. Furthermore, it was easy to learn. "A child of tender years can be taught this sublime art in one week," claimed one book of directions in 1830.[53] Girls could create their own patterns, but the profusion of designs suggests that stencils were made by teachers and distributed widely to students or were commercially manufactured. Students "painted" the composition by laying down one stencil at a time, applying color through its openings, and then removing it. The meticulous process was then repeated for each element until the picture was complete, a formula that assured even the pitifully untalented a small measure of aesthetic accomplishment. Similar techniques were applied to furniture as well (fig. 346).

Perhaps the earliest directions for theorem painting—also known as "Poonah Painting" and "Oriental Tinting"—came from *Hints to Young Practitioners in the Study of Landscape Painting,* an instruction book published in Edinburgh and London in 1805.[54] The practice must have been relatively new in America in 1810, when an advertisement in the *Albany Balance* boasted, "The numberless uses to which this art may be applied, the dispatch with which it is performed, its durability, and its superior beauty, must give it a decided preference to every kind of work hitherto performed by females."[55] By the 1820s, the practice was quite the rage and was further encouraged by English and American publishers who turned out a steady stream of instruction booklets to spread knowledge of the techniques. At its height, theorem painting was taught not only in schoolrooms, but in parlors and hotels as well. Frances Trollope, who in 1830 stopped at a hotel in Wheeling, (now West) Virginia, encountered a lady who taught "this invaluable branch of art." The lady, thinking she had met a naive foreign traveler, offered to teach her for a mere twenty-five dollars; Mrs. Trollope thanked her politely but declined the offer.[56]

FIGURE 346 Work table, Connecticut, 1810–1820. Maple and stenciled decoration with white pine. H. 28¼", W. 33", D. 20¾". (Courtesy, Shelburne Museum, Shelburne, Vermont.)

FIGURE 347 J. P. Hurlbert, bandbox with scraps, Boston, 1827–1829. Pasteboard, stereotype and wood-block scraps, and printed paper label. H. 4", W. 10⅜", D. 7½". (Courtesy, Old Sturbridge Village; photo, Henry E. Peach.)

FIGURE 348 Scraps box, America, ca. 1835. Pine, poplar, and painted and gilt decoration. H. 8⅝", W. 3⅜", D. 5⅝". (Courtesy, a New York collector; photo, Gavin Ashworth.)

The designs for Fancy theorems were generally simple. Still lifes or "fruit pieces" were most popular, but "flower pieces" also found an enthusiastic following—and both were consciously and subconsciously linked to themes of prosperity and fertility.[57] Between 1830 and 1845, when theorem painting was at its height, theorems were done in such quantity and—despite the stencils—often with such mediocrity that they discouraged professional artists from pursuing the technique. Animals, shells, and landscapes, along with patriotic and religious themes, were all popular subjects. As midcentury approached, schoolgirls often copied these subjects from lithographs, particularly from the works of Frances Flora Bond Palmers, whose pictures were widely published by Currier and Ives.[58]

Making colorful theorems was more than a mere childhood pastime; the act embodied the early nineteenth-century obsession with fanciful perception. The final goal was to carefully assemble the bits and pieces—whether of a cornucopia, a basket of fruit, or an imaginary scene—into an accessible storehouse of imaginative ideas and emotions. Schoolgirls honed this mode of fanciful perception by cutting up prints and gluing them in multitudes to everything in sight, a decorative technique that had been popular since the waning years of the eighteenth century (figs. 347 and 348). To help them along, printers composed sheets or rolls of small illustrations, called "scraps," especially for this purpose. In the 1820s and 1830s, the practice

FIGURE 349   J. C. Riker, title page in "Album of Sarah E. Whiting," New York City, 1835. (Private collection.)

FIGURE 350   Detail of a quilt, America, 1820–1830. Cotton. H. 91", W. 90". (Courtesy, Colonial Williamsburg Foundation.)

found a more concentrated focus in the emergence of a new pastime and a new word—pasting up "scrapbooks" that served as visual metaphors of female identity and carefully recorded life's most worthy moments. Compared to modern examples, these sometimes appear haphazard or random, composed of disconnected bits and pieces of information, including engravings or articles from newspapers or periodicals. Similarly, keeping an "album" filled with signatures of one's closest friends, accompanied by poetry, personalized notes, brief mementos, or quick sketches, carefully preserved these highly personal remembrances for future recollection (fig. 349). Homemade albums found competition from commercial examples, often beautifully bound in red morocco with gilt tooling.[59]

The new emphasis on scraps—and the aesthetic education they now symbolized—were also obvious in the art of Fancy quilt making after 1815. "We learned to sew patchwork at school, while we were learning the alphabet," wrote Lucy Larcom of a childhood experience from the 1830s, "and almost every girl, large or small, had a bed quilt of her own begun, with an eye to future house furnishing."[60] Historians have sometimes singled out quilts made of textile scraps (fig. 350) as examples of the economic use of materials, but patchwork became ever more popular as the cost of textiles spiraled downward in the early nineteenth century. There was little logic, at least in middling and upper-class homes, for women to save remnants of cloth from special dresses or favorite furnishings, cut them into tiny pieces, and then sew them back together in a different order when commercially available cloth was so inexpensive. Instead, making such Fancy quilts was a labor of love and a reflection of the way that women in the nineteenth century filled their minds with images and constructed their domestic realm.

The extensive range of Fancy wares made at home or available in stores after 1815 epitomizes the widespread visual and emotional allure of Fancy at the height of its style. Americans wholeheartedly indulged their taste for Fancy in ways that vividly reshaped the world around them, expanded their intellect, and pushed emotions to new heights. Yet, as delightful as they were, Fancy goods—like the feelings they engendered—were inevitably fleeting, and after 1840 the world of Fancy rapidly began to fade.

8 Farewell to Fancy

Fancy has an extensive influence in morals. Some of the most powerful and dangerous feelings . . . derive their principal nourishment from a cause apparently so trivial.

William Benton Clulow, *Aphorisms and Reflections,* 1843

Fancy reached new heights in the 1820s and 1830s but was soon to be eclipsed by more serious matters. Substantive changes in the national character, shaped by economic collapse and the growing trend toward industrialization, undermined the ebullience that had characterized Fancy at its peak. So too did the introduction of new technologies, most notably the 1839 invention of photography, which offered a stunningly new mode of visual representation. The popular Fancy style was further undermined by changing attitudes toward the faculty of fancy, most notably a growing belief in its secondary role to imagination in inspiring creativity. For more than a half century, Fancy's lively character had mirrored America's optimistic, youthful spirit, but as the nation matured, it outgrew both the spirit and the style.

The economic boom years of the mid-1830s came to an abrupt halt with the Panic of 1837, which precipitated the most destructive nationwide depression of the nineteenth century. The impact was devastating to the national spirit and affected Americans across the social spectrum (fig. 351). Businessmen—including those who sold Fancy goods—found themselves overstocked with inventory but insolvent, unable to extend further credit and unable to meet expenses. Consumers tightened their purse strings and their belts as they watched the economy shrink. Other factors contributed to America's changing attitude as well. The death that same year of eighty-nine-year-old Charles Carroll of Maryland, the last living signer of the Declaration of Independence, was symbolic of an era that was soon to come to an end. With the nation's heralded Revolutionary heroes now gone, it was time to focus on new issues that demanded immediate attention, particularly the devastated economy and the mounting furor over slavery and states' rights. This explosive situation exacerbated

FIGURE 351   Pie plate, New York or Connecticut, ca. 1835. Lead-glazed and slip-decorated earthenware. Diam. 12¼". (Courtesy, Allan Katz Americana, Woodbridge, Connecticut.) The plate reads, "it is Hard Times."

regional tensions and called into question the economic foundations of a huge segment of American society. In this new environment, the exuberance of the Fancy style seemed not only inappropriate but also outmoded.[1]

Enhanced methods of production and advances in technology further hastened the demise of Fancy. As mass production lowered the cost of Fancy goods, and the growth of transportation networks made goods available to larger markets, small-scale businessmen and independent artisans found they could not compete. Some, such as clockmaker Eli Terry (1772–1852), were able to change with the times. In 1806 he perfected a method of mass-producing tall clocks with durable gears made of wood rather than brass. Although replacing metal gears with wooden gears might seem like a giant step backward, the new process in fact was a major accomplishment, for it reduced prices and brought clocks within reach of middle-class consumers. Moreover, wooden parts were manufactured using newly developed cutters and lathes, significantly reducing the time needed to make the parts. Terry stunned his contemporaries by producing four thousand clock movements in assembly-line fashion and delivering them to a single client. Subsequently he made a handsome profit by selling the rights to his invention to Seth Thomas and Silas Hoadley of Plymouth, Connecticut, who then produced clocks by the thousands in a factory setting.

In 1814 Terry pulled another ace out of his sleeve when he turned his attention to perfecting an inexpensive wooden movement for ornate shelf clocks which took up far less space and were far less expensive than tall case clocks. The price of the average clock dropped from twenty-five dollars to four dollars within a decade, and what was once a costly status symbol was now proudly displayed on the shelves of countless American households (fig. 352). But the availability of cheap shelf clocks undermined the livelihood of traditional clockmakers and limited opportunities for cabinetmakers and ornamental painters who constructed and decorated the cases. The final blow to traditional methods of clock production came when Terry harnessed a coiled spring for power, supplanting weights, and invented the least expensive mechanism yet. By 1850 the last traditional clockmaker had closed his doors, and to the dismay of allied tradesmen who provided cabinetwork and ornamentation, every aspect of clockmaking now took place in factories.[2]

By midcentury, the character of Fancy painting had also changed irrevocably, due in large part to new tools that made it possible to suggest grained surfaces with a minimum of effort. Some artisans used stencils rather than their own creations to emulate woods, and others used tools of composition or rubber, which included stamps, rollers, and pressers that imitated burls, knots, and other natural configurations of wood (fig. 353). However, the free-flowing patterns of natural grain did not allow for mechanical reproduction, and the quality of the work suffered accordingly (fig. 354). "It is not claimed that these tools will do as good

FIGURE 352   Seth Thomas, shelf clock, Plymouth, Connecticut, 1818–1825. Wood, glass, and painted decoration with metal works. H. 31⅜", W. 17⅜", D. 4⅝". (Courtesy, Winterthur Museum. Partial funds for purchase from the Joyce Egan Memorial Fund.)

AMERICAN FANCY

FIGURE 353   Grain painter's kit, America, 1850–1900. Wood and mixed media. H. 5¼", W. 24⅞", D. 9¹⁄₁₆" (box). (Courtesy, Abby Aldrich Rockefeller Folk Art Museum, Colonial Williamsburg Foundation, Williamsburg, Virginia.)

FIGURE 354   Door, decoration attributed to Gustave Maul, Baird House, Waverly, Virginia, 1912. Yellow pine and painted decoration. H. 80". (Courtesy, Kenneth Coker; photo, Gavin Ashworth.) Mechanical means to produce grained surfaces were developed by the 1850s and continued into the early twentieth century.

work nor as varied as can be done by hand," cautioned one instruction manual. Yet if handwork was more visually engaging than tool work, the fiscal advantages of the latter were apparent. "Any ordinary painter can learn to do good graining in half a day," claimed a salesman of the new tools. "By this method exact imitation of different woods are made in the most perfect manner and so rapidly as to render all competition by handwork out of the question."3

Traditional American tinsmiths, or "tinkers," suffered a similar fate. Between 1825 and 1845 new machines were invented that could cut, stamp, bead, and turn tin, transforming the manufacture of tinware from a hand process to a machine-oriented one. "We learn of the difficulty in finding journeymen who could use the newly invented turning machine," wrote Oliver Filley of Connecticut, one of the leading manufacturers and brokers of ornamental tinware in the country. "The old men of the hand crafting order are not satisfactory." Ornamental painters who decorated tinware by the piece found their market shrinking as they competed with young women who sat at long tables in small factories painting identical pieces by the dozens.4

Other factors undercut the strength of traditional modes of artisanal production. The promotion of American manufacturing was encouraged by protective tariffs enacted in 1824 and 1829, which curbed foreign imports. Before 1830 independent artisans had been challenged to keep pace with imported goods—now they increasingly competed with native goods produced in American manufactories.

Moreover, while the protective tariffs may have kept foreign goods out of American stores, they could not stem the tide of innovative foreign technologies. In England, patents for James Hargreaves' spinning jenny in 1767 and Richard Arkwright's spinning frame in 1769 laid the foundations for a worldwide revolution in textile manufacture. Over the next half century, the production of cotton textiles in England was almost totally mechanized, while independent textile artisans watched their livelihoods disappear. Fabrics flowed from the new water-powered looms in unimaginable quantities and then ran through a series of cylinders that printed eye-catching designs and polished the surfaces to a high sheen.[5]

In America, the transition in textile production took place at a slower pace. Initially, for a brief period, the new looms gave a significant boost to domestic cloth production, particularly utilitarian textiles. Thomas Jefferson, writing in 1813 after traveling across much of America, was surprised to find "the number of carding and spinning machines dispersed through the whole country." He concluded, somewhat prematurely, that "the coarse and middling clothing of our families will forever hereafter continue to be made within ourselves."[6] In 1820 the production of textiles in American homes still outpaced factories by a factor of two to one. But by the 1830s steam-powered American factories were producing goods on a scale that nearly rivaled their British counterparts, and by midcentury small, commercial shops were all but gone. One of the last, a weaver of Jacquard coverlets working in the 1850s, incorporated misleading signa-

FIGURE 355 Coverlet, Chesterville, Ohio, 1853. Cotton warp and wool weft. H. 98¾", W. 82¼". (Courtesy, The Art Institute of Chicago. Gift of Dr. Frank W. Gunsaulus, 1911.225; photo, Bob Hashimoto, © The Art Institute of Chicago.)

FIGURE 356 Detail showing the corner of the coverlet illustrated in fig. 355.

ture blocks into his coverlets that read "MANUFACTURED EXPRESSLY FOR _____," deliberately leaving the last space blank so the new owner could stitch in his or her name (figs. 355 and 356).[7]

On the domestic front, women's Fancy needlework was diminished in importance by Berlin work patterns first introduced about 1804 by A. von Phillipson, a print seller in Germany. These commercially produced patterns were printed upon graph paper (fig. 357). Available through many Fancy stores, Berlin work patterns were sold with a piece of linen of the same size, with threads spaced equivalent to the lines on the paper. A schoolgirl or housewife could quickly transfer the pattern onto the cloth with minimal effort. Soon, larger threads and loosely woven canvases in which every tenth thread was colored made it faster to transfer the design and required fewer and larger stitches. Although women increased their efficiency by using Berlin patterns, the skills they had developed doing Fancywork were seriously eroded by these improvements.[8]

By the 1830s goods produced in large factories appeared ever more attractive and better suited to America's changing tastes than those made

FIGURE 357   Hertz and Wegener, Berlin work pattern, Berlin, ca. 1850. Watercolor on paper. (Courtesy, The Winterthur Library; Joseph Downs Collection of Manuscripts and Printed Ephemera, No. 89x10.10.)

in the home or produced on Jacquard looms in smaller textile operations. Some even retained the name Fancy. For example, the introduction of stable mineral dyes during the 1820s, as well as technological improvements to the printing process, resulted in fabrics adorned with complex background patterns that filled in the spaces between the larger figures. Called "fancy machine grounds," these patterns were composed of minute, repetitive dots, fine lines in diamond or honeycomb patterns, and trellis designs (fig. 358).[9] Similar advancements caused the price of "rich fancy prints" to drop to a fifth of their former price, which increased demand for raw materials and encouraged the expansion of cotton plantations across the South.[10]

FIGURE 358 Fancy machine ground textile, England, 1834. Printed cotton. H. 15", W. 27". (Courtesy, Winterthur Museum.) The design repeats every 13½ inches.

The same print technology used to make highly ornate textiles also was applied to the production of wallpapers. In 1799 Robert Louis, a French manufacturer, invented a machine that produced paper in continuous rolls, and over the next three decades the process of transferring ink from the printing cylinders to the paper was perfected. By 1839 machines were able to print four colors and, though hand operated, could embellish two hundred rolls of paper a day. By the time the first machine was imported to America in 1804, the best could produce dozens of different colors at a time. Traditional block printing continued in use for limited runs of wallpaper commissioned by wealthy clients, but most Fancy artisans who relied upon block printing for a living quickly found themselves out of work. Only those ornamental painters commissioned to create customized landscapes in imitation of French scenic papers had any real opportunity to support themselves using the old techniques, and their specialty had largely disappeared by midcentury.[11]

The deleterious effects of these changes on small-scale or independent Fancy producers were far-reaching. American artisans had once found security in pursuing trades that promised, with dedication and a little luck, to project them further up the social and economic ladder. Shop masters trained apprentices or hired journeymen to assist them as business grew, and eventually many came to oversee a small workforce. The most successful artisans often turned their shops over to trusted journeymen and went on to pursue even more lucrative businesses.[12] But by the 1820s tradesmen faced with the rising tide of industrialization realized that traditional modes of production and advancement were no longer a proven road to success. In order to succeed, artisans like Eli Terry had to adapt their old ways, which included learning "the science of manufactures" rather than "the art and mystery" of a trade that their forebears had known. This adaptation was reflected in the change in name from "artisan" to "mechanic." Keeping up with the trend, Rufus Porter, once one of the Fancy style's leading proponents, abandoned his career as a practicing artist and focused instead on the business of publishing and the study of science.[13]

By the 1820s mechanics perceived themselves, their workplaces, and their products in an entirely new light.[14] In cities and towns across America, small "factories" that placed an emphasis on efficiency emerged where "shops" had previously existed. Weaver Archibald Davidson advertised his highly patterned Jacquard coverlets during the 1820s and 1830s with his name and the descriptor "FANCY WEAVER" (figs. 359 and 360). In the late 1830s he still wove coverlets, but preferred to be known as the proprietor of a "Carpet Factory." His use of the word "factory" was a symbolic contraction of "manufactory," the dropped prefix "manu-" being Latin for "hand."

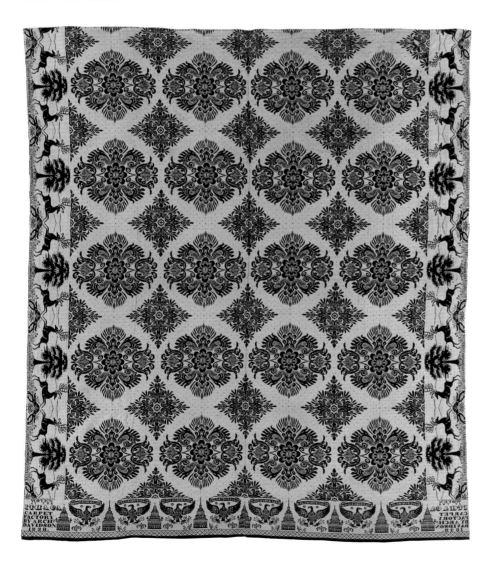

FIGURE 359   Archibald Davidson, coverlet, Ithaca, Tompkins County, New York, 1838. Wool and cotton. H. 91", W. 79". (Courtesy, Fenimore Art Museum, Cooperstown, New York; photo, Richard Walker.)

ARCHIBALD DAVIDSON,

FANCY WEAVER.

AT his Shop about 50 rods south of Otis Eddy's Cotton Factory, and a quarter of a mile east of the village of Ithaca, respectfully informs the publick that he has purchased a patent right for the town of Ithaca, superiour to any patent heretofore in the United States, for weaving Carpets and Carpet Coverlets of any pattern or figure that can be wove in the United States; and the work not inferiour to any in Europe or America.

He will weave the owners' name, date of the month and year, if required. If the yarn is good, and not cut, he flatters himself that he will show and give better work than has ever been by any patent loom heretofore invented. From his long experience and practice in the weaving line in Scotland and in the United States, and the great expense he has been at in procuring a patent so valuable, he hopes to merit the publick patronage.

Also, at his shop he weaves Broad Cloath, Sheeting, two and one half yards wide, in kersey or plain; Diaper of all kinds, and country work of every description done with punctuality and dispatch.

Yarn spun for coverlets ought to be spun 3 runs to the pound, doubled and twisted, and cotton, No. 7, doubled and twisted. Carpet yarn spun two runs to the pound, doubled and twisted, or one run to the pound, single. And he likewise, for their accommodation, will, if required, get their yarn coloured to suit the pattern.   Ladies are requested to call and examine the work before they engage their weaving.

FIGURE 360   "Archibald Davidson, Fancy Weaver," advertisement in *Ithaca Journal*, Ithaca, New York, November 9, 1831. (Courtesy, Cornell University Library.)

Like other artisans involved in the production of Fancy furnishings, the Finlay brothers of Baltimore adapted to the times in even more ambitious ways. In October of 1829, two months before the founding of the Baltimore and Ohio Railroad, and five months before the first passenger train in America left Baltimore for its inaugural journey, Hugh Finlay was granted a patent for one of the first "railroad carriages" in America. He died the following year, but by then his brother John had received a patent for iron wheels for railroad carriages; in 1837 he received a patent for a new system of propelling boats, and in 1838 another patent for a "spark catcher" for railroad engines. In 1837 John Finlay closed the doors of the Fancy furniture business forever, having made the leap from art to technology in less than a decade.[15]

One of the era's most significant technological achievements did little to alter methods of producing Fancy products but directly hastened the demise of the Fancy style. Photography was introduced to the world on a hot August day in 1839, when a member of the French Academy of Sciences stood before a large assembly and read the formula developed by his shy friend Louis J. M. Daguerre. Within thirty days every major newspaper in the Western world carried a report on the new process, and daguerrean images were displayed in Paris, London, New York, and Philadelphia. Never before, it seemed, had it been possible to capture visual reality so clearly.[16]

Within a year, artist Samuel F. B. Morse opened a school of photography in New York, and across America others honed their skills after reading detailed descriptions of the process in newspapers and journals. The camera, like the kaleidoscope two decades earlier, introduced a new way of seeing. But the colorful, abstract images that appealed to the fancy were subsumed by the startlingly realistic images that made a totally different impact upon the imagination. If the kaleidoscope had a certain scientific validity, the daguerrean process required a technical sophistication that made the kaleidoscope seem amateurish by comparison.

Photographic portraits known as "daguerreotypes" quickly became an economical way to record a person or family for posterity (fig. 361). But the literal representation produced by the camera came at the price of sacrificing the artistic spontaneity essential to painted portraits. Rigid restraints often were used to record the new images, and exposures sometimes lasted as long as twenty minutes, although the process was shortened to twenty or thirty seconds by midcentury. Early photographic sitters were required to pose in a chair with an attached "immobilizer"—a clamp that hooked around the back of the head to prevent body motion from blurring the likeness. This procedure left little to chance for either sitter or artist.

Portraits painted during this period began to reflect the aesthetic influence of the daguerrean process (fig. 362). Many echo the precise realism and stillness of the photographs, and many faces are similarly void of expression. Colors increasingly become muted and shadows pronounced—

FIGURE 361 *Portrait of a Daguerreotypist,* America, 1840–1850. Stereo daguerreotype. (Photographic History Collection, National Museum of American History, Smithsonian Institution.)

FIGURE 362   William Thompson Bartoll, *Girl with Cat*, probably Marblehead, Massachusetts, ca. 1840. Oil on canvas. 27½" x 22⅛". (Courtesy, Abby Aldrich Rockefeller Folk Art Museum, Colonial Williamsburg Foundation, Williamsburg, Virginia.)

as though a light source were nearby to increase the contrast of light and dark necessary for a time exposure. Each curl, each bit of lace, and each detail is rendered with a precision that suggests the detail captured in a photograph.

The legitimization of visual realism introduced by Daguerre was immensely destructive to the spontaneous vision that had helped to shape popular art in the previous two decades. Almost overnight Americans began to be surrounded by images fraught with minute detail that demanded close inspection, a far cry from the wild, more abstracted, and emotionally exuberant ornament found on works of Fancy. If the kaleidoscope helped to open the period when Fancy reached its height, the camera effectively closed it.

While scientific progress was redefining the marketplace and, in the process, undercutting the taste for Fancy goods, Americans were undergoing an intellectual revolution, as scholars and writers of the era reassessed mental faculties and the operations of the mind. Understanding of the word "fancy" was evolving yet again. By midcentury, Americans identified fancy, both in words and goods, as a concept solely linked to lighthearted expressions that merely pleased the eye. Imagination, on the other hand, increasingly was associated with more profound expressions of human creativity that were aesthetically and morally uplifting. Leading thinkers proposed that the trail of human progress from barbarism to civilization depended not upon the refinement of fancy, but rather on "the strengthening of the imagination by intellectual culture," which helped to tame the emotions.[17]

As the Fancy style pushed the limits of form and ornamentation in the material world, it steadily lost credibility in intellectual circles. Cultural critics implied that proponents of Fancy had lost their bearings and exceeded their intended purpose. "Fancy has an extensive influence on morals," wrote British clergyman William Benton Clulow. "Some of the most powerful and dangerous feelings, as ambition and envy, derive their principal nourishment from a cause apparently so trivial."[18] Imagination, on the other hand, was rising in stature as a valid means of thought and expression and was seen to soften excessive emotions and "strong antipathies" and to lessen "zeal"—helping to undermine the attributes that had made the concept of fancy so alluring at the beginning of the century.[19]

English writer and critic Leigh Hunt noted in 1844 that a distinction between the concepts of fancy and imagination had only been made "of late." Yet for many decades intuitive use of the words among English and American intellectuals, especially poets and philosophers, implied an unspoken difference. The poets William Wordsworth and Samuel Taylor Coleridge had debated the differences between fancy and imagination in the 1790s, and Wordsworth is generally credited with the first published comparison of the two concepts in the preface to his *Poems* in 1815, followed two years later by Coleridge's *Biographia Literaria*.[20] Wordsworth and Coleridge arrived rather late in the period concerned with the concepts of fancy. Yet they helped to bring greater focus to the distinction between fancy and imagination and to the moral relevancy of each. Growing segments of society had come to recognize that fancy responded to the surrounding world with greater immediacy than imagination, but its role was largely functional: namely to garner the images upon which creativity drew and, in turn, store them in the memory. Imagination was addressed as a "higher" faculty that guided the "creative" powers of the mind and performed the elevated role of giving substance and true meaning to the images provided by fancy.

In a letter to a friend in 1817, British poet John Keats compared creativity to a ship in which "fancy is the sails, and imagination the rudder."[21] Fancy harnessed the wind and gave motion to life, filling one's sails by collecting experiences. In the end, however, its potential was meaningless until consciously directed. In a ship, this was achieved by skillfully handling the rudder; in the mind, it was accomplished through the use of imagination. Leigh Hunt personified fancy when he wrote metaphorically:

Fancy . . . is the younger sister of Imagination, without the other's weight of thought and feeling. Imagination . . . is all feeling . . . [whereas] Fancy is sporting . . . with airy and fantastical creation. . . . One of the teachers of Imagination is Melancholy . . . [but Fancy's] tendency is to be childlike and sportive. She chases butterflies, while her sister takes flight with angels. She is the genius of . . . whatever is quaint and light, showy and capricious.[22]

At midcentury, British designer and aesthetic theorist John Ruskin further contributed to the discussion of the distinctions between fancy and imagination. "The fancy sees the outside. . . . The imagination sees the heart and inner nature, and makes them felt," he wrote.[23] Drawn to the debate was an influential circle of writers and philosophers including Ralph Waldo Emerson, Nathaniel Hawthorne, and Henry David Thoreau, men who lived in the vicinity of Boston, in the midst of an area that manufactured more Fancy things than any other place in America—a short distance from the Sandwich glassworks and the Lowell textile mills and less than a day's journey by train and wagon to the Connecticut factories that produced quantities of Fancy painted tinware and decorative window shades.

Hawthorne focused on the moral concern with fancy in his 1854 short story "A Select Party," in which "A Man of Fancy" entertains friends in a gilded castle with polished pillars of precious stone. Among the guests is an elderly but wise visitor who hastens to ask his host, "But are you sure that it is built of solid materials, and that the structure will be permanent?"[24] Although the question was purely rhetorical, in reality, Fancy's edifice was crumbling, both as an intellectual concept and as a mode of artistic expression. In addressing America's obsession with material things, including Fancy goods, Thoreau issued the concise but enduring dictum "simplify, simplify."[25]

Increasingly, society explored modes of expression deemed more appropriate for encouraging emotional and intellectual experiences that were profound and transcendent, not immediate and delightful, as with expressions of Fancy. In an 1869 essay entitled "Imagination in the Progress of Morals," W. E. H. Leckey encouraged reading and contemplation to build character and to divert attention from the insubstantial material world to the enduring transcendent:

Every book he reads, every intellectual exercise in which he engages, accustoms him to rise above the objects immediately present to his senses, to extend his realization into new spheres, and reproduce in his imagination the thoughts, feelings, and characters of others.[26]

The shifting emphasis away from delight and toward morality was reflected in the formal definition of the word "fancy." In 1860 Joseph E. Worcester in his *Dictionary of the English Language* first identified fancy as an adjective and defined it as "Ornamental, rather than useful."[27] This was a dramatic change from the belief only three decades earlier that fancy,

expressed in ornament, was essential for catching the eye, filling the storehouse of the mind, eliciting the positive emotions, and shaping good taste. The dismissal of Fancy as meaningless ornament echoes Johnson's ninth definition of the word a century before as "something that entertains or pleases without real use or value."

The shift away from fancy in favor of imagination is epitomized by two portraits dating from 1834: *Mrs. Keyser and Cat* (fig. 363) from Baltimore and *Jane Rumsey and Her Daughter Annie* (fig. 364) of Kentucky—both painted by unknown artists. The former was painted in watercolor on paper and probably was a relatively inexpensive picture. *Jane Rumsey,* in turn, was painted in oil on canvas and was therefore more expensive to create. To a significant number of Americans, the image of Mrs. Keyser would have been associated with fancy rather than imagination. The brilliant colors, profusion of ruffles, and endless attention to detail still delighted the eye but generally failed to elicit the deeper emotional responses provoked by the likeness of Jane Rumsey. She, too, has ruffles that tease the fancy, but the decorative details are relatively insignificant compared to the overall character of the painting. The darker palette suggests

FIGURE 364 *Jane Rumsey and Her Daughter Annie*, Kentucky, 1834. Oil on canvas. 30" x 25". (Courtesy, Mrs. Joseph M. Winston.)

a different tone and encourages more serious contemplation on the part of the viewer. Similarly, the expression on Jane Rumsey's face as she embraces her child elicits tenderness, empathy, and the essence of motherhood—all introspective themes that increasingly were linked to the imagination and deemed worthy of cultivation.

Such visually restrained expressions of tenderness and sentimentality found broad currency in America's material goods as midcentury approached (fig. 365). Printmakers flooded the market with a barrage of sentimental pictures, and cheap and plentiful prints and wall hangings replaced much of the Fancy needlework and other designs made by women a few decades earlier. These new images depicted beloved household pets, parents and children in endearing poses, or idealized family homes with ivy-draped porches and neatly fenced gardens. Lithographers like Nathaniel Currier and James Ives of New York, or the Kellogg family of Hartford, cashed in on the demand by creating an endless variety of sentimental prints and selling them for pennies apiece. Even printed mourning pieces, complete with weeping willows, tearful families, and maudlin poems, could be bought for a few cents at a local store by a

FIGURE 365 *God Bless Our Home*, America, 1860–1870. Cardboard and wool. 15¾" x 19¼". (Courtesy, Strong Museum, Rochester, New York.)

bereaved soul, who would pen in the name and dates of the deceased and drape the piece in black on the parlor wall.[28]

In keeping with the ascendancy of imagination, nineteenth-century Americans increasingly favored aesthetic styles that elevated the mind and built character by transporting the viewer to distant times and places, whether real or imagined. Revival styles in the Gothic, Elizabethan, and Renaissance tastes served as "imaginative repositories for the past."[29] Similarly, "exotic" styles from Egypt, China, Persia, and Turkey introduced new and evocative ways to nurture imaginative growth (fig. 366).[30] "Imagination expands and exalts us," wrote Ralph Waldo Emerson in 1875.[31]

FIGURE 366   Pl. 36 in Robert Lugar's *Fancy Architecture,* in *Architectural Sketches for Cottages, Rural Dwellings and Villas, in the Grecian, Gothic and Fancy Style,* London, 1825. (Courtesy, The Winterthur Library: Printed Book and Periodical Collection.)

Americans after 1840 sought clear distinctions between ornament that was acceptable and that which was not. Good decoration bespoke high moral standards and instructed its viewers in the most meaningful aspects of history and architecture. Unacceptable decoration merely titillated the senses and fueled base passions. The Gothic Revival style offers a clear example of how ornament became moralized. Unlike Fancy ornament of a generation earlier, Gothic details were not intended to elicit loud, outward expressions of uncontrolled delight; furnishings now resided in darkened interiors conducive to a reverential mood (fig. 367). Proponents of the Gothic style, whether A. W. N. Pugin in England or A. J. Downing

FIGURE 367 Center table, probably New York, ca. 1850. Rosewood, rosewood veneer, cherry, white marble, and brass casters. H. 30", W. 37", D. 43". (Courtesy, High Museum of Art, Atlanta, Georgia. Virginia Carroll Crawford Collection, 1983.190.)

in America, praised its ecclesiastical origins and high moral meaning. Its allusions to medieval cathedral architecture demonstrated "an unwavering faith, a most singular piety towards bygone ages" but also revealed a veneration for "the beauty of the courts of The Lord; an imagination glowing with the glories of the past."[32] In America, Downing's popular Gothic cottage designs embodied these ennobling ideas and were ill suited to fanciful displays that merely titillated the senses. The style inspired a quiet, studied appreciation rather than the ebullient spontaneity associated with Fancy.[33]

An emphasis on morality likewise shaped the art and ideas of the Shakers, a sect that splintered from English Quakerism in the eighteenth century and fled to America (fig. 368). Shakers considered superfluous decoration and

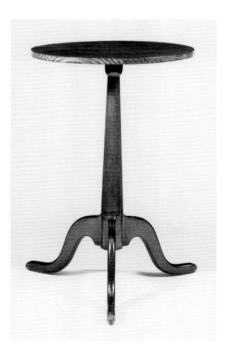

emotion unnecessary, viewing the world and all that filled it as gifts of God. Their most cherished gift, and also the title of the Shakers' most durable hymn, was "The Gift to Be Simple." In that, they mirrored Thoreau's secular view and his call to "simplify." From the Shaker perspective, the simple life was not only essential, it was holy law. Every man-made object should be "plain and simple," made of "good and substantial quality," and "unembellished by any superfluities, which add nothing to its goodness or durability" (fig. 369).[34] Not all outside observers were impressed. Charles Dickens remarked when he visited a Shaker settlement during his trip to America in 1840, "We walked into a grim room, where several grim hats were hanging on grim pegs, and the time was grimly told by a grim clock" (fig. 370).[35]

Initially, the furnishings of the Shakers did not differ significantly from the utilitarian goods of "the world" outside their isolated rural villages—the clean lines of their furniture reflect the practical styles indigenous to America at the end of the eighteenth century. Their "Millennial Laws" made little mention of material goods when written in 1821, yet America's ornamental fervor in the 1820s and 1830s forced the Shakers to articulate their beliefs to the contrary. In 1845 their laws underwent a major revision:

> Fancy articles of any kind, or articles which are superfluously finished, trimmed or ornamented are not suitable for Believers. Beadings, mouldings, and cornices, which are merely for fancy, may not be used by Believers. . . . Odd and fanciful styles of architecture may not be used among Believers. . . . Superfluously finished or flowery painted clocks, Bureaus, and Looking glasses, also super-fluously painted or fancy shaped sleighs . . . are also deemed improper.[36]

In general, by the 1840s the wild combinations of color and pattern that had characterized Fancy in the previous decade had fallen out of favor. D. R. Hay, the Scottish housepainter whose books were popular in America, observed in 1844 that "Many people of highly cultivated minds have a dislike for imitations of woods and marbles in house-painting," and warned of the "error of considering the arrangements of color as a matter of fancy."[37] Three American architects who compiled the popular *Village and Farm Cottages* in 1856 harshly chided the traditional preference for graining:

> This has become so common that we may almost call it a rage. Like other senseless fashions, it will have its day and pass away. It would be some satisfaction to us could we be instrumental in shortening its reign by a single hour.[38]

John Ruskin wasted no words in his outright criticism of the use of paint to suggest stone: "It is melancholy to think of the time and expense lost in marbling," he wrote, "and of the waste of our resources in absolute vanities, in things about which no mortal cares." His criticism of painted decoration extended far beyond his distaste for deceit or vanity. Like most Victorians who found beauty in the honest expression of nature, he looked to the character of heaven's creations for inspiration. "Bad decorators err as easily on the side of imitating nature as of forgetting her," he lamented. "All noble ornament is the expression of man's delight in God's work."[39] Over two decades later, an American critic used the same reasoning in an attempt to appeal to religious-minded Victorians. "The works of God are not built up. They are good throughout, from skin to the marrow; not surface and sham, but solid."[40]

Changing attitudes toward ornament brought into question the relevance of a host of Fancy objects and effected significant changes in their appearance. Edgar Allan Poe declared that the flickering lights so essential to the Fancy aesthetic were pleasing only "to children and idiots" and thought they should be scrupulously avoided in household decoration. Old-fashioned candles were replaced by cleaner materials like whale oil, camphene, and gas, which burned bright and clean, and pierced lanterns and Fancy sconces became obsolete. Worse yet, the twinkling light patterns

FIGURE 370   Isaac Young, clock, Shaker Community, Mount Lebanon, New York, ca. 1840. Butternut, white pine, and fruitwood. H. 31¼", W. 11", D. 4⅛". (Courtesy, Hancock Shaker Village, Pittsfield, Massachusetts.)

that enlivened Fancy interiors were now deemed harmful to the mind and body. Catherine Beecher suggested that all flames for giving light be surrounded with "glass chimneys" or "small shades," not only for aesthetic reasons but for health as well: "Nothing is more injurious to the eyes than a flickering, unsteady flame," she wrote.[41] Ideally, the best new shades should be frosted to diffuse the light, but otherwise they should be plain. "Plain shades do not injure the eyes, like cut ones." The fractured light that epitomized the Fancy taste of the 1820s and 1830s was replaced in the following decades by the soft, steady glow of oil and gas lamps with frosted shades.[42]

The insistence upon steady light also influenced window ornaments. As a child in 1841, poet Elizabeth Barrett Browning did not please her father when she hung an ornamented window shade in her room: "Papa insults me with the analogy of a back window in a confectioner's shop," she wrote a friend. Just a decade later, an article in *Godey's Lady's Book* advised its readers that the "most tasteful" shades were "perfectly plain buff." These were considered more "stylish" than "the most costly . . . painted shades as they are subdued in color and . . . harmonize with any style of furniture." By mid-century, painted or stenciled cornice boards were also on the way out. "There are no cornices," Poe wrote insistently of "tasteful apartments."[43]

FIGURE 371 *Water* (obverse), Staffordshire, England, ca. 1850. Earthenware and polychrome decoration. H. 8½". (Collection of Thomas A. Gray.)

FIGURE 372 *Gin* (reverse), Staffordshire, England, ca. 1850. Earthenware and polychrome decoration. H. 8½". (Collection of Thomas A. Gray.)

Poe was equally adamant when he criticized the popular taste for wildly painted floorcloths that had enlivened American households for over a century: "As for those antique floor cloths still occasionally seen in the dwellings of the rabble—cloths of huge, sprawling, and radiating devices, stripe interspersed, and glorious with all hues, among which no ground is intelligible—these are but the wicked inventions of a race of time servers and money lovers, worshipers of Mammon who, to spare thought and economize fancy, cruelly invented the kaleidoscope."[44]

Ceramic design was also transformed by new attitudes. The visual and emotional impact of abstract mocha wares was softened as designs lost their vibrancy and colors inclined toward dark or neutral tones: white, brown, black, and putty, in particular. Transfer-printed wares also underwent similar changes. The bold cobalt so popular in the 1820s and early 1830s gave way initially to softer pastels. Soon exotic scenes, sentimental or moral themes, and quiet landscapes replaced the American subjects that had aroused patriotic fervor in earlier decades and were so common on Fancy wares. Indeed, by the 1840s and 1850s many ceramic wares once associated with Fancy came to express not only a certain taste but a certain *class* of taste. In England, Charles Dickens observed that dipt wares were used principally in "cottages."[45]

Similarly maligned was the humorous and garish decoration typical of Fancy ceramic figures. Whimsey, formerly acceptable for ceramic figures, was superseded by a new emphasis upon sentimental and moral subjects. The American Sunday School Union and a growing number of temperance societies were raising American consciousness, and virtue and vice were sometimes illustrated by double-sided figures, such as the Staffordshire example with the words "Water" on one side and "Gin" on the other, where abstinence is contrasted with indulgence (figs. 371 and 372).[46] On rare occasions when the spirit of Fancy seemingly survived, it was of secondary importance to larger social or moral concerns. Figures depicting monkeys, some having racist overtones, often portrayed humans caught in excess and vice and reflected society's increasingly negative attitudes toward alcohol and tobacco (fig. 373).[47]

FIGURE 373 *Monkey Astride a Reclining Dog,* southeastern Pennsylvania, 1850–1870. Glazed red earthenware. H. 5¼", W. 5½", D. 2⅛". (Collection of the American Folk Art Museum, New York. Promised gift of Ralph Esmerian, P1.2001.144; photo © 2000 John Bigelow Taylor, New York.)

Eight FAREWELL TO FANCY

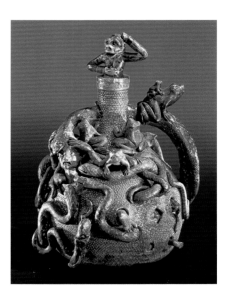

FIGURE 374   Kirkpatrick Pottery, jug, Anna, Illinois, ca. 1870. Salt-glazed stoneware and cobalt decoration. H. 13". (Courtesy, Abby Aldrich Rockefeller Folk Art Museum, Colonial Williamsburg Foundation, Williamsburg, Virginia.)

The same type of moralizing message is conveyed even more strongly by a group of ceramic jugs made at the Kirkpatrick Pottery in Anna, Illinois, during the third quarter of the nineteenth century (fig. 374). These were not ordinary productions. Serpents crawl in and out of them, waiting to devour the humans that desperately seek escape in indulgence. Frogs, reminiscent in form to those formerly used in whimsical tavern mugs, are applied to these ceramic jugs in very different ways than previously. They now sit curiously on the handle of the jug and at the nape of the neck, as though betting on the outcome. The spout is sealed with a monkey figure, representing a drunkard, trying without success to pat its head while rubbing its stomach. The overall effect is humorous yet unsettling.[48]

Paintings of the era also began to express new attitudes. Self-taught artist Henry Church infused moralism into his old-fashioned Fancy piece *The Monkey Picture,* giving another dimension to a traditional still-life composition (fig. 375). Here he depicted two escaped monkeys fighting over a banana and wreaking havoc in a Victorian dining room. The lion carpet on the floor grimaces beneath a falling glass of water, and the watermelon on the sideboard has a profile suggesting a human face. The policeman who appears through the window to the right seems to suggest that the artist believed those who indulged in excessive behavior should be restrained by society if unable to restrain themselves.[49]

To be sure, Fancy was a powerful and widespread phenomenon that did not simply fall prey to changing tastes. Rather, it faded in light of an array of evolving cultural norms, emotional, aesthetic, practical, and moral. During its heyday, Fancy captured the attention of Americans across all classes. As their needs and beliefs changed over time, Fancy became less alluring and less important. In 1848 Orson Fowler, the well-known phrenologist and designer, expressed a sentiment that by now had become generally accepted, "A fancy man will build a fancy cottage; a practical man, a convenient home."[50]

FIGURE 375   Henry Church, *The Monkey
Picture,* Chagrin Falls, Ohio, 1895–1900. Oil
on paper mounted on canvas. 32" x 47".
(Courtesy, Abby Aldrich Rockefeller Folk Art
Museum, Colonial Williamsburg Founda-
tion, Williamsburg, Virginia.)

FIGURE 376   Gustave Stickley's Craftsman Workshops, sideboard, Eastwood, New York, 1912–1915. White oak, oak veneer, and copper mounts. H. 48¾", W. 66", D. 23¾". (Courtesy, High Museum of Art, Atlanta, Georgia. Virginia Carroll Crawford Collection, 1984.141.)

By the end of the nineteenth century, the last vestiges of the Fancy style were all but gone. Gustave Stickley, the articulate proponent of the Arts and Crafts movement, espoused an entirely new outlook toward ornamentation that ushered in the new century. Above all else, he affirmed, "chasteness and restraint in form" and "simple, but artistic materials" were the proper expressions for furnishings of any kind (fig. 376). Stickley knew that the character of material goods reflected the people who made and used them, but it was not enough for him to look to the future to justify his point. "'Fancywork' was a cruelly right name for the old time decoration so labelled," he observed. "It was fancy, superfluous, and very hard work, and the burden fell alike upon those who made it and those who beheld it." He noted with pride that the craftsmen in his studios had started to call Fancywork textiles by their earlier name, "needlework." The practical and unadorned had returned to favor.[51]

Fancy's life cycle was complete. In less than a century and a half, the language and the philosophy that first defined fancy and then the Fancy style had moved from negative to positive and then back again. Fancy had made the novel transition from a concept that was explored solely in words and thoughts to one expressed primarily in material goods. Between 1790 and 1840, Americans across the social spectrum heartily embraced its perspectives and created lively interpretations of a dynamic style that reflected the country's optimism and youthful spontaneity. But by midcentury changes in economy, industry, and attitude challenged Americans to turn their attention to a different kind of world. No longer relevant to American lives, Fancy slipped back into the obscurity from which it had emerged.

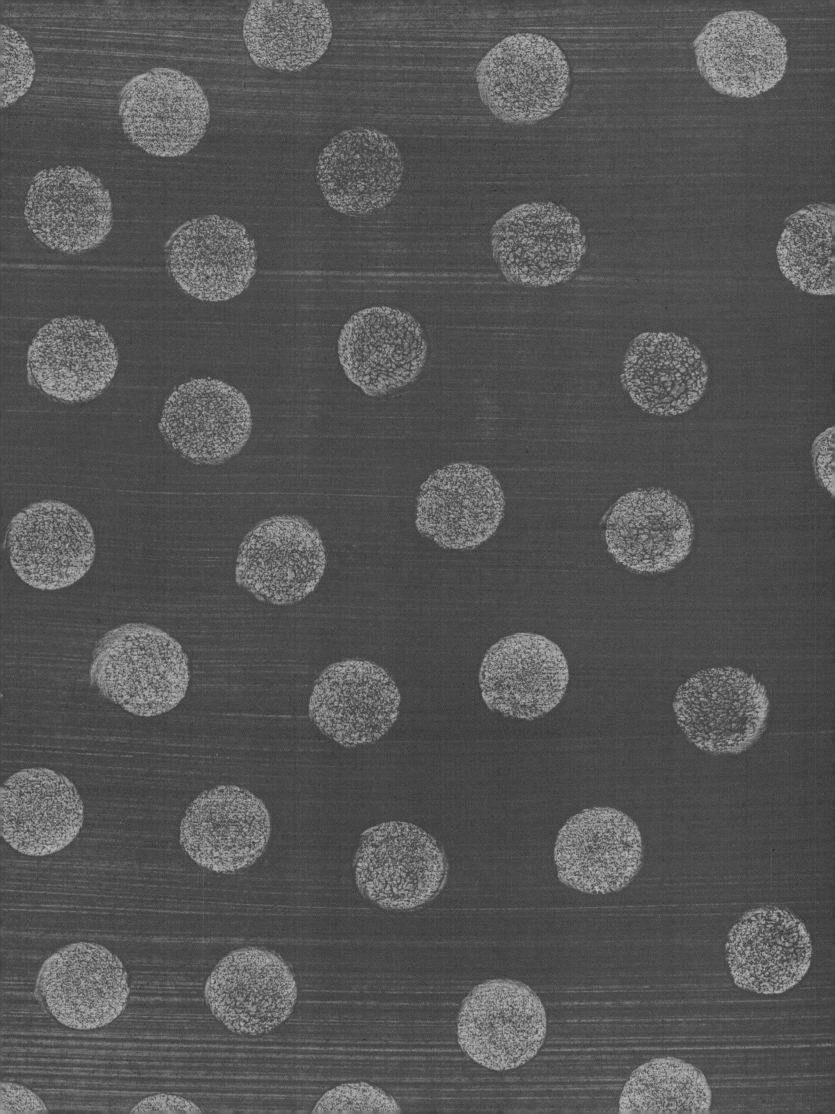

Notes

Preface

1. The author is grateful to Jeffrey Plank for his contributions to this paragraph.

Introduction

1. Richard J. Koke, Curator, New York Historical Society, to the author, May 8, 1981: "This study of double parlors with a screen of Ionic columns has a date ascribed of possibly ca. 1830, but it has also been cited as the parlor of the residence of John Cot Stevens, 1845, at the southeast corner or Murray Street and College Place (now West Broadway), New York City. This attribution is questionable, however, insofar as the room does not match the exterior plan of the house which is also in the Society's collection."
2. Charles Dickens, *American Notes* (1842; reprint, Gloucester, Mass.: Peter Smith, 1968), p. 90.
3. *The United States Illustrated; in View of City and Country,* edited by Charles Anderson Dana (New York: H. J. Meyer, [ca. 1853]), p. 9.
4. For further information on Joseph H. Davis, see Arthur and Sybil Kern, "Joseph H. Davis: Identity Established," *Clarion* 14, no. 3 (summer 1989): 49–53; Stacy Hollander et al., *American Radiance: The Ralph Esmerian Gift to the American Folk Art Museum, New York* (New York: American Folk Art Museum in association with Harry N. Abrams, Inc., 2001), pp. 59, 392–395.
5. James Hewitt, sheet music, "Delighted Fancy Hails the Hour" (New York: James Hewitt, 1807), New York State Library, Manuscripts and Special Collections; Sheet music, "Tell Me, Where is Fancy Bred?" (n.p., n.d., ca. 1820), New York State Library, Manuscripts and Special Collections.
6. Thomas Reid, "Of Simple Apprehension in General," in *Essays on the Intellectual Powers of Man* (Edinburgh: John Bell; London: G. G. and J. Robinson, 1785), p. 374.
7. *The Oxford English Dictionary, Being a Corrected Re-Issue with an Introduction, Supplement and Bibliography of a A New English Dictionary on Historical Principles Founded Mainly on the Materials Collected by the Philological Society,* edited by James A. H. Murray et al., 12 vols., 2d ed. (Oxford: Clarendon Press, 1961), s.v. "fancy and fantasy"; Joseph T. Shipley, *Dictionary of World Literary Terms* (1943; reprint, Boston: The Writer, Inc., 1970), s.v. "fancy," "fantasy," "imagination"; *Oxford English Dictionary* (1961), s.v. "fancy" and s.v. "fantasy."

8. Samuel Johnson, *A Dictionary of the English Language*, 2d ed. (1755; London: W. Strahan, 1773), s.v. "fancy." In the 1773 edition of his *Dictionary*, Johnson updated his definitions for fancy from his original conceptions of 1755. He added "In Shakespeare it signifies love"; he substituted the term "false notion" for "Frolick; idle scheme; vagary"; and he added the words "without real use or value" at the end of the ninth definition.

9. Thomas Dyche and William Pardon, *A New General English Dictionary* (1740; reprint, New York: George Olms Verlag Hildesheim, 1972), s.v. "fancy."

10. Alexander Gerard, *An Essay on Taste, to which are annexed Three Dissertations on the same Subject by Mr. De Voltaire, Mr. D'Alembert, and Mr. De Montesquieu*, 2d ed. (1764; reprint, New York: Garland, 1970), p. 190. The first edition was published in 1759. Gerard's *Essay on Taste*, with an introduction by Walter J. Hipple, Jr., 3d ed. (1780; Delmar, N.Y.: Scholars' Facsimiles & Reprints, 1978), also contains his brief essay "Observations concerning the Imitative Nature of Poetry," but lacked the three accompanying essays by Voltaire, Montesquieu, and D'Alembert. Hipple's modern introduction provides valuable insights into the 1755 competition and into Gerard's philosophy.

11. [François Marie Arouet] de Voltaire, "Mr. De Voltaire's Essay on Taste," in Gerard, *An Essay on Taste*, p. 215.

12. All quotes are from Leigh Hunt, *Wit and Humor, Selected from the English Poets, with an Illustrative Essay, and Critical Comments* (New York: Wiley and Putnam, 1847), pp. 5–6.

13. *An Addition to the Present Melancholy Circumstances of the Province Considered* (Boston: S. Kneeland, 1719), p. 7.

14. Rufus Porter, *A Select Collection of Valuable and Curious Arts*, 2d ed. (Concord, N.H.: J. B. Moore, 1826), p. 100.

Chapter One A BRIEF HISTORY OF FANCY

1. William Park, *The Idea of Rococo* (Newark: University of Delaware Press; London and Toronto: Associated University Presses, 1993), p. 11.

2. Samuel Johnson, *Rambler*, no. 162 (October 5, 1751).

3. Samuel Johnson, *The History of Rasselas, Prince of Abissinia*, from *Samuel Johnson: Rasselas, Poems and Selected Prose*, edited by Bertrand H. Bronson (New York: Holt, Rinehart and Winston, Inc., 1958), p. 526. The poet Imlac, who speaks these lines, is widely acknowledged to express Johnson's outlook on life. Johnson's admiration of poetry is clarified in Imlac's further commentary: "The Province of poetry is to describe Nature and Passions," and "To a poet nothing can be useless. Whatever is beautiful, and whatever is dreadful, must be familiar to his imagination: he must be conversant with all that is awfully vast or elegantly little" (*Rasselas*, p. 526).

4. Nicholas Bretton, "A Foole, Dame Fancies man, speaketh in Defence of his Mistress, Fancie," in *School and Forte of Fancie* (1582), in *The Works in Verse and Prose of Nicholas Breton, for the First Time Collected and Edited: With Memorial Introduction, Notes and Illustrations, Glossarial Index, Facsimiles, &c.*, by the Rev. Alexander B. Grosart, 2 vols. (1879; reprint, New York: AMS Press, Inc., 1966), p. 20.

5. The link between the eye and the imagination was long acknowledged by 1600 when Shakespeare posed, and answered, the question: "Tell me where is fancy bred, / Or in the heart or in the head? / How begot, how nourished? / Reply, reply. / It is engendered in the eye." William Shakespeare, *The Merchant of Venice*, in *The Annotated Shakespeare*, edited by A. L. Rowse, 3 vols. (New York: C. N. Potter, 1978), 3: ii, 63–64.

6. Samuel Johnson to James Boswell, undated (probably March 19, 1774) in *Letters of Samuel Johnson*, edited by Bruce Redford, 5 vols. (Princeton, N.J.: Princeton University Press, 1994), 2: 132–34. Courtesy Frank Lynch.

7. John Dryden, preface to *Religio Laici* (1682), in *The Oxford Authors: John Dryden*, edited by Keith Walker (Oxford and New York: Oxford University Press, 1987), p. 227.

8. William Hogarth, *A Rake's Progress, in Eight Plates* (London: William Hogarth, 1735; retouched by the artist, 1763), pl. 8; Johnson, *The History of Rasselas*, p. 596.

9. Ralph Waldo Emerson, *Society and Solitude and Poems* (Boston and New York: Houghton, Mifflin, 1929), p. 50.

10. It is obvious that not all classical subjects were rational: Cupid's love antics, Jupiter's rape of Europa, Sirens luring sailors to their deaths—these and other fictitious events involving the superhuman creatures of ancient mythology could not possibly represent the classical ideal. Of the story of Diana's visit to the sleeping Endymion, Thomas Sheraton observed that this "and a thousand others of the same kind" were merely the "fabrications" of ancient poets and idolaters created "according to their vain imagination." As with most people in any period, the early British looked selectively to the past for that which reinforced their perceptions of themselves in their own time. Thomas Sheraton, *An Accompaniment to the Cabinet-Maker and Upholsterer's Drawing-Book,* 3d ed. (1802; reprint, New York: Dover Publications, Inc., 1972), p. 24.

11. *The Spectator* was published daily from March 1711 to December 1712, and "The Pleasures of the Imagination" appeared in *Spectator* numbers 411 to 421, spanning June 21, 1712, to July 3, 1712. Addison served in the House of Commons from 1708 to 1719, and his text is significant in its attempt to heighten the public's intellectual and moral comprehension of life and thus to advance British character and taste. Addison's prefatory comments appeared in *Spectator* 409 (June 19, 1712), in which he addressed the importance of taste "as the utmost perfection of an accomplished man" and advised the reader of the impending essays. The author is grateful to Jeffrey Plank for his contributions to this paragraph.

12. Addison, "Pleasures of the Imagination," *The Spectator,* no. 411 (Saturday, June 21, 1712).

13. Ibid. Addison separated the pleasures of sight into two categories: "primary," in which the delight arises from objects immediately visible, and "secondary," where it results from images stored unaltered in the memory or "recombined to form visions of things that are either absent or fictitious." Addison, "The Pleasures of the Imagination," *The Spectator,* no. 411 (Saturday, June 21, 1712).

14. Addison, "Pleasures of the Imagination," *The Spectator,* no. 412 (Monday, June 23, 1712). Eighteenth-century philosophers often observed the instinctive human attraction to beauty in one's species, as did Voltaire: "It does not seem to have been the intention of nature, that the generality of mankind should acquire by custom and experience those sensations and perceptions which are necessary to their preservation." See [Francois Marie Arouet] de Voltaire, "Mr. De Voltaire's Essay on Taste," in Gerard, *An Essay on Taste,* p. 212.

15. Addison, "Pleasures of the Imagination," *The Spectator,* no. 412 (Monday, June 23, 1712).

16. During the medieval period, the word "sublime" referred to the loftiest peaks in a Gothic structure, *Oxford English Dictionary* (1961), s.v. "sublime." Among the emotions associated with the sublime, the "terror" elicited when confronting the overwhelming power of nature was widely considered to confer an intuitive understanding of the Creator.

17. Beginning in the eighteenth century, the sublime was given particular credence in Britain by the European "rediscovery" of an ancient text "On the Sublime" attributed, at that time, to the Greek philosopher Cassius Longinus (A.D. 213–273). That text is now widely acknowledged to antedate Longinus.

18. Addison, "Pleasures of the Imagination," *The Spectator,* no. 412 (Monday, June 23, 1712).

19. Edmund Burke, "Introduction on Taste," in *A Philosophical Enquiry into the Origin of our Ideas of the Sublime and Beautiful,* edited with an introduction and notes by James T. Boulton (Notre Dame, Ind., and London: University of Notre Dame Press, 1958), pp. 11–27. Burke, like Addison, was a Member of Parliament (1765–1795) and shared a concern for elevating British character. The *Enquiry* (1757) addressed the virtues of the sublime and beautiful in great detail. Unlike later proponents of fancy, Burke added the "Introduction on Taste" in his second edition (1759) to deflect criticism for failing to inform his readers that the refinement of imagination was essential to the development of taste, and thereby indispensable to shaping life's most important decisions. Burke addressed novelty with great caution. Although he acknowledged its role in instinctive human attraction to the beautiful and sublime, he considered novelty to be a corrupting force if not moderated by more elevating powers.

20. William Hogarth, *Analysis of Beauty, Written with a view of fixing the fluctuating ideas of taste,* edited with an introduction and notes by Ronald Paulson (1753; New Haven and London: Yale University Press, 1997). Hogarth distinguished two types of beauty: "Nature's more superficial beautys, of sportiveness, and Fancy, . . . which differ so greatly from her other beautys, of order, and usefulness," p. 116. Hogarth promoted the latter. Hogarth's proposed timeless style drew from classical design, the unalterable laws of geometry, and the beauties of nature—particularly the graceful cyma or S-shaped curves of the human figure (pp. 7–12, 43, 48, 102–13). Hogarth satirized Britain's indulgent aristocracy in his "Modern Moral Subjects." The print *Taste, or Burlington's Gate* is widely thought to be Hogarth's work; it mocked William Kent's overly ambitious designs for Lord Burlington. Hogarth's disparaging commentary on British classical design emerged not from a disdain for ancient sources, but for modern aristocrats who misused them to elevate their status instead of their morals. Ronald Paulson, *Hogarth's Graphic Works,* 2 vols. (New Haven and London: Yale University Press, 1970), 1: 299–300.

21. Hogarth, *Analysis of Beauty,* p. 12. A positive perspective on Chinese and Gothic subjects was expressed in Robert Sayer, *The Ladies Amusement: or Whole Art of Japanning Made Easy* (1762; reprint, Newport, Eng.: Ceramic Book Company, 1966), p. 4: "With Indian and Chinese Subjects . . . Liberties may be taken, because Luxuriance of Fancy recommends their production more than Propriety." Courtesy Philip Zea.

22. Sir Joshua Reynolds, "Discourse VII," in *Seven Discourses on Art* (New York: Cassell, 1888), pp. 268–70. Reynolds' annual discourses were delivered to the Royal Academy between 1769 and 1776. Discourse VII, concerned principally with the vagaries of taste, was presented on December 10, 1776.

23. Thomas Chippendale, *The Gentleman and Cabinet-Maker's Director,* 3d ed. (1762; reprint, New York: Dover Publications, 1966), title page and preface.

24. Voltaire, "Essay on Taste," p. 215. Although French by birth, Voltaire lived in Britain between 1726 and 1729, spoke English fluently, and was an astute observer of British culture. Voltaire's essay is translated from his contribution to "Gout, (Gramm. Littérat & Philos.)," in Denis Diderot, *Encyclopédie ou Dictionnaire Raisonné des Sciences, des Arts et des Métiers,* 28 vols. (Paris, 1757), 7: s.v. "gout."

25. A. Browne, "Ars Pictoria or an academy teaching painting, drawing . . ." (1669), quoted in the *Oxford English Dictionary* (1961), s.v. "phantasy."

26. Addison, "Pleasures of the Imagination," *The Spectator,* no. 412 (Monday, June 23, 1712): 331.

27. Addison, "Pleasures of the Imagination," *The Spectator,* no. 411 (Saturday, June 21, 1712): 324–25.

28. For a seventeenth-century English view of the variable perception of color, see John Locke, *An Essay Concerning Human Understanding,* edited by A. S. Pringle Pattison (Oxford: Clarendon Press, 1924), 2: xxiii, 11.

29. Addison, "Pleasures of the Imagination," *The Spectator,* no. 413 (Tuesday, June 24, 1712).

30. Addison, "Pleasures of the Imagination," *The Spectator,* no. 412 (Monday, June 23, 1712).

31. Addison alludes to the motion of a waterfall as impressing the fancy, both for its motion (*The Spectator,* no. 413, p. 334) and its sound (*The Spectator,* no. 412, p. 331). He also observed the appeal of meteors to the imagination. Similarly, Samuel Johnson compared "reason to the sun, of which the light is constant, uniform, and lasting; and fancy to a meteor, of bright but transitory luster, irregular in its motion, and delusive in its direction." Johnson, *Rasselas,* p. 545.

32. Locke, *An Essay Concerning Human Understanding,* 2: xxiii, 19. Locke considered human motion to have a sacred stature, viewing it as an extension of mind and spirit expressed through the body.

33. Ibid.

34. Gerard, *An Essay on Taste,* 2d ed. Gerard's essay won an international competition sponsored in 1755 by the Philosophical Society of Edinburgh for the best essay on taste. It was notable for emphasizing association as an imaginative power and its role in shaping taste. Association—also known as the "Association of Ideas"—was first acknowledged in the seventeenth century by Thomas Hobbes, and then by John

Locke. Voltaire similarly observed the importance of association to taste: "Taste then, in general, is a quick discernment, a sudden perception . . . it relishes what is good with an exquisite and voluptuous sensibility, and rejects the contrary with loathing and disgust." Voltaire, "Essay on Taste," p. 209.

35. The moral philosopher Dugald Stewart was a professor at the University of Edinburgh and an associate of poet Robert Burns. Stewart found imagination to include several faculties: "Conception or simple Apprehension, which separates the selected materials . . .; and Judgment or Taste, which selects the material. . . . To these powers, we may add, that particular habit of association to which I formerly gave the name of Fancy; as it is this which presents to our choice, all the different materials which are subservient to Imagination." Dugald Stewart, *Elements of the Philosophy of the Human Mind* (London: printed for A. Strahan, and T. Cadell in the Strand; Edinburgh: W. Creech, 1792), pp. 477–78.

36. Addison, "Pleasures of the Imagination," *The Spectator,* no. 416 (June 28, 1712); David Hume, *A Treatise of Human Nature,* with an introduction by A. D. Lindsay (1740; reprint, New York: Dutton, 1970), p. 31.

37. John Dryden, *Dramatic Essays,* edited by William Henry Hudson (London and Toronto: J. M. Dent & Sons; New York: E. P. Dutton, 1921), pp. 72–73.

38. Montesquieu concurred that "marvelous, new, or unexpected" things acted quickly upon the mind. See Montesquieu, "Essay on Taste," in Gerard, *An Essay on Taste,* p. 274.

39. Addison on novelty, "Pleasures of the Imagination," *The Spectator,* no. 412 (Monday, June 23, 1712).

40. Hogarth, *Analysis of Beauty,* pp. 27, 39, 145.

41. Nancy V. McClelland, *Historic Wallpapers from Their Inception to the Introduction of Machinery* (Philadelphia and London: J. B. Lippincott, 1924), p. 270.

42. Many early philosophers acknowledged a hierarchy within humor, farce, and wit. John Locke, a perennial humanist, marked the difference between men of wit and men of judgment. "Men who have a great deal of wit, and prompt memories, have not always the clearest judgment or deepest reason," he observed. After all, wit is an "assemblage of ideas" put together with "quickness and variety" and contributes to "pleasant pictures and agreeable visions in the fancy." A man of judgment, on the other hand, is rarely misled by "similitude" and seldom confuses "one thing for another." Locke, *An Essay Concerning Human Understanding,* 2: ix, 2. John Dryden observed that humor required an understanding of the "folly or corruption" that characterized the human condition," and therefore had social value (Dryden, *Dramatic Essays,* p. 78). Wit was seen to reflect a quick mind, but initially was thought to have little merit. Addison expressed his skepticism of its powers, "Our general taste in England is for epigram, turns of wit, and forced conceits, which have no manner of influence . . . for the bettering or enlarging the mind of him who reads them." (Addison, "Taste," *The Spectator,* no. 409 [June 19, 1712].) This later changed, for wit gained in stature as British society embraced the powers of imagination. Eventually, those who embraced fancy at century's end saw wit as integral to association and thought it reflected the quickness and receptivity of the mental faculties. In contrast, farce was generally seen to have little redeeming merit beyond mere diversion. As Dryden noted, "I detest . . . farces . . . I am sure I have reason on my side." (Dryden, *Dramatic Essays,* p. 78.)

43. Montesquieu, "An Essay on Taste," pp. 274–77.

Chapter Two FANCY TAKES FORM

1. Philip Freneau of New Jersey, roommate of James Madison at Princeton, wrote *The Power of Fancy* in 1770, while at university. An accomplished poet and essayist, he was persuaded by Thomas Jefferson to found the *National Gazette,* and he shared the future president's Republican values. Other writings concerned with fancy include Richard Alsop, *The Charms of Fancy: A Poem in Four Cantos with Notes,* edited by Theodore Dwight (1788; New York: D. Appleton, 1856). Not published until seventy years after

it was written, the poem's 2,300 lines stand as a major testimony to the pervasive influence of fancy at the end of the eighteenth century.

2. Occasionally, prior to the 1760s, the noun fancy was used in an *objective* context, immediately in front of another noun and sounding, upon first impression, as though it were an adjective. It was generally hyphenated in such cases, though not always. In *As You Like It* (III, ii, 381), Shakespeare wrote: "If I could meet that Fancie-monger, I would give him some good counsel." Such usage helped to introduce a pattern, to accustom the ear to hearing fancy in this context, and to establish a precedent for placing it in front of other nouns. The adjective "fanciful," meaning "full of fancy," was an early outgrowth but was neither as brief nor as conveniently spoken as fancy, and was uncommonly used in its stead. Samuel Johnson, *A Dictionary of the English Language,* 4 vols., 9th ed. (London: Longman, Hurst, Rees, and Orme, 1805), s.v. "fanciful."

3. One of the first uses of the term "fancy chair" appears in the advertisement of William Challen of New York in the *Gazette and General Advertiser* (New York), February 22, 1797, quoted in Dean A. Fales, *American Painted Furniture 1660–1880* (New York: E. P. Dutton, 1972), p. 102.

4. Fancy does not appear in the dictionary as an adjective until the mid-nineteenth century. The first such entry found by the author is in Joseph E. Worcester's *A Dictionary of the English Language* (Cambridge: H. O. Houghton, 1860), s.v. "fancy," p. 537.

5. Stewart, *Elements of the Philosophy of the Human Mind,* p. 309.

6. Fanny Burney, *The Early Diary of Madame D'Arblay* [Fanny Burney], *1768–1778, with a selection from her correspondence, etc.* 2 vols. (London: George Bell, 1889), see entry for January 10, 1770, quoted in the *Oxford English Dictionary* (1961), s.v. "fancy dress." Madame D'Arblay was a confidant of Dr. Johnson and Sir Joshua Reynolds. A circa 1765 London trade card for "The Manufactory for Paperhangings" advertised "designs for Gentlemen's Different fancies"; see Ambrose Heal, *London Tradesmen's Cards of the XVIII Century* (1925; New York: Dover Reprints, 1968), pl. 70.

7. *Virginia Gazette,* October 26, 1769; *Virginia Gazette,* April 30, 1772; *Virginia Gazette,* October 14, 1773; *Virginia Gazette Supplement,* April 19, 1770; *Virginia Gazette,* October 31, 1771. Courtesy Mildred Lanier.

8. *Commercial Advertiser,* October 18, 1790. Courtesy Susan B. Swan.

9. In *Hamlet,* William Shakespeare, noting the quality of a smock or "habit" worn by one of his characters, commented, "Costly thy habit as thy purse can buy; but not express'd in fancy; rich not gawdy." In the mid-seventeenth century, ribbons worn on suits with open-legged breeches were sometimes known as "fancies"; see Shakespeare, *Hamlet* (I, iii , 71); Voltaire, "Essay on Taste," p. 215.

10. Florence M. Montgomery, *Printed Textiles: English and American Cottons and Linens, 1700–1850* (New York: Viking Press for the Winterthur Museum, 1970), p. 102.

11. *New York Gazette Supplement,* September 6, 1772. *Maryland Journal and Baltimore Advertiser* (Baltimore), May 22, 1789. Courtesy Arlene Palmer Schwind. Quoted in *The Dictionary of Americanisms,* edited by Milford M. Mathews (Chicago: University of Chicago Press, 1951), p. 584.

12. *Columbian Centennial* (Boston), May 12, 1792, quoted in *Supplement to the Oxford English Dictionary,* edited by R. W. Burchfield (Oxford: Clarendon Press, 1972), s.v. "fancy."

13. Nathan Bailey, *Dictionarum Britannicum* (London: T. Cox, 1736), s.v. "fancy."

14. *Oxford English Dictionary* (1961), s.v. "trifle"; Horace Walpole to Richard Bentley, September 18, 1755, quoted in Therle and Bernard Hughes, *English Painted Enamels* (1951; reprint, Feltham, Middlesex, Eng.: Hamlyn Publishing Group Ltd., 1967), p. 54. Bentley was a skilled draughtsman who worked closely with Walpole on a number of design projects. The author is grateful to Taylor B. Williams for his contributions to these paragraphs. An American sampler wrought by Albina L. Morgan in 1815 (private collection) bears the verse "Trifles such as these, the ingenious fancy please."

15. H. Mackenzie et al., *The Mirror* (1779), quoted in the *Oxford English Dictionary* (1961), s.v. "trifle."

16. Thomas Sheraton, appendix, in *The Cabinet-Maker and Upholsterer's Drawing-Book,* 3d ed. (1802; reprint, New York: Dover Publications, 1972), p. 3.

17. Wendell D. Garrett, "John Adams and the Limited Role of the Fine Arts," *Winterthur Portfolio*, vol. 1 (Winterthur, Del.: Winterthur Museum, 1964), pp. 247, 252.

18. Benjamin Rush, "Thoughts upon Female Education . . . ," *The Universal Asylum and Columbian Magazine* (May 1790): 292, quoted in Susan Burrows Swan, *Plain and Fancy, American Women and Their Needlework, 1700–1850* (New York: Holt Rinehart and Winston, 1977), p. 13.

19. Hester Mulso Chapone, *Letters on the Improvement of the Mind, Address to a Young Lady*, 2 vols. (1772; reprint, London: C. Whittingham, 1801), p. 157. Chapone's *Letters* was also published in Boston and Worcester, Massachusetts, in 1783, in Philadelphia in 1786, and in New York in 1793. Courtesy Tori Eberline.

20. The author is grateful to Jeffrey Plank for his contributions to this paragraph and section.

21. Rudolph Ackermann, "Observations on Fancy-work," *The Repository of Arts, Science, Literature, Commerce, Manufactures, Fashions, and Politics*, no. 15 (March 1810): 192–95; continued under the same name in no. 16 (April 1810): 397. This quote is taken from page 397. An engraved page with the title "Patterns of Fancy Papers and Borders," with samples of embossed, gilt, and printed papers for ornamenting fancy furniture, etc., appears on page 193. Courtesy Carol Baker and Kathryn McKenney.

22. Stewart, *Elements of the Philosophy of the Human Mind*, p. 521.

23. I am indebted to Davida Deutsch of New York City for sharing her insights on the skills taught at school. For further information about the Folwell School, see Davida Deutsch, "Samuel Folwell of Philadelphia: An Artist for the Needleworker," *Antiques* 119, no. 2 (February 1981): 420–23; "Collectors' Notes," *Antiques* 128, no. 3 (September 1985): 526–27; "Collector's Notes: A follow-up on our man Folwell," *Antiques* 135, no. 3 (March 1989): 616, 620, 624. Samuel Folwell's son, Godfrey, also served as an instructor at the school, and though his work is similar to that of his father, it can be distinguished. Deutsch, "Collectors' Notes," *Antiques* 130, no. 4 (October 1986): 646–47.

24. Sarah Anna Emery, *Reminiscences of a Nonagenarian* (Newburyport, Mass.: William H. Huse & Co., 1879), p. 223. Quoted in Charles F. Montgomery, *American Furniture, the Federal Period, in the Henry Francis du Pont Winterthur Museum* (New York: Viking Press, 1966), p. 462.

25. Edward Young, *Night Thoughts* (IV, 71), in *Edward Young Poems*, selected and introduced by Brian Hepworth (Cheadle, Eng.: Carcanet Press, 1975). A closely related dressing table by another daughter of the Lombard family is in the collection of the Shelburne Museum, Shelburne, Vermont.

26. For illustrations of other early quilts with appliqué designs, see Gloria Seaman Allen, *First Flowerings: Early Virginia Quilts* (Washington, D.C.: D.A.R. Museum, 1987).

27. The first poem, of unknown origin, appears on the 1806 sampler of Ann Gilliam Blunt (1793–1836), Warren County, North Carolina. The sampler was documented by the Museum of Early Southern Decorative Arts [hereafter cited as MESDA], Winston-Salem, North Carolina, Research File S-3763. Courtesy Dywana M. Saunders. The circa 1805 mourning piece depicted, dedicated to Shakespeare, bears a poem from Mark Akenside, "The Pleasures of Imagination: A Poem in Three Books" (1744), in *The Poetical Works of Mark Akenside: Collated with the Best Editions by Thomas Park, Esq. F.S.A.*, 2 vols. (London: Printed at the Stanhope Press, by Charles Whittingam for J. Sharpe, 1805), 1: 15. The embroidery is also pictured in Betty Ring, *American Needlework Treasures: Samplers and Silk Embroideries from the Collection of Betty Ring* (New York: E. P. Dutton in association with the Museum of American Folk Art, 1987), p. 70, fig. 115. I am grateful to Betty Ring for her frequent assistance with this project.

28. I am grateful to the late Michael Berry, former Curator for the Museum of the Daughters of the American Revolution in Washington, D.C., for first bringing these observations to my attention. For further insights into mourning jewelry, see Davida Deutsch, "Jewelry for Mourning, Love and Fancy, 1770–1830," *Antiques* 155, no. 4 (April 1999): 566–75. For further information on mourning embroidery, see Anita Schorsch, *Mourning Becomes America, Mourning Art in The New Nation* (Clinton, N.J.: Main Street Press, 1976); Jane Nylander, "Some Print Sources of New England Schoolgirl Art," *Antiques* 110, no. 2 (August 1976): 292; Betty Ring, "Memorial

Embroideries by American Schoolgirls," *Antiques* 100, no. 4 (October 1971): 570–77; Robin Jaffe Frank, *Love and Loss: American Portrait and Mourning Miniatures* (New Haven: Yale University Press, 2000). I am grateful to Elle Shushan for sharing her insights on the history of mourning.

29. Mark Twain, *Adventures of Huckleberry Finn* (New York: Grosset & Dunlap, 1948), p. 83. For further insights into Twain's observations on mourning, see Carol Colclough Strickland, "Emmeline Grangerford, Mark Twain's Folk Artist," *Bulletin of the New York Public Library* 79, no. 2 (winter 1976): 225–33.

30. Emery, *Reminiscences of a Nonagenarian*, p. 221.

31. Charles Carter, *The Complete Practical Cook: or, a New System of Cookery* (London, 1730; facsimile, Devon, Eng.: Prospect Books, 1984), introduction.

32. "Desserts were made to please the eye as well as the palate," wrote colonial food historian Helen Bullock in 1939, "and sometimes, one might suspect, the eye had the preference." Helen Bullock, *The Art of Williamsburg Cookery* (Williamsburg, Va.: Colonial Williamsburg Foundation, 1939), p. 70. Hannah Glasse, *The Art of Cookery Made Plain and Easy* (London: Printed for the author, 1747).

33. John Farley, *London Art of Cookery* (London: Scatcherd and Letterman, 1807; facsimile, Lewes, East Sussex, Eng.: Southover Press, 1988), p. 308.

34. Elizabeth Raffald, *The Experienced English Housekeeper, for the Use and Ease of Ladies, Housekeepers, Cooks, & c.,* 13th ed. (London, 1806). Raffald's book was first published in 1769.

35. Bullock, *The Art of Williamsburg Cookery,* p. 185.

36. Raffald, *The Experienced English Housekeeper,* p. 98. Thanks to Nancy Carter Crump for her research and keen observations into the origins of Fancy cookery.

37. "Observations on Fancy-Work," in Rudolph Ackermann's *Repository*, p. 397.

Chapter Three   EARLY FANCY FURNISHINGS

1. Elisabeth Donaghy Garrett, *At Home: The American Family 1750–1870* (New York, Harry N. Abrams, Inc., 1998), p. 33.

2. *The American* (Baltimore), December 5, 1811, quoted in Stiles Tuttle Colwill, *Francis Guy: 1760–1820* (Baltimore, Md.: Maryland Historical Society, 1981), p. 32.

3. Ibid., January 11, 1812, quoted in Colwill, *Francis Guy,* p. 33.

4. "Letters from New York, No. 1," *The New Monthly Magazine,* 26, no. 104 (August 1829): 153, quoted in Garrett, *At Home,* p. 18.

5. James Fenimore Cooper, *Notions of the Americans Picked up by a Travelling Bachelor* (1829; New York: Frederick Ungar Publishing Co., 1929) quoted in Garrett, *At Home,* p. 17.

6. Ralph Izard to George Dempster, Naples, January 21, 1775, quoted in Maurie D. McInnis et al., *In Pursuit of Refinement, Charlestonians Abroad, 1740–1860* (Charleston, S.C.: Gibbes Museum of Art with the cooperation of the Historic Charleston Foundation, 1999), p. 18.

7. "Diary of Samuel Sewall," in *Collections of the Massachusetts Historical Society,* 5th ser., vol. 5 (1878), p. 413, quoted in Abbott Lowell Cummings, "Decorative Painters and House Painting at Massachusetts Bay, 1630–1725," in *American Painting to 1776: A Reappraisal,* edited by Ian M. G. Quimby (Charlottesville: University Press of Virginia for the Winterthur Museum, 1971), p. 72.

8. For further information on Robert Adam, see John Fleming, *Robert Adam and His Circle in Edinburgh and Rome* (Cambridge, Mass.: Harvard University Press, 1962); Geoffrey Beard, *The Work of Robert Adam* (New York: Arco, 1978); and Damie Stillman, *The Decorative Work of Robert Adam* (New York: Transatlantic Arts, 1966).

9. George Hepplewhite, *The Cabinet-Maker and Upholsterer's Guide,* 3d ed. (1794; reprint, New York: Dover Publications, 1969), p. 2.

10. Ibid., preface; Thomas Sheraton, *An Accompaniment to the Cabinet-Maker and Upholsterer's Drawing-book* (1794; reprint, New York: Dover Publications, 1972), p. 7; Sheraton, appendix in *The Cabinet-Maker and Upholsterer's Drawing-Book,* 3d ed., p. 3; Thomas Sheraton, *Cabinet Dictionary,* with an introduction by Wilford P. Cole and

Charles F. Montgomery, 2 vols. (1803; reprint, New York: Praeger, 1970). See frontis-piece.

11. Massachusetts, Hampshire County Probate Court, Inventory of Joseph Barnard, Hampshire County Probate Records (Greenfield, March 1, 1790, pp. xvi, 135).

12. Montgomery, *American Furniture,* p. 449.

13. The use of hardwoods such as maple made it possible to work on a delicate scale not generally permitted by Honduran mahogany, which was stunning to behold but gen-erally porous and therefore less durable.

14. William Bentley, *The Diary of the Rev. William Bentley, D.D. Pastor of the East Church, Salem, Massachusetts,* 2 vols. (1907; reprint, Gloucester, Mass.: Peter Smith, 1962), 2: 100.

15. Sheraton, *The Cabinet-Maker and Upholsterer's Drawing Book,* 3d ed., no. 1, pl. 36.

16. Zilla Lea, *The Ornamented Chair: Its Development in America 1700–1890* (Rutland, Vt.: Charles E. Tuttle Co., 1960), p. 37. Challen also advertised "wangee" finishes, proba-bly a corruption of the word "wenge," the period term for the wood purpleheart, pop-ular for exotic inlays. I am grateful to James Millard for this insight.

17. Milton Grigg of Grigg, Wood, Brown, Eichman and Dagleish Architects, Charlottes-ville, Virginia, to the author, October 8, 1979. The letter is now on deposit in the Colo-nial Williamsburg Foundation Archives, Williamsburg, Virginia. The house stood in the 100 block of Prince Street, Alexandria. For such a tented treatment, see Jane Webb Smith, "The Wickham House in Richmond: Neoclassical Splendor Restored," *Antiques* 155, no. 2 (February 1999): 308.

18. Nancy Goyne Evans, "The Christian M. Nestell Drawing Book: A Focus on the Orna-mental Painter and His Craft in Early Nineteenth-Century America," in *American Fur-niture,* edited by Luke Beckerdite (Hanover, N.H.: University Press of New England for the Chipstone Foundation, 1998), pp. 99–163.

19. *American and Commercial Daily Advertiser* (Baltimore), November 7, 1805.

20. Frances Trollope, *Domestic Manners of the Americans,* 2 vols. (London: Whittaker, Treacher & Co., 1832), 2: 99.

21. Gregory R. Weidman and Jennifer F. Goldsborough, *Classical Maryland 1815–1845 Fine and Decorative Arts from the Golden Age* (Baltimore: Maryland Historical Society, 1993), p. 90.

22. Francis Guy's employment with the Finlay brothers is explored in Colwill, *Francis Guy,* pp. 24–27. Related pieces are explored in Lance Humphries, "Provenance, Patronage, and Perception: The Morris Suite of Baltimore Painted Furniture," in *American Fur-niture,* edited by Luke Beckerdite (Hanover, N.H.: University Press of New England for the Chipstone Foundation, 2003), pp. 138–212.

23. *The American* (Baltimore), August 11, 1804, quoted in Colwill, *Francis Guy,* p. 24.

24. Thomas Reid, *Essays on the Intellectual Powers of Man* (Edinburgh: John Bell, 1785), p. 365.

25. Massachusetts, Suffolk County Probate Court, Inventory of John Hancock, no. 20215. Suffolk County Probate Records (Boston, 1794); Alfred Coxe Prime, *The Arts and Crafts in Philadelphia, Maryland, and South Carolina, 1786–1800,* 2d. ser. (Topsfield, Mass.: The Walpole Society, 1932), p. 306; *Virginia Chronicle* (Norfolk), May 18, 1793. Advertisement of Moses Grant Junior, Boston, 1813, quoted in McClelland, *Historic Wallpapers,* p. 270.

26. John Holverson to Sumpter Priddy, February 4, 1977. The author thanks Donald R. Walters for bringing the inscription on the Codman painting to his attention; Rembrandt Peale quoted in Colwill, *Francis Guy,* p. 20.

27. *Evening Post* (New York) December 28, 1821, quoted in Colwill, *Francis Guy,* p. 95; Documentation of deBeet's association with the Finlays is found in a letter from Rembrandt Peale to Thomas Jefferson, December 7, 1825: "For a while he was engaged in Baltimore ornamenting Windsor chairs for Messrs. Finlay when I became acquaint-ed with him and it is only of late that he has attempted to make pictures or landscapes. I cannot but think his practice on the chairs have been injurious to his taste," quoted in Colwill, *Francis Guy,* p. 25.

28. Montgomery, *American Furniture,* pp. 457–58; For more information on furniture made for *Cleopatra's Barge,* see Walter Muir Whitehill, *George Crowninshield's Yacht*

"Cleopatra's Barge" and a Catalogue of the Francis B. Crowninshield Gallery (Salem, Mass.: Peabody Museum, 1959).

29. Alexandra Alevizatos Kirtley, "Survival of the Fittest: The Lloyd Family's Furniture Legacy," in *American Furniture,* edited by Luke Beckerdite (Hanover, N.H.: University Press of New England for the Chipstone Foundation, 2002), pp. 32–33, 52 n. 55; Alexandra Alevizatos Kirtley, "New Discoveries in Baltimore Painted Furniture," *Catalog of Antiques and Fine Art* 3, no. 2 (spring 2002): 204–9. I am grateful to Ms. Kirtley for sharing her insights into furniture from early Baltimore and Philadelphia. Papers surviving from Governor Edward Lloyd V's occupancy of Wye record that he paid Hugh Finlay $14.75 for the two cornices in 1828, a total of $7.00 each, plus another $.75 to pack them for shipping. Their exceptional quality is best understood when compared to his next purchases in 1833, when receipts record a set of a half dozen fancy Windsor chairs for $7.00 or slightly more than $1.15 each; an armchair with a cane seat for $3.25, and an unspecified number of "cabbin stools" for the family's private schooner, the group costing $3.75.

30. For further information on Latrobe's architectural designs, see Jeffrey A. Cohen and Charles E. Brownell, *The Architectural Drawings of Benjamin Henry Latrobe,* 2 vols. (New Haven and London: Yale University Press for the Maryland Historical Society and the American Philosophical Society, 1994).

31. Jack L. Lindsey, "An Early Latrobe Furniture Commission," *Antiques* 139, no. 1 (January 1991): 209–19; Gregory R. Weidman, "The Painted Furniture of John and Hugh Finlay," *Antiques* 143, no. 5 (May 1993), pp. 744–55. Dolley Madison to her sister Anna Payne Cutts Causten, August 23, 1814, in "The Papers of Dolley Madison (1794–1852)," microfilm reel 18, 940, call number MMC-3373, on deposit in the Manuscripts Division, Library of Congress.

32. In 1806 Latrobe apprised Congress of his ideals for taste—though one can only surmise they applied to public structures, rather than private dwellings: "As the arts continue to be improved, simplicity gains daily more admirers. Indeed nothing appears so clear from the general assent of all ages, as that a graceful and refined simplicity is the highest achievement of taste and of art; not only in architecture, but in poetry, in rhetoric, in dress and in manners. . . . Nothing is so easy as to ornament. . . . And on this account we find ornaments increase in proportion as art declines, or as ignorance abounds." B. Henry Latrobe to the . . . Members of Congress, November 28, 1806, in *The Correspondence and Miscellaneous Papers of Benjamin Henry Latrobe,* edited by John C. Van Horne and Lee W. Fromwalt, 3 vols. (New Haven: Yale University Press for the Maryland Historical Society, 1986), 2: 306. It should be observed that Latrobe was known in his lifetime as Henry and signed his name "B. Henry Latrobe." The preference for Benjamin is mistaken and modern. Courtesy Charles Brownell, Richmond, Virginia.

33. Lindsey, "An Early Latrobe Furniture Commission," pp. 209–19; Weidman, "The Painted Furniture of John and Hugh Finlay," p. 747.

34. Bridport's interiors for the Waln house in 1808 and for the Wickham House, Richmond, in 1812, incorporated griffin ornaments closely related to those on the Waln chairs and pieces from the Finlay shops.

35. The Yellott family of Woodville, in Baltimore, owned a table with decorative details closely related to those of the Waln set. See Baltimore Museum of Art, *Baltimore Furniture: The Work of Baltimore and Annapolis Cabinetmakers from 1760 to 1810* (Baltimore, Md.: By the Museum, 1947), p. 158, fig. 99.

36. Wendy A. Cooper, with Tara Louise Gleason and Katharine A. John, *An American Vision, Henry Francis du Pont's Winterthur Museum* (Washington, D.C.: National Gallery of Art; Wilmington, Del.: Winterthur Museum, 2002), p. 177. The Yellott family table mentioned in note 25 is related in numerous details to this example. I am grateful to Alexandra Kirtley for sharing her insights into the complex layering of distinct, mid-Atlantic ornament upon furniture forms usually associated with New England. See Alexandra Kirtley, unpublished manuscript, Philadelphia Museum of Art.

37. Weidman, "The Painted Furniture of John and Hugh Finlay," p. 747.

38. Thomas Renshaw's former partner remains unidentified, but it may have been his

kinsman, William Renshaw, who appeared in Baltimore later as a "turner"—one of the tradesmen essential to producing Fancy chairs. Courtesy MESDA.

39. Anne Castrodale Golovin, "Cabinetmakers and Chairmakers of Washington, D.C., 1791–1840," *Antiques* 107, no. 5 (May 1975): 918; *Museum and Washington and George-Town Advertiser* (Georgetown), August 31, 1801, and October 26, 1801; *Journal of Early Southern Decorative Arts* 26, no. 1 (summer 2000): 49; *Journal of Early Southern Decorative Arts* 24, no. 2 (winter 1998): 57. Unknown is John Barnhart's relationship to Henry Barnhart, who apprenticed in 1807 to Baltimore Windsor chair maker Robert Fisher, or to Hosea Renshaw, a Baltimore County "nailer" who died in 1795.

40. *Oxford English Dictionary* (1961), s.v. "elastic." Springs were employed occasionally in exercise "horses" during the eighteenth century, but they were not used for seating furniture until the late 1820s. See David Conradsen, "The Stock-in-Trade of John Hancock and Company," in *American Furniture*, edited by Luke Beckerdite (Hanover, N.H.: University Press of New England for the Chipstone Foundation, 1993), pp. 39–54; "Very comfortable . . . ," from Samuel Gragg's patent certificate now owned by James Madison University, is quoted in Michael Podmaniczky, "The Incredible Elastic Chairs of Samuel Gragg," *Antiques* 163, no. 5 (May 2003): 138–45. See also Karla Klein Albertson, "The Incredible Elastic Chairs of Samuel Gragg," *Antiques and the Arts Weekly* (Newtown, Conn.), April 4, 2003, pp. 1, 40–41. The author is grateful to Michael Podmaniczky of Winterthur for sharing his insights into Samuel Gragg's chairs.

41. For more information on the Samuel Gragg family of chair makers, see Montgomery, *American Furniture,* p. 469; Nancy Goyne Evans, "Genesis of the Boston Rocking Chair," *Antiques* 123, no. 1 (January 1983): 246–53; Podmaniczky, "The Incredible Elastic Chairs of Samuel Gragg," pp. 138–45; and Patricia Kane, "Samuel Gragg: His Bentwood Fancy Chairs," Yale University Art Gallery *Bulletin* 33, no. 2 (fall 1971): 26–37.

42. The term *verre églomisé,* or simply *églomisé,* now often used to designate a wide variety of transparent painting with gold leaf on glass, is a poor choice. According to Paul J. Foley, *Willard's Patent Time-Pieces, A History of the Weight Driven Banjo Clock 1800–1900* (Norwell, Mass.: Paul J. Foley, 2002), p. 184: "In the 18th century in Paris, Jean Baptiste Glomy popularized gilt and black painted glass mat frames for prints that became known as 'verre eglomise' (glass in the manner of Glomy)." Cited from Frieder Ryser, *Reverse Paintings on Glass: The Ryser Collection* (Corning, N. Y.: Corning Museum of Glass, 1992). The author is also grateful to Peter Kenny, Curator of American Decorative Arts, Metropolitan Museum of Art, for sharing his insights into this topic.

43. *Evening Gazette* (Charleston, S.C.) October 20, 1785. Courtesy MESDA.

44. Montgomery, *American Furniture,* pp. 204–5.

45. Carol Damon Andrews, "John Rito Penniman (1782–1841): An Ingenious New England Artist," *Antiques* 120, no. 1 (July 1981): 147–70.

46. Information from the New York and Boston City Directories courtesy MESDA; William Pinchbeck, *The Expositor: or Many Mysteries Unraveled* (Boston: privately printed, 1805). Pinchbeck also published a book intended to reveal the secrets of witchcraft; see William Pinchbeck, *Witchcraft: Or the Art of Fortune-Telling Unveiled* (Boston: privately printed, 1805).

47. Nathaniel Whittock, *The Decorative Painters' and Glaziers' Guide* (London: Isaac Taylor Hinton, 1827), p. 20. Whittock's books had a significant impact on the arts of the era. These include *The Youth's New London Self-Instructing Drawing Book* (London: George Virtue, 1836); *The Complete Book of Trades* (London: John Bennett, 1837); and *The Miniature Painter's Manual* (London: Sherwood, Gilbert and Piper, 1844).

48. Advertisement of William Boyle and Company from the *Baltimore Daily Repository,* May 18, 1792, lists "House, Ship, Sign, Carpet and Fancy Painting." Quoted in Prime, *Arts and Crafts in Philadephia, Maryland and South Carolina, 1786–1800,* p. 303; and Nina Fletcher Little, *American Decorative Wall Painting, 1700–1850* (1952; reprint, New York: E. P. Dutton, 1989), p. 6.

49. The word "marbling" was in use by the late seventeenth century to describe the process of emulating marble on wood, although more frequently employed to describe the process of staining papers for books or of cutting marble in quarries. The words "graining" and "grainer" do not commonly appear until the early years of the nine-

teenth century, the latter word being relatively scarce. See the *Oxford English Dictionary* (1961), s.v. "marbling" and "marbler"; s.v. "graining" and "grainer."

50. Edward Hazen, *Panorama of Professions and Trades* (Philadelphia: Uriah Hunt and Sons, 1837), s.v. "painter," p. 217.

51. William Mullinger Higgins, *The House Painter; or Decorator's Companion* (London: Thomas Kelly, 1851), p. 154.

52. Whittock, *The Complete Book of Trades,* p. 360.

53. Higgins, *The House Painter,* p. 154.

54. D. R. Hay, *Laws of Harmonious Colouring,* 4th ed. (London: W. S. Orr and Co., 1838), quoted in Little, *American Decorative Wall Painting,* p. 6.

55. Barry worked intermittently at the Capitol and the President's House when not employed at Monticello. His work is recorded in *Thomas Jefferson's Memorandum Books: Accounts, with Legal Records and Miscellany, 1767–1826,* edited by James A. Bear, Jr., and Lucia C. Stanton (Princeton, N.J.: Princeton University Press, 1997), pp. 1149, 1150, 1163, 1167, 1177, 1182, 1232, 1237, 1264, and 1274. Payments to Barry continued over a period of nearly six years, finally ending on March 15, 1812, and totaled $572.50. Frank Welsh, historic paint consultant of Bryn Mawr, Pennsylvania, revealed the original surfaces of the doors at Monticello. See Frank Welsh, "The Art of Painted Graining," *Historic Preservation* 29, no. 3 (July–September, 1977): 33–37.

56. The term "whirligig" appears in English by the mid-fifteenth century. *Oxford English Dictionary* (1961), s.v. "whirligig"; Charles L. Granquist, "Thomas Jefferson's 'Whirligig' Chairs," *Antiques* 109, no. 5 (May 1976): 1056–60.

57. See William B. O'Neal, *Jefferson's Fine Arts Library* (Charlottesville: University Press of Virginia, 1976), p. 2.

58. Thomas Jefferson to William J. Coffee, July 10, 1822, on deposit in the Massachusetts Historical Society.

59. See Thomas Jefferson to Charles Brockden Brown, January 15, 1800: "Some of the most agreeable moments of my life have been spent in reading works of imagination which have this advantage over history that the incidents of the former may be dressed in the most interesting form, while those of the latter must be confined to fact." From the collections of the Library of Congress, courtesy Diane Ehrenpreis, The Thomas Jefferson Memorial Foundation, Charlottesville.

60. According to neighbors' recollections, the Trower house, now destroyed, had a brick dated 1812 in the chimney. See Ralph A. Whitelaw, *Virginia's Eastern Shore: A History of Northampton and Accomack Counties,* edited by George Carrington Mason, 2 vols. (Gloucester, Mass.: Peter Smith, 1968), 1: 59–61. After the loss of the house in the mid-twentieth century, much of the interior woodwork was installed in "Sylvan Scene." For further information on Sylvan Scene, see Whitelaw, *Virginia's Eastern Shore,* 1: 347–49.

61. Addison, "Pleasures of the Imagination," *The Spectator* (June 25, 1712).

62. Ibid., June 24, 1712.

63. *New York Gazette Supplement,* September 6, 1772. Courtesy Arlene Palmer Schwind.

64. *South Carolina State Gazette* (Charleston, S.C.) January 15, 1793. Courtesy MESDA.

65. *Daily Advertiser* (Alexandria, Va.), April 12, 1808. Courtesy MESDA.

66. Many of these ornamental wares are now known as "Pratt" ware after a Staffordshire firm by that name. In reality, scarcely a handful of pieces signed by Pratt are recorded, and the style reflects a broader trend in Staffordshire and beyond, in the years between 1780 and 1840. See John Lewis and Griselda Lewis, *Prattware: English and Scottish Relief Decorated and Underglaze Coloured Earthenware 1780–1840* (Woodbridge, Suffolk, Eng.: Antique Collectors' Club, in association with Alan Kaplan, 1993).

67. "Turners List of Prices for Common Ware," undated broadside, Staffordshire, England, [ca. 1810–1840], now on deposit in the Local Collections Division of the University of Keele Library, Staffordshire, England. Courtesy Jonathan Rickard.

68. Donald Carpentier and Jonathan Rickard, "Slip Decoration in the Age of Industrialization," in *Ceramics in America,* edited by Robert Hunter (Hanover, N.H.: University Press of New England for the Chipstone Foundation, 2001), p. 117.

69. *Journal, & Patriotic Register* (New York City), July 20, 1790, quoted in Rita Susswein,

Arts & Crafts in New York, 1777–1799 (New York: New-York Historical Society, 1954), entry 497. Courtesy Margaret Pritchard.

70. I am grateful to Christopher Ohrstrom of Adelphi Paper Hangings for sharing his insights and scholarship in this area. For further information see <www.adelphipaper hangings.com>. Émigré Anthony Chardon arrived in Philadelphia from Nantes, France, in 1795. Courtesy Christopher Ohrstrom.

71. Such repetitive diamond patterns may have been inspired, in part, by an optical device that was popularized in the 1790s. Consisting of a conical tube capped by a lens with diamond facets, the instrument replicated any image viewed therein in multiples, set within adjoining diamonds. I am grateful to Lou Storey for bringing this device to my attention.

Chapter Four   THE KALEIDOSCOPE

1. Sir David Brewster, *A Treatise on the Kaleidoscope* (Edinburgh: Archibald Constable and Co., 1819), pp. 1–2. Brewster's publication was greatly heralded. Ackermann, *Repository of the Arts* 6, no. 34 (October 1, 1818): 243, announced that "Dr. Brewster's Treatise on the Kaleidoscope, including an account of the various forms of that curious and entertaining instrument, will appear very shortly." A subsequent article entitled "Origin of the Kaleidoscope" with a subtitle "To the Editor" appeared in *Repository of the Arts* (April 1, 1822): 205–7. A brief description of the invention is also included in Sir David Brewster, *A Treatise on Optics* (1831; reprint, Philadelphia: Carey, Lea and Blanchard, 1844), pp. 262–63. A subsequent edition of Brewster's original publication appeared as *The Kaleidoscope: Its History, Theory, and Construction, with Its Application to the Fine and Useful Arts* (London: John Murray, 1858). This edition, which is widely available, is cited as the source for Brewster's *Treatise* (1819).

2. Brewster began his book by observing that the word Kaleidoscope was formed from three Greek words, καλό, *beautiful*; ειδος, *form*; and σκοπέω, *to see,* cited in Brewster, *A Treatise,* p. 1. Also cited in Ernst H. Gombrich, *The Sense of Order, The Wrightsman Lectures Delivered under the Auspices of The New York University Institute of Fine Arts* (New York: Phaidon, 1979), p. 149.

3. Certain design elements of the kaleidoscope existed a century before in an optical device designed by David Bradley, first professor of Botany at Cambridge University. Bradley recommended using cojoined mirrors to facilitate garden design, and addressed their use in part 2 of his *New Improvement of Planting and Gardening* (London, 1718). He there included a chapter entitled "Descriptions and use of a new invention for the more speedy designing of garden platts." In the nineteenth century, Bradley's designs were published anew, and anonymously, as *Descriptions and Use of the Instrument now called a Kaleidoscope, as published by its original inventor, Richard Bradley* (London: E. L. Simons, 1818). Bradley's invention, which he never named, had minimal impact in its time—the mind-set of eighteenth-century Britain was not yet sufficiently primed to absorb its lesson in abstraction. David Brewster addressed the differences between the two inventions in the appendix at the end of his *Treatise.* I am grateful to Caroline Davidson, the British historian of gardens and food ways, for sharing these insights. Caroline Davidson to Sumpter Priddy, November 21, 1980.

4. Joseph Addison, "Pleasures of the Imagination," *The Spectator* (June 30, 1712); E. H. Gombrich, *The Sense of Order: A Study in the Psychology of Decorative Art* (Oxford, Eng.: Phaidon, 1979), p. 151.

5. Brewster patented his invention in 1817 as "Specifications for Brewster's Patent No. 4136, A new optical instrument called the Kaleidoscope," cited in the *Oxford English Dictionary* (1961), s.v. "kaleidoscope"; Brewster, *The Kaleidoscope*, p. 7.

6. The cone-shaped kaleidoscope was known as a polyangular kaleidoscope, in which it was possible to adjust both the angle of the opening between the mirrors, and the angle of the mirrors themselves, thereby maximizing the possible variations. Such kaleidoscopes were expensive to produce and, therefore, extremely scarce outside of scientific circles. Brewster devoted chapter 11 to the subject, "On the Construction and

Use of the Polyangular Kaleidoscope, in which the Reflectors can be fixed at any Angle," *The Kaleidoscope*, pp. 88–97.

7. Brewster, *A Treatise on Optics*, p. 263. Brewster's interests lay not only in the principles of science but in theories of sight and perception, as well. Three decades later, he invented the stereoscope, thereby providing to the Victorian era the capacity to visualize two dimensional images, including photographs of distant places, in three dimensions. Stereoscopes, which appeared in parlors across America, helped to shape the aesthetic sensibilities of the Victorian era. See Sir David Brewster, *The Stereoscope: Its History, Theory and Construction*, 2d ed. (1856; reprint, Hastings-on-Hudson, N.Y.: Morgan and Morgan; London: Fountain Press, 1977).

8. "The Kaleidoscope," *The Idiot* (Boston), September 12, 1818.

9. "A Kaleidoscope—On A Large Scale," *The Idiot* (Boston), October 31, 1818. *The Idiot* was published by Haws and Doss, who also published a new literary magazine in November 1818 called *The Kaleidoscope*. The name of the magazine was expanded to *The Boston Kaleidoscope and Literary Rambler* in January 1819. Another magazine called *The Kaleidoscope* appeared briefly in Nashville, Tennessee, in 1833.

10. "Pasteboard" was the forerunner of modern cardboard and served much the same purpose. As the name suggests, pasteboard was made by using paste to laminate three or more sheets of cotton paper. See the *Oxford English Dictionary* (1961), s.v. "pasteboard." An undated entry, June 1818, Business Ledger of Ephraim Gilman, Merchant, 1805–1822, Alexandria, Virginia, on deposit in the library of Historic Alexandria, notes that Gilman paid two dollars wholesale for a kaleidoscope; advertisement for Daniel Pierce, *Gazette* (Alexandria), August 11, 1819. "Umbrella and Trunk Manufactory . . . likewise a good assortment of fancy and common trunks . . . corset bones, pocketbooks . . . kaleidoscopes, &." Courtesy Elaine Hawes, Alexandria, Virginia.

11. James Flint, *Letters from America, containing Observations on the Climate and Agriculture of the Western States, the Manners of the People, the Prospects of Emigrants, &c. &c.* (Edinburgh: W & C Tart, 1822; reprint, New York: Johnson Reprint Corp., 1970), p. 20.

12. Brewster, *The Kaleidoscope*, p. 160; Dr. Roget's entry for "Kaleidoscope" in the *Encyclopaedia Britannica*, quoted in Brewster, *The Kaleidoscope*, p. 7; ibid., p. 5.

13. A related engraving, entitled "CALEIDOSCOPES, or Paying for Peeping," was published in June 1818 by S. W. Fores of London. A copy is now on deposit at Yale University's Lewis Walpole Library, Farmington, Connecticut.

14. Brewster, *The Kaleidoscope*, p. 8.

15. I am grateful to Jeffrey Plank for his contributions to this paragraph.

16. "The Literary Kaleidoscope," *Boston Kaleidoscope and Literary Rambler*, January 23, 1819.

17. Gombrich, *The Sense of Order*, p. 151.

18. "The Literary Kaleidoscope," *Boston Kaleidoscope and Literary Rambler*, January 23, 1819.

19. "Kaleidoscopes," *Boston Kaleidoscope and Literary Rambler*, October 31, 1818.

20. Brewster, *The Kaleidoscope*, p. 136.

21. Ibid., pp. 131, 137. The camera obscura was an invention nearly a thousand years old that consisted of a "darkened chamber or box, into which light is admitted through a double convex lens, forming an image of external objects on a surface of paper, glass, etc. placed at the focus of the lens." The camera lucida, an improvement on the earlier device, was invented in 1825 by Dr. William Hyde Wollaston of Britain. It differed in using "a peculiarly-shaped prism, and produced an image on paper placed beneath the instrument, whilst the eye at the same time can see directly the pencil, with which the image is being traced . . . and came into popular use for copying and reducing drawings." *Oxford English Dictionary* (1961), s.v. "camera obscura" and "camera lucida."

22. See Brewster, chapter 20, "On the Application of the Kaleidoscope to the Fine and Useful Arts," *The Kaleidoscope*, pp. 134–47.

23. Brewster, *The Kaleidoscope*, p. 144.

24. In 1999 Nancy E. Davis, Curator of Textiles at the Maryland Historical Society, suggested in her study *The Baltimore Album Quilt Tradition* (Baltimore: Maryland Historical Society, 1999), pp. 33–35, that "possibly" those "who created these complicated geometric stars found inspirations for the quilt designs in the kaleidoscope." The

author first made this observation in 1981, received assistance from photographer Hans Lorenz of Colonial Williamsburg in recording kaleidoscopic images that parallel quilt designs, and has frequently lectured on the subject since that time. The author is grateful to Sarah Cantor for brining this publication to his attention.

25. It is unlikely that a radiating star composed of multiple tiny pieces of fabric was used as a central design for American quilts prior to 1816, although eight pointed stars are recorded in needlework and bed rugs prior to 1816. A quilt made by Frances Washington of Virginia has a large star design and can be documented to the period 1790–1800 but is constructed of large squares and is quite unlike the later examples inspired by the kaleidoscope. See Gloria Seaman Allen, *First Flowerings, Early Virginia Quilts* (Washington, D.C.: Daughters of the American Revolution Museum, 1987), p. 31. That quilt is now at Mount Vernon.

26. Philadelphia Museum of Art, *Three Centuries of American Art* (Philadelphia: By the museum, 1976), pp. 305–6. Other examples by Rebecca Scattergood Savery can be found in the collections of the Winterthur Museum and the American Folk Art Museum. For images of the Savery quilt at the American Folk Art Museum, see Stacy Hollander, *American Anthem: Masterworks from the American Folk Art Museum, New York* (New York: American Folk Art Museum in association with Harry N. Abrams, Inc., 2001), p. 89. Such starburst quilts existed in Britain but were scarce there until the 1870s and seem to have been made principally in the northern midlands. For further information and for an example made in Weardale, County Durham, and now in the collection of the North of England Open Air Museum, see James Ayres, *Two Hundred Years of English Naive Art 1700–1900* (Alexandria, Va.: Art Services International, 1996), p. 77, fig. 22; see also Rosemary E. Allan, *North Country Quilts and Coverlets from the Beamish Museum* (Beamish, Eng.: The North of England Open Air Museum, 1987). Courtesy Paige Inslee.

27. The author is grateful to Jeffrey Plank and Glenn Adamson for their contributions.

28. Edgar Allan Poe, "The Philosophy of Furniture," in the *Works of Edgar Allan Poe in One Volume,* edited by Hervey Allen (New York: P. F. Collier & Son Co., 1927), p. 919.

29. Many of the quilt designs of the post-1820 period bear a remarkable kinship to the eye-catching, mosaic floors excavated in the eighteenth century at ancient sites on the shores of the Mediterranean. Whether this is coincidental, or the result of published designs, it is worthy of further exploration. Few designs for ancient floors were published until after 1820 — and it appears that they had little impact until the kaleidoscope had whetted an appetite for such patterns. I am grateful to Toby Fitzgerald for sharing her enthusiasm on this subject with me.

30. Quoted in Patsy Orlofsky and Myron Orlofsky, *Quilts in America* (New York: McGraw-Hill, 1974), p. 90.

31. The author is grateful to Edward Maeder, Director of Collections for Historic Deerfield, for bringing this quilt to his attention.

32. Variants of the eight-pointed star can be documented in Caucasian and Turkish carpets as early as the fourteenth and fifteenth centuries. For illustrations, see *Turkish Handwoven Carpets,* catalog no. 2, 2d ed. (Istanbul and Ankara: Turkish Republic Ministry of Culture, 1992), and Ian Bennett, *Oriental Rugs, Volume 1, Caucasian* (London: Antique Collectors' Club, 1981). The "Maltese Cross," a similar design in which the points of the star are extended and the sides concave, is often associated with the Eastern Orthodox Church and was also an early motif.

33. One variation of this design was simpler to execute because "the shape of every piece is the same." This was called the "Chinese Pattern" in *Peterson's Magazine* 35, no. 13 (April 4, 1859): 306–7, quoted in Birmingham and Montgomery Museums of Art, *Black Belt to Hill Country: Alabama Quilts from the Robert and Helen Cargo Collection* (Birmingham, Ala.: Birmingham Museum of Art, 1981), p. 31.

34. The impact of the kaleidoscope upon the color schemes for woodwork is discussed in David Van Zanten, *The Architectural Polychromy of the 1830s* (New York and London: Garland Publishing, 1977).

35. Rufus Porter, "Art of Painting: Chrystaline [*sic*] Changeable Painting," *Scientific American* 1, no. 16 (January 1, 1846).

Chapter Five SPIRITED ORNAMENTATION

1. The complex issues facing Americans in this period, and the sometimes fiery rhetoric that accompanied the populist "revolution" of the era, has been addressed by numerous scholars, among them Edmond Pessen, *Jacksonian America: Society, Personal and Politics* (1969; reprint, Urbana, Ill.: University of Illinois Press, 1985); Lee Benson, *The Concept of Jacksonian Democracy: New York as a Test Case* (1961; reprint, Princeton, N.J.: Princeton University Press, 1973); and Douglas T. Miller, *The Birth of Modern America 1820–1850* (1970; reprint, Indianapolis and New York: Bobbs Merrill Company, 1979). I am grateful to Professor James C. Curtis for sharing his insights into the Jacksonian era.

2. Alexis de Tocqueville, *Democracy in America,* edited by Andrew Hacker (New York: Washington Square Press, 1964), pp. 156, 150.

3. De Tocqueville, *Democracy in America,* pp. 118, 206.

4. Whittock, *The Decorative Painters' and Glaziers' Guide,* p. 46.

5. The discovery in 1797 of an inexpensive commercial process for creating a brilliant chrome yellow pigment revolutionized the color palette of homes in Europe and America. For further discussions of pigments and historic paint colors, see Roger W. Moss, *Paint in America: The Colors of Historic Buildings* (Washington, D.C.: National Trust for Historic Preservation, 1994).

6. Rufus Porter, "Imitation Painting," *Scientific American* 1, no. 17 (January 8, 1846): 2.

7. A. J. Downing, *The Architecture of Country Houses; including Designs for Cottages, Farm-houses, and Villas* (New York: D. Appleton and Co., 1850), p. 38.

8. Downing, *The Architecture of Country Houses,* p. 368. Specimen cards showing many of these marbled and grained surfaces can be found in Whittock, *The Decorative Painters' and Glaziers' Guide,* p. 182. According to the *Oxford Drawing Book* (1840; reprint, New York: Collins, Keese and Co., 1842), which he also authored, Whittock was "teacher of drawing and perspective, and lithographist [*sic*] to the University of Oxford"; Downing, *The Architecture of Country Houses,* p. 368.

9. D. R. Hay, *The Laws of Harmonious Colouring Adapted to Interior Decorations, Manufacturers, and Other Useful Purposes,* 6th ed. (1828; reprint, Edinburgh and London: W. Blackwood and Sons, 1847), p. 134.

10. Some chests with decoration similar to that illustrated in fig. 174 have been attributed in the past to Thomas Matteson and other family members of South Shaftesbury, Vermont. See Hollander, *American Anthem,* pp. 64 and 315; and Caroline Hebb, "A Distinctive Group of Early Vermont Painted Furniture," *Antiques* 104, no. 3 (September 1973): 458–61. For other recent scholarship that addresses the Matteson attributions, see Kenneth Zogry, *The Best the Country Affords, Vermont Furniture 1765–1850* (Bennington, Vt.: Bennington Museum, 1995), p. 46.

11. Waldo Tucker, *The Mechanics Assistant* (Windsor, Vt., 1837).

12. Reid, "Of Simple Apprehension in General," p. 374.

13. According to one source, megilp consisted of linseed oil thickened with a mixture of turpentine or mastic varnish and was used in both fine art and decorative painting. See the *Oxford English Dictionary* (1961), s.v. "megilp." Another recipe—composed of beeswax, linseed oil, turpentine, sugar of lead [lead acetate], and rotten stone—is found in Whittock, *The Decorative Painters' and Glaziers' Guide,* p. 22. The earliest use of the noun "scumble" to define the glaze thus created with megilp dates to 1798. "To scumble" defined the process as applied to Fancy painting and fine art. For other references see the *Oxford English Dictionary* (1961), s.v. "scumble."

14. The Eaton sample kit is illustrated and further discussed in Sandra Tarbox, "Fanciful Graining: Tools of the Trade," *The Clarion* 6, no. 3 (fall 1981): 34–37; Hollander, *American Anthem,* pp. 62, 314 .

15. Carolyn Weekley, *The Kingdoms of Edward Hicks* (New York: Harry N. Abrams, Inc., 1999), p. 215.

16. Quoted in Fales, *American Painted Furniture,* p. 236.

17. For further information on chimney boards and fireboards, see Little, *American Decorative Wall Painting,* pp. 66–79. For an image of a related fireboard with two cats sitting inside the fireplace, now used as an overmantel, see Julie Eldridge Edwards,

"The Brick House, the Vermont Country House of Electra Havemeyer Webb," *Antiques* 163, no. 1 (January 2003): 200, pl. x.

18. Details of Porter's life are abstracted from Jean Lipman, *Rufus Porter Rediscovered* (New York: Clarkson N. Potter, 1980). A bibliography of Porter's published works can be found in Lipman, *Rufus Porter Rediscovered*, p. 192; Rufus Porter, *A Select Collection of Valuable and Curious Arts* (Concord, N.H.: J. B. Moore, 1825). *Curious Arts* subsequently went through second and third Concord editions, both printed by Moore in 1826, as well as a fourth and fifth Concord edition that same year, both printed by William Brown, as outlined by Lipman, *Rufus Porter Rediscovered*, p. 192. Porter's career as a journalist and pamphleteer is explored in ibid., pp. 49–62, 192.

19. See Lipman, *Rufus Porter Rediscovered*, pp. 27–53, 192. Porter published the weekly newspaper, *The New York Mechanic*, from 1840 to 1841 and subsequently founded *Scientific American* on August 28, 1845, eventually selling his interest in the paper in 1847.

20. Rufus Porter, "Art of Painting: Ornamental Gilding and Bronzing," *Scientific American* 1, no. 9 (November 13, 1845): 2.

21. This house has now been moved and re-erected at the Shelburne Museum, Shelburne, Vermont. For a brief discussion, see Little, *American Decorative Wall Painting*, pp. 146–47.

22. Rufus Porter, "Art of Painting: Ornamental Gilding and Bronzing," p. 2.

23. Deborah Lambeth, "Rufus Cole: A Mohawk Valley Decorator," *The Decorator* 35, no. 2, (spring 1981): 4–11. The related clock by J. D. Green is pictured in Fales, *American Painted Furniture*, p. 406, and in David A. Schorsch, "Living with Antiques, A Collection of American Folk Art in the Midwest," *Antiques* 138, no. 4 (October 1990): 776.

24. Quoted in John Obed Curtis and William H. Guthman, *New England Militia Uniforms and Accoutrements—A Pictorial Survey* (Sturbridge, Mass: Old Sturbridge Village, 1971), p. 5. For illustrations of related militia material, see Sotheby's January 19, 2003, sales catalog, *To Arms! Uniforms, Painted Knapsacks, Canteens, Hat Plates and Other Related Militia Accoutrements from the Private Collection of William H. Guthman* (New York: Sotheby's, 2003). A bibliography at the end of the sales catalog lists three articles published for *Antiques* with many of the same illustrations.

25. Although known as "tinware," the pieces actually consisted of rolled sheet iron with a tin coating.

26. Asphaltum was also known as "asphalt" or "mineral pitch" in the period, "a bituminous [coal derived] substance, found in many parts of the world, a smooth, hard, brittle, black or brownish-black resinous material, consisting of a mixture of different hydrocarbons." *Oxford English Dictionary* (1961), s.v. "asphaltum." A coat of asphaltum was applied to tinware both for its protective qualities, being largely impervious to water, and its slightly translucent qualities, which allowed the brilliant metal beneath to subtly glisten through the finish.

27. *Maine Enquirer*, June 5, 1827, quoted in Nina Fletcher Little, "William Matthew Prior: Travelling Artist and His In-Laws the Painting Hamblens," *Antiques* 53, no. 1 (January 1948): 44.

28. Everett N. Robinson, "The Country Tin of Oliver Filley," in *Decorator Digest: Chapters in the History of Early American Decoration and its European Background Selected from the "Decorator,"* edited by Natalie Ramsey (Rutland, Vt.: Charles E. Tuttle Co., 1965), p. 116; Shirley Spaulding Devoe, *The Tinsmiths of Connecticut* (Middletown, Conn.: Wesleyan University Press for the Connecticut Historical Society, 1968), pp. 11–21.

29. Rufus Porter, "Art of Painting: Landscape Painting on Walls," *Scientific American* 1, no. 24 (February 26, 1846): 2.

30. Ibid.; and Porter, *Scientific American* 1, no. 28 (March 26, 1846): 2.

31. Ibid.; advertisement for "Landscape Scenery Painting. RUFUS PORTER," *The Gazette* (Providence, Rhode Island), November 20, 1822, illustrated in Ann Eckert Brown, *American Wall Stenciling, 1790–1840* (Hanover, N.H.: University Press of New England, 2003), p. 141.

32. Porter, "Art of Painting: Landscape Painting on Walls," *Scientific American* 1, no. 27 (March 19, 1846): 2; ibid., *Scientific American* 1, no. 29 (April 2, 1846): 2; Lipman, *Rufus Porter Rediscovered*, pp. 165–67.

33. Ibid.; Porter, *Scientific American* 1, no. 26 (March 12, 1846): 2; Rufus Porter, "Claro Obscuro or Light and Shade Painting on Walls," *Scientific American* 1, no. 30 (April 9, 1846): 2.

34. McClelland, *Historic Wallpapers,* p. 270.

35. Advertisement, "Landscape Scenery Painting. RUFUS PORTER," *Gazette* (Providence), November 20, 1822, quoted in Brown, *American Wall Stenciling, 1790–1840,* p. 141. In 1819 Ephriam Gilman, import merchant from Alexandria, Virginia, paid wholesale prices of $35 for an imported set of French block-printed wallpapers entitled "The Ports of France" and $40 for a set of the "Bay of Naples." See Ed Polk Douglas, "French Panoramic Wallpaper: Historical Background, Characteristic Development and Architectural Application" (master's thesis, University of Virginia, 1976), pp. 59–60. The prices seem to have decreased over the next decade, for in 1831, Humbertson Skipwith of Prestwould Plantation, Mecklenberg County, Virginia, again paid $35 each for three sets of imported landscape papers, this time retail, from Richmond, Virginia, merchant Francis Regnault. The cost of installation doubled his final price. Richard C. Nylander, "Prestwould Wallpapers," *Antiques* 147, no. 1 (January 1995): 168–70.

36. Rufus Porter, "Art of Painting: Transferring Prints," *Scientific American* 1, no. 15 (December 25, 1845): 2. For insights into the practice of transferring prints to glass during the seventeenth century, see John Stalker and George Parker, *A Treatise on Japanning and Varnishing* (1688; reprint, London: Alec Tiranti, 1971), pp. 30, 69, 73.

37. Porter, "Art of Painting: Transferring Prints," p. 2; William Tell, the Swiss hero who defied Austrian authority and was forced to shoot an apple from his son's head, was the subject of an 1832 poem by William Cullen Bryant and briefly, it seems, a symbol of the anti-slavery movement. Bryant's poem begins: "Chains may subdue the feeble spirit, but thee, Tell, of the iron / heart! They could not tame!" Courtesy Jolie Kelter and Michael Malce.

38. See chapter 3, note 42.

39. De Tocqueville, *Democracy in America,* p. 155.

40. Twain, *The Adventures of Huckleberry Finn,* pp. 130–31.

41. Charles Coleman Sellers, *Charles Willson Peale* (1947; New York: Charles Scribners Sons, 1969), pp. 194–97. The author is grateful to June Sprigg for this and other insights concerning transparent window shades.

42. *Maryland Journal,* April 13, 1792, quoted in Arthur Cox Prime, *Arts and Crafts of Philadelphia, Maryland and South Carolina 1786–1800,* ser. 2, p. 302. Ornamental shades were documented in Britain a half century earlier, where examples "Curiously Painted on Canvas, Silk or Wire" had been advertised by John Brown of London between 1728 and 1744. From Ambrose Heal, *London Tradesmen's Cards of the XVIII Century* (London: B. T. Batsford, 1925), p. 69, quoted in Janet R. MacFarlane, "Shades of Our Forefathers," *Antiques* 76, no. 2 (August 1959): 123; *Federal Gazette* (Philadelphia), March 9, 1796, quoted in Prime, *The Arts and Crafts of Philadelphia,* p. 304. See also the advertisement for Ignatius Snydore in *Daily Advertiser* (New York), June 6, 1788, quoted in *The Arts and Crafts of New York 1777–1779,* compiled by Rita Susswein Gottesman (New York: New-York Historical Society, 1954), p. 345.

43. MacFarlane, "Shades of Our Forefathers," p. 122; Samuel F. Bartol, *Practical Hints on the Subject of Window Ornaments* (New York: C. Willets, printer, 1849), p. 15.

44. Bartol, *Practical Hints,* pp. 9, 14, 15.

45. Mrs. Trollope and the *Rochester Republic* are both quoted in MacFarlane, "Shades of Our Forefathers," p. 122.

46. Rufus Porter, "Art of Painting: Transparent Painting on Cambric," *Scientific American* 1, no. 12 (December 4, 1845): 2.

47. Juliette Tomlinson, *Paintings and Journal of Joseph Whiting Stock* (Middletown, Conn.: Wesleyan University Press, 1976), p. 44, entry for May 7, 1845; Bartol, *Practical Hints,* p. 13. Edgar Weld King, "Painted Window Shades," *Antiques* 36, no. 6 (December 1939): 288–91.

48. King, "Painted Window Shades," p. 289.

49. "Nabob" was introduced to the English language upon Britain's explorations in India

and formally referred to an official of the Mogul Empire. In nineteenth-century Britain and America it was often used to connote an individual of great wealth. See the *Oxford English Dictionary* (1961), s.v. "nabob"; King, "Painted Window Shades," pp. 290–91.

50. Bartol, *Practical Hints,* pp. 10–14; King, "Painted Window Shades," p. 289.

51. Bartol, *Practical Hints,* p. 10; King, "Painted Window Shades," p. 289.

52. Porter, "Art of Painting: Transparent Painting on Cambric," p. 2; Bartol, *Practical Hints,* p. 8; Emily Dickinson to Mrs. Martin, 1841, quoted in MacFarlane, "Shades of Our Forefathers," p. 122.

53. Twain, *The Adventures of Huckleberry Finn,* p. 135.

54. King, "Painted Window Shades," p. 289.

55. *Aurora* (New York), June 11, 1844, quoted in William Jedlick, "Landscape Window Shades of the Nineteenth Century in New York State and New England" (master's thesis, State University of New York at Oneonta, 1967), p. 39; *Godey's Lady's Book* 43, no. 6 (December 1851): 369; King, "Painted Window Shades," pp. 288–91; Bartol, *Practical Hints,* p. 13.

56. Bartol, *Practical Hints,* p. 8; Emily Dickinson, quoted in MacFarlane, "Shades of Our Forefathers," p. 122; Bartol, *Practical Hints,* p. 8.

Chapter Six BOLD FURNISHINGS FOR ALL AMERICANS

1. For further information on the chair from the Union Street Methodist Church, see Jonathan Prown, "A Cultural Analysis of Furniture Making in Petersburg, Virginia, 1760–1820," *Journal of Early Southern Decorative Arts* 18, no. 1 (May 1992): 69; for Fancy Windsor chairs, see Nancy Goyne Evans, *American Windsor Chairs* (New York: Hudson Hills Press; Winterthur, Del.: Winterthur Museum, 1996); Nancy Goyne Evans, *American Windsor Furniture, Specialized Forms* (New York: Hudson Hills Press; Winterthur, Del.: Winterthur Museum, 1997); "Seven Marble Windsor chairs" were documented in a Pennsylvania inventory in 1835, Margaret Schiffer, *Chester County, Pennsylvania, Inventories* (Atglen, Pa.: Schiffer Publishing Ltd., 1974), p. 108.

2. For further information on Huey, see Jean Sikes Hageman, *Ohio Furniture Makers,* 2 vols. (Cincinnati, Ohio: privately printed, 1984), 1: 123. According to Hageman, Pennsylvania-born James Huey moved to Zanesville, Ohio, in 1828 and remained in business until 1851, possibly longer. See also Evans, *American Windsor Chairs,* p. 614. As Evans notes, in the 1850 industrial census, Huey employed twenty men in his steam powered factory, and produced $8,000 worth of furniture on an annual basis.

3. Donna R. Braden, *Leisure and Entertainment in America, Based on the Collections of Henry Ford Museum & Greenfield Village* (Dearborn, Mich: Henry Ford Museum, 1988), p. 137.

4. Eleanor Gustafson, "Museum Accessions," *Antiques* 123, no. 5 (May 1983): 950.

5. Although rocking was generally associated with women and the elderly in the 1800s, there existed simultaneously a somewhat similar behavior enjoyed by healthy adult men—the uncouth practice of "tilting" backward in chairs. As Kenneth Ames observes, early paintings verify that tilting was normally practiced by men in informal circumstances outside of the home, usually in the presence of other men. The development of the rocking chair may well have been an attempt to domesticate one of the informal privileges of male behavior. See Kenneth L. Ames, "Posture and Power," in *Death in the Dining Room and Other Tales of Victorian Culture* (Philadelphia: Temple University Press, 1992), pp. 216–32.

6. Evans, *American Windsor Furniture, Specialized Forms,* p. 56.

7. Among the exceptions is a large rocking cradle, significant enough in scale to contain an adult invalid, and now exhibited at the Memorial Hall Museum, Deerfield, Massachusetts. For more information on the development of the rocking chair, see Bert Denker and Ellen P. Denker, *The Rocking Chair Book* (New York: Mayflower Books, 1979). For information on the rocking chair in the Victorian period, see Kenneth L. Ames, "Posture and Power," pp. 216–32.

8. Manuscript bill from the Hitchcock Company to Mr. Samuel Crocker, dated June 10, 1828, on deposit in 1979 at the Hitchcock Chair Company Museum, Lambertville,

Connecticut; Rocking chairs sometimes had cushions, as cited in Schiffer, *Chester County, Pennsylvania, Inventories,* p. 106.

9. Evans, *American Windsor Furniture, Specialized Forms,* p. 56.

10. Nancy Goyne Evans, "The Genesis of the Boston Rocking Chair," *Antiques* 123, no. 1 (January 1983), p. 252. The Hitchcock Chair Company sponsored a museum at its factory in Lambertville, Connecticut, from the 1970s until 2000 with a collection of chairs produced by the company in its early years, and a fine collection of other Fancy furniture and related material. Among the pieces exhibited there was a bill from the Hitchcock Company to Mr. Samuel Crocker, dated June 10, 1828, in which the customer was charged $1.75 for a rocking chair. The location of that bill is currently unknown.

11. Denker and Denker, *The Rocking Chair Book,* p. 39.

12. Ibid., p. 38.

13. Ibid.

14. Ibid., pp. 38–39.

15. *Advertiser* (Albany, N.Y.), February 16, 1815, and May 19, 1815.

16. *Albany Institute of History and Art: 200 Years of Collecting,* edited by Tammis K. Groft and Mary Alice Mackay, with an introduction by Christine M. Miles (New York: Hudson Hills Press in association with Albany Institute of History and Art, 1998), pp. 223–24. The Winterthur Museum owns a Buttre Fancy chair, accession number 52.50.1, closely related to the example from the Albany Institute, although it was later redecorated. According to conservator Michael Podmaniczky, the Winterthur chair appears to have been red and blue with a white seat and gilt ornament.

17. *Albany Register* (New York), February 16, 1815, and May 19, 1815. Quoted in Fales, *American Painted Furniture, 1660–1880,* p. 167, and in Montgomery, *American Furniture,* pp. 458–59. The Treaty of Ghent was announced on December 24, 1814. The senate passed the treaty on February 16, 1815—the day of Buttre's advertisement—and within twenty-four hours the president signed the document. Victory was formally proclaimed on February 18, 1815.

18. The advertisement for Wheaton and Davis appeared in the *Evening Post* (New York) July 28, 1817; John Cowperthwaite, invoice to Stephen Wheeler, April 29, 1816, on deposit in the Downs Manuscript Collection, Winterthur Museum, (No. 61 x 92), in Montgomery, *American Furniture,* pp. 457 and 479, n. 12; Cowperthwaite's advertisement also appeared in *The Picture of New York* (New York, 1817), appendix.

19. The advertisement for Wheaton and Davis, "Fancy Chair Manufacturers" appeared in the *Evening Post* (New York) July 28, 1817, as cited in Montgomery, *American Furniture,* pp. 457 and 479, n. 12.

20. Evans, *American Windsor Chairs,* pp. 217–19.

21. Ibid., pp. 210, 217–19.

22. John T. Kenney, *The Hitchcock Chair* (New York: Clarkson N. Potter, Inc., 1971), pp. 43, 52–56, 91–95.

23. Ibid., pp. 53–54.

24. Ibid., pp. 43, 52–56, 91–95.

25. Ibid., pp. 46–52, 94.

26. Ibid., p. 157.

27. Ibid., pp. 129–33.

28. Ibid., pp. 129–33, 135–36; appendix 3, pp. 308–10.

29. For further information on David Alling, see Don C. Skemer, "David Alling's Chair Manufactory: Craft Industrialization in Newark, New Jersey, 1801–1854," in *Winterthur Portfolio,* vol. 22 (Winterthur, Del.: Winterthur Museum, 1987), pp. 1–22.

30. William N. Hosley, Jr., "Wright, Robbins, & Winship and the Industrialization of the Furniture Industry in Hartford, Connecticut," *Connecticut Antiquarian* 35, no. 2 (December 1983): 12–19.

31. For further information on the Finlays, and illustrations of several of their later products, see Gregory Weidman, "The Painted Furniture of John and Hugh Finlay," pp. 744–55.

Chapter Seven WARES TO ENRICH THE HOME AND THE MIND

1. Many aspects of the "consumer revolution" that began in the eighteenth century, and later helped to shape the Fancy style, are addressed in a series of articles that appear in *Of Consuming Interests: The Style of Life in the Eighteenth Century,* edited by Cary Carson, Ronald Hoffman, and Peter J. Albert (Charlottesville, Va.: United States Capitol Historical Society, 1994). See also Colin Campbell, *The Romantic Ethic and the Spirit of Modern Consumerism* (New York and London: Basil Blackwell, 1987).

2. Anne Royall, *Mrs. Royall's Pennsylvania, or Travels Continued In the United States,* 2 vols. (Washington, D.C.: privately printed, 1829), 1: 9.

3. *Wealth and Biography of the Wealthy Citizens of Philadelphia* (Philadelphia, 1840), s.v. "Isaac DeYoung."

4. In expressing the outlooks of his time, Johnson had identified fancy as a "false notion." However, attitudes toward the concepts of imagination had changed dramatically in the ensuing years, and now the word "notion" was widely recognized for its virtues. Samuel Johnson, *Dictionary* (1755), s.v. "fancy."

5. "Notions," *Boston Kaleidoscope and Literary Rambler,* April 24, 1819.

6. James Alexander's account book survives at the New York State Historical Association at Cooperstown. Virginia D. Parslow, "James Alexander, Weaver," *Antiques* 69, no. 4 (April 1956): 346–49. Among other weavers who advertised Fancy weaving prior to the introduction of the Jacquard loom in America was Joseph Reeve of Burlington, New Jersey. John W. Heisey, *A Checklist of American Coverlet Weavers* (Charlottesville: University Press of Virginia, 1980), p. 96. Even relatively simple patterns like twill weaves were known as "fancy," such as the pattern "Irish Fancy" that appears in John Hargrove, *Weaver's Draft Book and Clothiers Assistant,* with an introduction by Rita J. Adrosko (Baltimore, Md.: I. Hagerty, 1792; reprint, Worcester, Mass.: American Antiquarian Society, 1979), no. 80, p. 8. Overshot coverlets with abstract designs have been attributed to dates in the early eighteenth century, such as one made by Lydia Spofford of Kingston, New Hampshire, in the 1740s and now in the American Textile History Museum in Lowell, Massachusetts. See Paul E. Rivard, *A New Order of Things: How the Textile Industry Transformed New England* (Hanover and London: University Press of New England, 2002), p. 6. Overshot coverlets were widely produced in the South. An example documented to have been woven by plantation slaves is preserved in the collection of the Old Slave Mart Museum in Charleston, South Carolina.

7. Thomas Webster and Mrs. William Parks, *The American Family Encyclopaedia of Useful Knowledge,* edited by David M. Reese, 2d ed. (1845; New York: Derby and Jackson, 1858), pp. 254–55.

8. For further information on the development of the Jacquard loom, see Pauline Montgomery, *Indiana Coverlet Weavers and Their Coverlets* (Indianapolis, Ind.: Hoosier Heritage Press, 1974), pp. 117–22.

9. Advertisement of Mathew Rattray in the Richmond (Indiana) *Palladium,* October 2, 1841, reproduced in Montgomery, *Indiana Coverlet Weavers,* p. 85.

10. The term "Fancy Weaver" was adopted in numerous variations by dozens of artisans. See Heisey, *Checklist of American Coverlet Weavers.* An example called "Farmer Fancy" is pictured in *Heirlooms From Old Looms: A Catalogue of Coverlets Owned by the Colonial Coverlet Guild of America and Its Members,* edited by Mrs. Luther M. Swygert (Chicago: privately printed, 1955), p. 231. "Fancy Patent" appears on a coverlet by P. Warner of Carroll County, Maryland, illustrated in Clarita Anderson, *"No Man Can Better It": Maryland Coverlets and Their Weavers* (College Park: University of Maryland Press, 1981), p. 11. This coverlet is marked P. WARNER / CARROLL. / COUNTY. / 1851 / M. / SHERMAN / FANCY PATENT. Another Fancy Patent coverlet is in the collection of the Carroll County, Maryland, Historical Society.

11. *The Freeman and Messenger* (Lodi, N.Y.), November 22, 1841. Quoted in Heisey, *Checklist of American Coverlet Weavers,* p. 45.

12. For more information on Argand's inventions, see John J. Wolf, *Balloons, Brandy & Lamps, Ami Argand, 1750–1803* (Carbondale and Edwardsville, Ill.: Southern Illinois University Press, 1999). For a further discussion of nineteenth-century advances in

lighting, see William T. O'Dea, *The Social History of Lighting* (London: Routledge and Pue, 1958), pp. 52–54; Malcolm C. Watkins, "Artificial Lighting in America 1830–1860," *Smithsonian Institution Annual Report, 1951* (Washington, D.C.: Smithsonian Press, 1952); and *Lighting in America,* edited by Lawrence S. Cooke (New York: Main St. / Universe Books, Antiques Magazine Library, 1975), pp. 76–80. *Oxford English Dictionary* (1961), s.v. "sinumbra," and s.v. "astral."

13. O'Dea, *The Social History of Lighting,* p. 54.

14. Ibid.

15. Lanterns with piercings are documented as early as 1500. See *American Collector* 6, no. 4 (May 1937): 1; and Edward A. Rushford, "Patented Lamps date 1830–1880," *American Collector* 6, no. 7 (August 1937): 1.

16. John Bivins, Jr., and Paula Welshimer, *Moravian Decorative Arts of North Carolina: An Introduction to the Old Salem Collection* (Winston-Salem, N.C.: Old Salem, Inc., 1981), p. 79.

17. Schiffer, *Chester County, Pennsylvania, Inventories,* p. 19. Manuscript Bill for Atkins and Homer, Importers of Crockery, China and Glass, Boston, 1826, manuscript #63 x 83.9, the Joseph Downs Manuscript Collection, Winterthur Museum, Winterthur, Del.

18. For further insights into the use of mocha and other related wares, see David Barker, "'The Usual Classes of Useful Articles': Staffordshire Ceramics Reconsidered," in *Ceramics in America,* edited by Robert Hunter (Hanover, N.H.: University Press of New England for the Chipstone Foundation, 2001), pp. 73–93; "The 'Moco' pattern on the outside of basons [*sic*] makes them appear as if delicate branches of seaweed had been laid upon their surfaces," noted one observer who visited the factories in 1833, as quoted in Carpentier and Rickard, "Slip Decoration," p. 122. See also Susan Van Rensselaer, "Banded Creamware," *Antiques* 90, no. 3 (September 1966): 340; George L. Miller, "A Revised Set of CC Index Values for Classification and Economic Scaling of English Ceramics from 1787 to 1880," *Historical Archaeology* 25, no. 1 (1991): 1–25.

19. Van Rensselaer, "Banded Creamware," p. 340; Carpentier and Rickard, "Slip Decoration," p. 122.

20. Carpentier and Rickard, "Slip Decoration," pp. 126–29.

21. The mottled ornament of yellow and green bears some resemblance to Chinese earthenwares made for the Chinese domestic market, having a mottled ground referred to in the West as an "egg and spinach" ground. Those Asian examples usually employ a purple or aubergine color that distinguishes them from British productions, which also include whimsical "eyelets" to enliven the design.

22. American wares having mocha designs are relatively scarce, the few that survive generally dating from the period after Fancy had reached its height. A buff colored mug at the Winterthur Museum (acc. # 60.556) has mocha tree or "dendritic" designs. It is signed by John Bell of Waynesboro, Pennsylvania, and dates 1840–1880. For an illustration, see Kenneth L. Ames, *Beyond Necessity: Art in the Folk Tradition* (New York: W. W. Norton for the Winterthur Museum, 1977), p. 82. See Barker, "'The Usual Classes of Useful Articles': Staffordshire Ceramics Reconsidered," pp. 73–93. I am grateful to Mr. Barker for further sharing his insights into the comparative availability of mocha wares in Britain and America.

23. For further information on hand painted wares, see John A. Shuman, III, *The Collector's Encyclopedia of Gaudy Dutch & Welsh* (Paducah, Ky.: Collector Books, 1991); and Eleanor J. Fox and Edward G. Fox, *Gaudy Dutch* (Pottsville, Pa.: privately printed, 1968).

24. Kevin McConnell, *Spongeware and Spatterware,* 3d ed. (Atglen, Pa.: Schiffer Publishing Ltd., 2001). Arlene Greaser and Paul H. Greaser, *Homespun Ceramics: A Study of Spatterware* (Des Moines, Iowa: Wallace-Homestead Co., 1973).

25. Michael Gibson, *Nineteenth Century Lustreware* (London: Antique Collectors' Club, 1999). The firm of Henshaw and Jarves, ceramic merchants of Boston, advertised "fancy luster" and "fancy luster teapots" for sale upon the dissolution of their partnership in the May 20, 1818, issue of the *Columbian Centinel*. A lustre-trimmed jug made between 1815 and 1818 for Henshaw and Jarves by the ceramics manufacturers Wood and Caldwell of Staffordshire is in the collection of the Winterthur Museum. See F. Munroe Endicott, "English Lustreware: Two Inscribed Wares," *Antiques* 20, no. 3 (September 1946): 146–47. Courtesy Arlene Palmer Schwind.

26. A. W. Coysh and Frank Stephano, Jr., *Collecting Ceramic Landscapes: British and American Landscapes on Printed Pottery* (London: Lund Humphries, 1981), pp. 12–13, quoted from *Penny Magazine* (May 1843).

27. Society of Architectural Historians, Decorative Arts Chapter *Newsletter* 2, no. 2 (spring 1976): 23. Coysh and Stephano, *Collecting Ceramic Landscapes,* pp. 12–14.

28. Coysh and Stephano, *Collecting Ceramic Landscapes,* p. 68.

29. Puzzle jugs were produced both in England and America. A Philadelphia-made example of red earthenware with a manganese glaze was excavated in the vicinity of Independence Hall by the National Park Service. See Robert Lewis Giannini, III, "Ceramics and Glass from Home and Abroad," in *Treasures of Independence: Independence National Historical Park and Its Collections,* edited by John C. Milley (New York: Mayflower Books, A Main Street Press Book, 1976), p. 63.

30. G. Bernard Hughs, "Tricks in the Tavern," *Country Life* 121, no. 3138 (March 7, 1957): 424–26.

31. Ibid.

32. The chamber pot is inscribed in full as follows: "PRESENT. / Dear lovely Wife pray rise &P:ss. / Take you that handle & I'll take this, / Let's use the Present which was sent. / To make some mirth is only meant, / So let it be as they have said, / We'll laugh and P:ss and then to Bed." The opposite side is inscribed "MARRIAGE. / This Pot it is A Present Sent. / Some mirth to make is only Meant. / We hope the same you'll not Refuse. / But keep it safe and oft it Use. / When in it you want to P:ss, Remember them who sent you / THIS." The interior is also inscribed "Keep me Clean and use me well, / And what I see I will not tell."

33. For further information on chamber pots, see Ivor Noël Hume, "Through the Lookinge Glasse: Or, The Chamber Pot as a Mirror of Its Time," in *Ceramics in America,* edited by Robert Hunter (Hanover, N.H.: University Press of New England for the Chipstone Foundation, 2003), pp. 138–71.

34. For other variants of whimsical pipes, see John Lewis and Griselda Lewis, *Prattware: English and Scottish Relief Decorated and Underglaze Coloured Earthenware 1780–1840* (Woodbridge, Suffolk, Eng.: Antique Collectors' Club in association with Alan Kaplan, 1993), pp. 246–48, 254.

35. Broadside, "Bennington Stone-Ware Pottery," 1852, illustrated in Donald Blake Webster, *Decorated Stoneware Pottery of North America* (Rutland, Vt.: Charles E. Tuttle, 1971), p. 210.

36. Broadside for "Clark & Fox, At Athens (New York), Opposite the City of Hudson," n.p. dated 1837, in the collections of the New York State Historical Association, Cooperstown, New York.

37. Jerry Oberwager, *Chalkware Tools and Methods, prepared as a complement for a talk by Jerry Oberwager before the Early Trades and Crafts Society* (n.p.: privately printed, April 1981) [p. 2]). A copy of the pamphlet is now on deposit in the Crowninshield Library at the Winterthur Museum.

38. *The Cries of New York,* cited in Oberwager, *Chalkware: Tools and Methods,* [pp. 3–4].

39. Twain, *The Adventures of Huckleberry Finn,* p. 131. "Squeak toys" were commonly made of papiér-mâché rather than plaster.

40. Broadside, "Astonishing! Beautiful! Splendid!," n.d., the Joseph Downs Manuscript Collection, Winterthur Museum, Winterthur, Del.; Memorandum by Eliza Susan Quincy, 1879, #PH 959, the Joseph Downs Manuscript Collection, Winterthur Museum, Winterthur, Del.

41. *The Courier* (New Orleans), January 10, 1832; January 19, 1832; February 7, 1832; May 7, 1832; February 26, 1833. Courtesy Arlene Palmer Schwind.

42. H. F. du Pont Winterthur Museum, *Glass in Early America, Selections from the H. F. du Pont Winterthur Museum* (Winterthur, Del.: By the museum, 1993); Kenneth M. Wilson, *American Glass 1760–1930* (New York: Hudson Hills Press for the Toledo Museum of Art, 1994); Lowell Inness, *Pittsburgh Glass, 1791–1891, A History and Guide for Collectors* (Boston: Houghton Mifflin Co., 1976); Helen McKearin and George S. McKearin, *Two Hundred Years of American Blown Glass* (New York: Crown Publishers, 1966).

43. Schiffer, *Chester County, Pennsylvania, Inventories,* p. 154.

44. Jane Shadel Spillman, *American and European Pressed Glass in the Corning Museum of Glass* (Corning, N.Y.: Corning Museum of Glass, 1981), pp. 13–14.

45. For further information on mold blown flasks and an extensive representation of the patterns made in America, see Helen McKearin and Kenneth Wilson, *American Bottles and Flasks and Their Ancestry* (New York: Crown Publishers, Inc., 1978).

46. Spillman, *American and European Pressed Glass,* p. 17.

47. Ibid.

48. Ibid.; Marshall Davidson, *American Antiques,* 3 vols. (New York: American Heritage, 1968), 2: 174.

49. Spillman, *American and European Pressed Glass,* p. 118.

50. For further information on structures with commercial space on the first floor and residential on the second, see Anne Smart Martin, "Commercial Space as Consumption Arena: Retail Stores in Early Virginia," in *People, Power, Places: Perspectives in Vernacular Architecture VIII,* edited by Sallie McMurray and Annemarie Adams (Knoxville: University of Tennessee Press, 2000), pp. 201–18. Courtesy Camille Wells.

51. *A Series of Progressive Lessons, Intended to Elucidate the Art of Flower Painting in Water Colors* (Philadelphia: M. Thomas, 1818); Fielding Lucas, *The Progressive Drawing Book* (Baltimore, Md.: Fielding Lucas, [n.d. ca. 1828]). The latter was illustrated by B. Henry Latrobe with plates colored by Anna Claypoole Peale. Among the other popular books in the field was Nathaniel Whittock, *The Oxford Drawing Book, a New and Improved Edition* (New York: Collins, Keese & Co., 1840).

52. For further information on tinsel painting, see Marilyn G. Karmason, "Shimmering and Brilliant: American Victorian Tinsel Painting," *The Clarion* 16, no. 4 (winter 1991–1992), pp. 73–79. For Grecian painting, see B. F. Gandee, *The Artist or, Young Ladies' Instructor in Ornamental Painting, Drawing, etc.* (London: Chapman and Hall; New York: W. Jackson, 1835). The author is grateful to Wayne Fisher's American Design, Alexandria, Virginia, for bringing the Grecian painting of Mt. Vernon to his attention.

53. Matthew D. Finn, *Theorematical System of Painting, or Modern Plan, Fully Explained in Six Lessons* (New York: James Ryan, 1830), title page. B. F. Gandee devoted an entire chapter to theorem painting or "oriental tinting" in his work *The Artist or, Young Ladies' Instructor,* pp. 126–62.

54. J. William Alston, *Hints to Young Practitioners in the Study of Landscape Painting,* 3d ed. (1805; London: Printed for Longman, Hurst, Rees & Orme, 1820). The British sometimes used the term "Poonah painting," in reference to Poonah, a city in Bombay Province, India, to describe the technique. Poonah was frequently visited by foreigners and credited as the source of theorem painting in nineteenth-century Britain, even though stencils had been documented in Britain as early as the fifteenth century. The term "Poonah painting" was frequently used synonymously with theorem painting, as indicated by an advertisement in the *Lynchburg Virginian,* April 3, 1837, courtesy Barbara Luck, Colonial Williamsburg Foundation. The term "Oriental Tinting" was also frequently employed, as in Gandee, *The Artist or, Young Ladies' Instructor,* pp. 126–62. *Oxford English Dictionary* (1961), s.v. "stencil."

55. *Albany Balance* (Albany, N.Y.), September 4, 1810, courtesy Barbara Luck.

56. Trollope, *Domestic Manners of the Americans,* 1: 264. At the time that Mrs. Trollope was offered a course in theorem painting, the fair market rate was closer to five dollars, or for a full semester of instruction in "Scientific Painting and Drawing" at a female seminary, about fifteen dollars, according to an advertisement for the Bedford (Virginia) Female Seminary in the *Lynchburg Virginian,* December 11, 1834. Courtesy Barbara Luck.

57. Alexander Nemerov, *The Body of Raphaelle Peale: Still Life and Selfhood 1812–1824* (Berkeley: University of California Press, 2001); Jonathan Prown and Richard Miller, "The Rococo, The Grotto, and The Philadelphia High Chest," in *American Furniture,* edited by Luke Beckerdite (Hanover, N.H.: University Press of New England for the Chipstone Foundation, 1996), pp. 105–36.

58. William H. Gerdts and Russell Burke, *American Still-life Painting* (New York: Praeger, 1971), pp. 55–59.

59. *Oxford English Dictionary* (1961), s.v. "scrapbook," notes the first use of the word scrapbook in 1825.

60. T. S. Arthur, *Trials and Confessions of an American Housekeeper* (Philadelphia: Lippincott, Grambo & Co., 1854), p. 122. Lucy Larcom was a character in Arthur's popular book.

Chapter Eight FAREWELL TO FANCY

1. For further information on the Panic of 1837, see Bray Hammond, *Banks and Politics in America from the Revolution to the Civil War* (Princeton, N.J.: Princeton University Press, 1957); James Roger Sharp, *The Jacksonians Versus the Banks: Politics in the States After the Panic of 1837* (New York: Columbia University Press, 1970); and James C. Curtis, *The Fox at Bay: Martin Van Buren and the Presidency, 1837–1841* (Lexington, Ky.: University Press of Kentucky, 1970). In Britain, the 1837 coronation of Queen Victoria (1819–1901) began an extended reign that coincided with a remarkable age of industrial and social change and is forever linked to her in the name "Victorian."

2. Kenneth D. Roberts, *Eli Terry and the Connecticut Shelf Clock* (Bristol, Conn.: Kenneth Roberts Publishing Co., 1973); Leslie Allen Jones, *Eli Terry: Clockmaker Of Connecticut* (New York: Farrar and Rinehart, 1942).

3. Frederick Maire, *Graining and Marbling; A Series of Practical Treatises on Material, Tools and Appliances Used* (Chicago: F. J. Drake and Company, [ca. 1910]), p. 31; *Daily Advertiser* (Auburn, N.Y.), October 21, 1873, pp. 2–3, quoted in Ruby Rogers, "Terance J. Kennedy" (master's thesis, State University of New York, Oswego, 1971), p. 18.

4. "Letters of Oliver Filley," in *Decorator Digest,* pp. 116, 126.

5. Rivard, *A New Order of Things,* pp. 7–8; Montgomery, *Printed Textiles.*

6. Thomas Jefferson to John Melish, January 13, 1813, quoted in *The Best Letters of Thomas Jefferson,* selected and edited by J. G. de Roulhac Hamilton (New York and Boston: Houghton, Mifflin Co., 1926), pp. 173–74.

7. Rivard, *A New Order of Things,* p. 19; the weaver of the Chesterville coverlet is not known; for further description, see Mildred Davidson and Christa Mayer-Thurman, *Coverlets: A Handbook of the Collection of the Art Institute of Chicago* (Chicago: Art Institute of Chicago, 1973), p. 98.

8. Swan, *Plain and Fancy,* p. 205.

9. Montgomery, *Printed Textiles,* pp. 35, 307.

10. *The Connoisseur Period Guide to the Houses, Decoration, Furnishing and Chattels of the Classic Period, No. 5. Regency Period 1810–1830,* edited by Ralph Edwards and L. G. Ramsay (London: Connoisseur, 1956–1958), p. 6, quoted in Montgomery, *Indiana Weavers and their Coverlets,* p. 3; "Rich Fancy Prints" sold for $.27/yard from Gordon & Stoddard, State St., Boston. Manuscript invoice, October 1, 1834, Joseph Downs Manuscript Collection, Winterthur Museum Library.

11. For further information on the mechanization of wallpaper production, see Lilian Baker Carlisle, *Hat Boxes and Bandboxes at the Shelburne Museum* (Shelburne, Vt.: Shelburne Museum, 1960), pp. 109–10; Richard Nylander, *Wallpapers for Historic Buildings* (Washington, D.C.: National Trust for Historic Preservation, 1992).

12. Douglas T. Miller, *Birth of Modern America, 1820–1850* (New York: Pegasus, 1970), pp. 107–9.

13. The Panic of 1837 probably hastened Porter's pursuit of science and publishing. He became publisher of *The New York Mechanic* in 1840 and thereafter devoted much of his professional life to science and invention. See Lipman, *Rufus Porter Rediscovered,* pp. 49–53, 192. For further information on scientists who began their careers as artists, see Harry Kloss, *Samuel F. B. Morse* (New York: Harry N. Abrams, in association with the National Museum of American Art, Smithsonian Institution, 1988) and Cynthia Owen Philip, *Robert Fulton, A Biography* (New York and Toronto: Franklin Watts, Inc. in association with the Hudson River Maritime Museum, 1985).

14. Ibid.; Pessen, *Jacksonian America,* p. 94. As methods of production changed, many artisans who produced Fancy goods began to view themselves as "mechanics," "That branch of mathematics which considers motion and moving powers, their nature and laws, with their effects in machines." James Scott et al., *A New General Dictionary of Arts and Sciences, or, Compleat System of Universal Knowledge,* 3 vols. (London: J. Cooke,

1767), s.v. "mechanics." New outlooks toward production were further bolstered by the introduction of the word "technology." This word was given popular currency by Harvard professor Jacob Bigelow, who held an endowed chair for the "application of science to the art of living." Bigelow noted that he had "adopted the general name of technology, a word sufficiently expressive, which is found in some of the older dictionaries, and is beginning to be revived in the literature of practical men at the present day." Jacob Bigelow, *Elements of Technology* (Boston: Hilliard, Gray, Little and Wilkins, 1829), p. iv; Miller, *Birth of Modern America*, p. 32, n.

15. The Finlays advertised early in their career "Coach, Sign, and all other kinds of Ornamental Painting," *The American* (Baltimore) August 11, 1804. Although the Baltimore and Ohio Railroad was founded in 1827 and received its charter in 1829, it did not carry the first revenue passengers until January 7, 1830. The first regularly scheduled passenger service began on May 24, 1830, two months after John Finlay received his patent for railroad wheels. During the first year and one half of service, the railroad used horse drawn carriages, due to the poor reliability of steam engines. The first steam engine, the *York,* went into regular service in August 1831; *List of Patents for Inventions and Designs Issued by the United States from 1790 to 1840,* compiled by Edmund Burke (Washington, D.C: Government Printing Office, 1847), s.v. "land conveyance." Timothy Jacobs, *The History of The Baltimore and Ohio Railroad* (New York: Crescent Books, 1989), pp. 15–25.

16. Matthew D. Horan, *Matthew Brady, Historian with a Camera* (New York: Bonanza Books, 1955), pp. 4–7. For further information on the invention of the daguerrean process, see Helmut Gernsheim and Alison Gernsheim, *L.J.M. Daguerre: The History of the Diorama and the Daguerreotype,* 2d ed. rev. (New York: Dover Publications, 1968).

17. W. E. H. Leckey, "Imagination in the Progress of Morals," *Appleton's Journal: A Magazine of General Literature* 1, no. 6 (May 8, 1869): 184.

18. William Benton Clulow, *Aphorisms and Reflections: Miscellany of Thought and Opinion* (London: John Murray, 1843), p. 253.

19. Leckey, "Imagination in the Progress of Morals," p. 184.

20. William Wordsworth, *Poems, Including Lyrical Ballads,* 2 vols. (London: Longman, Hurst, Rees, Orme, and Brown, 1815), 1: preface; and Samuel Taylor Coleridge, *Biographia Literaria; or, Biographical Sketches of My Literary Life and Opinions* (New York: Kirk and Merein, 1817). The first American edition of Coleridge's *Biographia Literaria* was published within months of the London edition. William Wordsworth (1770–1850) and Samuel Taylor Coleridge (1772–1834) were born at the beginning of the 1770s, when positive attitudes toward fancy were in the ascent. Both men reached their maturity in the early 1790s and began their inquiry into the distinctions between imagination and fancy at the same time that fancy goods filtered into fashionable households. It is logical to suggest that both men knew the material culture of fancy and that it played a role in shaping their perspectives on the distinctions between the faculties. By the time Wordsworth and Coleridge articulated their refined observations for a literary audience in 1815 and 1817, respectively, they were expressing observations visible in the material goods made by some of the era's most astute, although not necessarily literate, artisans. With the distinctions now clarified in both literature and the material arts, the products of imagination hereafter gained credence, while those of fancy increasingly raised suspicions and went into gradual decline, particularly within educated circles.

21. John Keats to Benjamin Bailey, October 8, 1817, cited in *The Complete Poetical Works and Letters of John Keats* (New York and Boston: Houghton Mifflin Company, 1899), p. 228; Keats' poem "Fancy" can be found in ibid., p. 124. Period authors who frequently attempted to decipher the distinctions between fancy and imagination have been carefully studied by modern literary scholars. Although these subtle, and purely subjective, distinctions are helpful in comprehending the perspectives of the individual authors, the significance of the debate lies not in attempting to resolve subjective differences, but in identifying how perceptions of the distinctions affected the lives, the writings, and the products of those who articulated them, whether expressed in literature or in other media.

22. Leigh Hunt, "What is Poetry," in *Imagination and Fancy, or Lessons from the English Poets* (1844; reprint, New York: Wiley and Putnam, 1845), pp. 20–21. Leigh Hunt (1784–1859), was the son of an American clergyman who settled in Southgate, Middlesex, England, and became one of the leading editors and writers of British romanticism. He introduced Shelley to Keats and served as the inspiration for the character Skimpole in Charles Dickens' *Bleak House*. See the *Cambridge History of English and American Literature,* vol. 12, *The Romantic Revival,* edited by A. W. Ward and A. R. Waller (Cambridge: Cambridge University Press: 1907–1921). The debate about imagination and fancy voiced in intellectual circles occasionally drew critics, among them Edgar Allan Poe. Poe lamented that "As, by metaphysicians and in ordinary discourse, the word fancy is used with very little determinateness of meaning." He nonetheless felt the difference between fancy and imagination, "is a distinction without a difference—even a difference of a degree." Edgar Allan Poe, "N. P. Willis," in "The Literati of New York," in *Complete Works of Edgar Allan Poe,* edited by James A. Harrison, 16 vols. (New York: Thomas Y. Crowell, 1902), 15: 12. Courtesy Larry Gobrecht.

23. John Ruskin, *Modern Painting* (1843), in *The Works of John Ruskin,* edited by E. T. Cook and Alexander Wedderburn, 38 vols. (London: George Allen; New York: Longman, Green and Company, 1903), 4: 253.

24. Nathaniel Hawthorne, "A Select Party" (1844), in *The Centenary Edition of the Works of Nathaniel Hawthorn,* edited by William Charvat et. al. (Columbus: Ohio State University Press, 1974), 10: 57–73.

25. Henry David Thoreau, "Where I Lived and What I Lived For," in *Walden and Other Writings by Henry David Thoreau,* edited and with an introduction by Joseph Wood Krutch (New York: Bantam Books, 1962), p. 173.

26. Leckey, "Imagination in the Progress of Morals," p. 184.

27. Joseph E. Worcester, *A Dictionary of the English Language* (Cambridge, Mass.: H. O. Houghton & Co., 1860), s.v. "fancy."

28. For an extensive list of images printed by Currier and Ives, see Frederic A. Conningham, *Currier & Ives Prints; an Illustrated Checklist* (New York: Crown Publishers, 1970).

29. Bryan J. Wolf, *Romantic Revision: Culture and Consciousness in Nineteenth-Century American Painting and Literature* (Chicago: University of Chicago Press, 1982), p. 168.

30. Many of these mysterious Eastern styles were referred to, briefly, as "Fancy" styles when they first emerged in avante garde British circles during the 1820s and 1830s, but that descriptor quickly disappeared as distinctions between fancy and imagination solidified. These exotic styles were later associated with the more general nineteenth-century rubric "the picturesque," which provided a key subset of literary and artistic Romanticism, and were discussed as falling principally within the powers of imagination. See Robert Lugar, *Architectural Sketches for Cottages, Rural Dwellings, and Villas, in the Grecian, Gothic, and Fancy Styles, with Plans; Suitable to Persons of Genteel Life and Moderate Fortune* (London: J. Taylor, 1823).

31. Ralph Waldo Emerson, "Poetry and Imagination" (1875), in *The Complete Writings of Ralph Waldo Emerson, Containing All of His Inspiring Essays, Lectures, Poems, Addresses, Studies, Biographical Sketches, and Miscellaneous Works,* 2 vols. (New York: William H. Wise & Co., 1929), 2: 735.

32. E. S. Purcell on A. W. N. Pugin, 1861, cited in Megan Aldrich, *Gothic Revival* (London: Phaidon Press, 1997), p. 129.

33. For further information, see Calder Loth and Julius Trousdale Sadler, Jr., *The Only Proper Style: Gothic Architecture in America* (Boston: New York Graphic Society, 1975), and Museum of Fine Arts, Houston, *Gothic Revival Style in America: 1830–1870* (Houston, Tex.: By the museum, 1976).

34. Cited in Edward Deming Andrews and Faith Andrews, "The Holy Laws of Zion," in *Shaker Furniture* (New York: Dover Publications, Inc., 1950), pp. 49–50.

35. Charles Dickens, *The Life and Adventures of Martin Chuzzlewit and American Notes,* 2 vols. (Boston and New York: Houghton Mifflin and Co., 1894), 2: 56, quoted in June Sprigg, *By Shaker Hands* (New York: Alfred Knopf, 1975), p. 63.

36. Father Joseph Meacham, "Millennial Laws or Gospel Statutes and Ordinances," in Edward Deming Andrews, *The People Called Shakers* (1953; reprint, New York: Dover Publications, 1963), pp. 282–85.

37. D. R. Hay's *The Laws of Harmonious Colouring* (1828) underwent a number of editions during the 1830s and 1840s. His fourth London edition (London: W.S. Orr; Edinburgh: W. & R. Chambers, 1838) had been revised at the height of the craze for Fancy. It differed from the fifth edition of 1844, which, through subtle word changes, began to cast aspersions on the concept of fancy. D. R. Hay, *Laws of Harmonious Colouring*, 5th ed. (London: W. S. Orr and Co.; Edinburgh: Fraser and Co., 1844), introduction; D. R. Hay, *Laws of Harmonious Colouring*, 6th ed. (London: W. Blackwood, 1847), p. 133.

38. Henry W. Cleaveland, William Backus, and Samuel D. Backus, *Village and Farm Cottages, The Requirements of American Village Homes Considered and Suggested; with Designs for Such Houses of Moderate Cost* (New York: D. Appleton and Co., 1856), p. 11.

39. John Ruskin, *The Seven Lamps of Architecture* (1851; reprint, New York: D. Appleton and Co., 1899), pp. 52, 311.

40. Walter Smith, *Art Education, Scholastic and Industrial* (Boston: James R. Osgood and Company, 1872), p. 195.

41. Poe, "Philosophy of Furniture," p. 921. Fluid lamps, first introduced in the 1830s, burned a volatile, but inexpensive, mixture of turpentine and alcohol. For further information on fluid lamps, see Leroy Thwing, *A History of Domestic Lighting Through the Ages* (Rutland, Vt.: Charles E. Tuttle Company, 1958), pp. 59–62; Catherine Beecher and Harriet Beecher Stowe, *American Home; or Principles of Domestic Science* (New York: J.B. Ford and Company, 1869), quoted in Maj. L. B. Wyant, "The Etiquette of Nineteenth-Century Lamps," *Antiques* 30, no. 1 (September 1936): 79.

42. Poe, "Philosophy of Furniture," pp. 919–20; Catherine Beecher, *A Treatise on Domestic Economy* (New York: Harper and Bros., 1842), p. 283.

43. Elizabeth Barrett Browning to Mrs. Martin, 1841, quoted in Janet R. Macfarlane, "Shades of Our Forefathers," *Antiques* 76, no. 2 (August 1959): 122; *Godey's Lady's Book* (December 1851): 369; Poe, "Philosophy of Furniture," p. 921.

44. Poe, "Philosophy of Furniture," pp. 919–20.

45. Charles Dickens, on visiting the Copeland works in 1852, from *Martin Chuzzlewit and American Notes,* quoted in Geoffrey A. Godden, *British Pottery and Porcelain, 1780–1850* (London: Arthur Barker Ltd., 1963), p. 143.

46. For a further discussion of the temperance movement in America, see Joseph R. Gusfield, *Symbolic Crusade: Status Politics and the American Temperance Movement,* 2d ed. (1963; Carbondale: University of Illinois Press, 1986).

47. Monkeys have been used since medieval times to express the lower nature of humans or their pursuit of base instincts. For further insights, see Ames, *Beyond Necessity: Art in the Folk Tradition,* pp. 55, 60, 62.

48. For further information on the Kirkpatrick Pottery and its production, see Ellen Paul Denker, "Forever Getting Up Something New: The Kirkpatrick's Pottery and Anna, Illinois, 1859–1896" (master's thesis, University of Delaware, 1978); and Ellen Paul Denker, *Kirkpatrick's Pottery at Anna, Illinois* (Urbana-Champaign, Ill.: Krannert Art Museum, 1986).

49. For further information on Henry Church and *The Monkey Picture,* see Sam Rosenberg, "Henry Church," in *American Folk Painters of Three Centuries,* edited by Jean Lipman and Tom Armstrong (New York: Hudson Hills Press for the Whitney Museum of Art, 1980), pp. 175–81.

50. Orson S. Fowler, *A Home for All, or The Gravel Wall and Octagon Mode of Building* (New York: Samuel R. Wells, 1853), p. 12.

51. Gustave Stickley quoted in Lizabeth A. Cohen, "Embellishing a Life of Labor: An interpretation of the Material Culture of American Working-Class Homes, 1885–1915," in *Material Culture Studies in America,* compiled by Thomas J. Schlereth (Nashville, Tenn.: American Association for State and Local History, 1982), p. 289; Fowler, *A Home for All,* p. 12; Gustav Stickley, ed., *The Craftsman, An Illustrated Monthly Magazine in the Interest of Better Art, Better Work, and a Better More Reasonable Way of Living* 10, no. 2 (May 1906): 270, 273, 275.

Select Bibliography

Primary Books

Addison, Joseph. "The Pleasures of the Imagination." In *Critical Essays from The Spectator, with Four Essays by Richard Steele,* edited by Donald F. Bond. New York and Oxford, Oxford University Press, 1970.

Akenside, Mark. *The Pleasures of Imagination, A Poem in Three Books* (1744). In *The Poetical Works of Mark Akenside: Collated with the Best Editions: by Thomas Park, Esq. F.S.A.* 2 vols. London: Printed at the Stanhope Press by Charles Whittingham for J. Sharpe, 1805.

Alsop, Richard. *The Charms of Fancy: A Poem in Four Cantos with Notes.* Edited by Theodore Dwight. 1788. New York: D. Appleton, 1856.

Alston, J. William. *Hints to Young Practitioners in the Study of Landscape Painting.* 3d ed. 1805. London: Printed for Longman, Hurst, Rees & Orme, 1820.

Arthur, T. S. *Trials and Confessions of an American Housekeeper.* Philadelphia: Lippincott, Grambo & Co., 1854.

Bartol, Samuel F. *Practical Hints on the Subject of Window Ornaments.* New York: C. Willets, printer, 1849.

Bigelow, Jacob. *Elements of Technology.* Boston: Hilliard, Gray, Little and Wilkins, 1829.

Bretton, Nicholas. *School and Forte of Fancie.* 1582. In *The Works in Verse and Prose of Nicholas Breton, for the First Time Collected and Edited: With Memorial Introduction, Notes and Illustrations, Glossarial Index, Facsimiles, &c.,* by the Rev. Alexander B. Grosart. 2 vols. 1879. New York: AMS Press, 1966.

Brewster, Sir David. *A Treatise on the Kaleidoscope.* Edinburgh: Archibald Constable and Co., 1819.

———. *The Kaleidoscope: Its History, Theory, and Construction, with Its Application to the Fine and Useful Arts.* London: John Murray, 1858.

Burke, Edmund. "Introduction on Taste." In *A Philosophical Enquiry into the Origin of Our Ideas of the Sublime and Beautiful,* edited with an introduction and notes by James T. Boulton. Notre Dame, Ind. and London: University of Notre Dame Press, 1958.

Chippendale, Thomas. *The Gentleman and Cabinet-Maker's Director.* 3d ed. 1762. New York: Dover Publications, 1966.

Cleaveland, Henry W., William Backus, and Samuel D. Backus. *Village and Farm Cottages, The Requirements of American Village Homes Considered and Suggested; with Designs for Such Houses of Moderate Cost.* New York: D. Appleton and Co., 1856.

Clulow, William Benton. *Aphorisms and Reflections: Miscellany of Thought and Opinion.* London: John Murray, 1843.

Coleridge, Samuel Taylor. *Biographia Literaria; or, Biographical Sketches of My Literary Life and Opinions.* New York: Kirk and Merein, 1817.

Downing, A. J. *The Architecture of Country Houses; including Designs for Cottages, Farm-houses, and Villas.* New York: D. Appleton and Co., 1850.

Dryden, John. *Religio Laici.* 1682. In *The Oxford Authors: John Dryden,* edited by Keith Walker. Oxford and New York: Oxford University Press, 1987.

Emerson, Ralph Waldo. "Poetry and Imagination." 1875. In *The Complete Writings of Ralph Waldo Emerson, Containing all of His Inspiring Essays, Lectures, Poems, Addresses, Studies, Biographical Sketches, and Miscellaneous Works.* 2 vols. New York: William H. Wise & Co., 1929.

Finn, Matthew D. *Theorematical System of Painting, or Modern Plan, Fully Explained in Six Lessons.* New York: James Ryan, 1830.

Fowler, Orson S. *A Home for All, or The Gravel Wall and Octagon Mode of Building.* New York: Samuel R. Wells, 1853.

Freneau, Philip. "The Power of Fancy." In *American Literature Survey, Colonial and Federal to 1800,* edited by Milton R. Stern and Seymour L. Gross. New York: Viking Press, 1966.

Gandee, B. F. *The Artist or, Young Ladies' Instructor in Ornamental Painting, Drawing, etc.* London: Chapman and Hall; New York: W. Jackson, 1835.

Gerard, Alexander. *An Essay on Taste, to which are annexed Three Dissertations on the same Subject by Mr. De Voltaire, Mr. D'Alembert, and Mr. De Montesquieu.* 1759. 2d ed. 1764. Reprint, New York: Garland, 1970.

Gerard, Alexander. *An Essay on Taste, together with Observations concerning the Imitative Nature of Poetry.* 1780. 3d ed. Facsimile reprint, with an introduction by Walter J. Hipple, Jr. Delmar, N.Y.: Scholars' Facsimiles & Reprints, 1978.

Hargrove, John. *Weaver's Draft Book and Clothiers Assistant.* 1792. With an introduction by Rita J. Adrosko. Worcester, Mass.: American Antiquarian Society, 1979.

Hay, D. R. *The Laws of Harmonious Colouring Adapted to Interior Decorations, Manufacturers, and Other Useful Purposes.* 1828. 4th ed. London: W. S. Orr and Co.; Edinburgh: W. & R. Chambers, 1838.

———. *The Laws of Harmonious Colouring Adapted to Interior Decorations, Manufacturers, and Other Useful Purposes.* 1828. 5th ed. London: W. S. Orr and Co.; Edinburgh: Fraser and Co., 1844.

———. *The Laws of Harmonious Colouring Adapted to Interior Decorations, Manufacturers, and Other Useful Purposes.* 1828. 6th ed. Edinburgh and London: W. Blackwood and Sons, 1847.

Hazen, Edward. *Panorama of Professions and Trades.* Philadelphia: Uriah Hunt and Sons, 1837.

Hepplewhite, George. *The Cabinet-Maker and Upholsterer's Guide.* 1794. 3d ed. New York: Dover Publications, 1969.

Higgins, William Mullinger. *The House Painter; or Decorator's Companion.* London: Thomas Kelly, 1851.

Hogarth, William. *Analysis of Beauty, Written with a view of fixing the fluctuating ideas of taste.* 1753. Edited with an introduction and notes by Ronald Paulson.

New Haven and London: Yale University Press, 1997.

Hume, David. *A Treatise of Human Nature.* 1740. With an introduction by A. D. Lindsay. London and Toronto: J. M. Dent & Sons; New York: Dutton, 1970.

Hunt, Leigh. "What is Poetry." In *Imagination and Fancy, or Lessons from the English Poets.* 1844. New York: Wiley and Putnam, 1845.

_____. *Wit and Humor, Selected from the English Poets, with an illustrative Essay, and Critical Comments.* New York: Wiley and Putnam, 1847.

Johnson, Samuel. *The History of Rasselas, Prince of Abissinia.* In *Samuel Johnson: Rasselas, Poems and Selected Prose*, edited by Bertrand H. Bronson. New York: Holt, Rinehart and Winston, 1958.

Keats, John. *The Complete Poetical Works and Letters of John Keats.* New York and Boston: Houghton Mifflin Co., 1899.

Locke, John. *An Essay Concerning Human Understanding.* 1690. Edited by A. S. Pringle Pattison. Oxford: Clarendon Press, 1924.

Lucas, Fielding. *The Progressive Drawing Book.* Baltimore: Fielding Lucas, n.d. [ca. 1821–1828].

Lugar, Robert. *Architectural Sketches for Cottages, Rural Dwellings, and Villas, in the Grecian, Gothic, and Fancy Styles, with Plans; Suitable to Persons of Genteel Life and Moderate Fortune.* London: J. Taylor, 1823.

Maire, Frederick. *Graining and Marbling; A Series of Practical Treatises on Material, Tools and Appliances Used.* Chicago: F. J. Drake and Co., n.d. [ca. 1910].

Pinchbeck, William. *The Expositor: or Many Mysteries Unraveled.* Boston: privately printed, 1805.

Poe, Edgar Allan. "The Philosophy of Furniture." In the *Works of Edgar Allan Poe in One Volume,* edited by Hervey Allen. New York: P. F. Collier & Son Co., 1927.

Porter, Rufus. *A Select Collection of Valuable and Curious Arts.* Concord, N.H.: J. B. Moore, 1825.

_____. *A Select Collection of Valuable and Curious Arts,* 2d ed. Concord, N.H.: J. B. Moore, 1826.

Reid, Thomas. *Essays on the Intellectual Powers of Man.* Edinburgh: John Bell; London: G. G. and J. Robinson, 1785.

Reynolds, Sir Joshua. "Discourse VII." In *Seven Discourses on Art.* 1769–1776. New York: Cassell, 1888.

Royall, Anne. *Mrs. Royall's Pennsylvania, or Travels Continued in the United States.* 2 vols. Washington, D.C.: privately printed, 1829.

Ruskin, John. *Modern Painting.* 1843. In *The Works of John Ruskin,* edited by E. T. Cook and Alexander Wedderburn. 38 vols. London: George Allen; New York: Longman, Green and Co., 1903.

_____. *The Seven Lamps of Architecture.* 1851. New York: D. Appleton and Co., 1899.

A Series of Progressive Lessons, Intended to Elucidate the Art of Flower Painting in Water Colors. Philadelphia: M. Thomas, 1818.

Sheraton, Thomas. *The Cabinet-Maker and Upholsterer's Drawing-Book.* 1802. 3d ed. New York: Dover Publications, 1972.

_____. *Cabinet Dictionary.* 1803. With an introduction by Wilford P. Cole and Charles F. Montgomery. 2 vols. New York: Praeger, 1970.

Smith, Walter. *Art Education, Scholastic and Industrial.* Boston: James R. Osgood and Co., 1872.

Stalker, John, and George Parker. *A Treatise on Japanning and Varnishing.* 1688. London: Alec Tiranti, 1971.

Stewart, Dugald. *Elements of the Philosophy of the Human Mind.* London: printed for A. Strahan and T. Cadell in the Strand; Edinburgh: W. Creech, 1792.

Stickley, Gustave, ed. *The Craftsman, An Illustrated Monthly Magazine in the Interest of Better Art, Better Work, and a Better More Reasonable Way of Living.* Vol. 10, no. 2 (May 1906).

Tocqueville, Alexis de. *Democracy in America.* Edited by Andrew Hacker. New York: Washington Square Press, 1964.

Trollope, Frances. *Domestic Manners of the Americans.* 2 vols. London: Whittaker, Treacher & Co., 1832.

Whittock, Nathaniel. *The Decorative Painters' and Glaziers' Guide.* London: Isaac Taylor Hinton, 1827.

_____. *The Complete Book of Trades, or the Parent's Guide and Youth's Instructor.* London: John Bennett, 1837.

_____. *The Oxford Drawing Book, A New and Improved Edition.* New York: Collins, Keese & Co., 1840.

Wordsworth, William. *Poems, Including Lyrical Ballads.* 2 vols. London: Longman, Hurst, Rees, Orme, and Brown, 1815.

Primary Articles / Essays

Ackermann, Rudolph. "Observations on Fancy-work." *The Repository of Arts, Science, Literature, Commerce, Manufactures, Fashions, and Politics*, no. 15 (March 1810): 192–95; no. 16 (April 1810): 397.

Hawthorne, Nathaniel. "A Select Party." 1844. In *The Centenary Edition of the Works of Nathaniel Hawthorn,* edited by William Charvat, et al. Columbus: Ohio State University Press, 1974.

Leckey, W. E. H. "Imagination in the Progress of Morals." *Appleton's Journal: A Magazine of General Literature* 1, no. 6 (May 8, 1869): 184–86.

Montesquieu, Baron de. "Essay on Taste." In Alexander Gerard, *An Essay on Taste, to which are annexed Three Dissertations on the same Subject by Mr. De Voltaire, Mr. D'Alembert, and Mr. De Montesquieu.* 1759. New York: Garland, 1970.

Voltaire, François Marie Arouet de. "Mr. De Voltaire's Essay on Taste." In Alexander Gerard, *An Essay on Taste, to which are annexed Three Dissertations on the same Subject by Mr. De Voltaire, Mr. D'Alembert, and Mr. De Montesquieu.* 1759. New York: Garland, 1970.

Dictionaries

The Dictionary of Americanisms. Edited by Milford M. Mathews. Chicago: University of Chicago Press, 1951.

Johnson, Samuel. *A dictionary of the English language: in which the words are deduced from their originals, and illustrated in their different significations by examples from the best writers; to which are prefixed, A history of the language, and an English grammar.* London: Printed by W. Strahan for J. and P. Knapton, 1755.

_____. *A Dictionary of the English Language.* 2d ed. London: W. Strahan, 1773.

The Oxford English Dictionary, Being a Corrected Re-Issue with an Introduction, Supplement and Bibliography of A New English Dictionary on Historical Principles Founded Mainly on the Materials Collected by the Philological Society. Edited by James A. H. Murray et al. 12 vols. 2d ed. Oxford: Clarendon Press, 1961.

A Supplement to the Oxford English Dictionary. Edited by R. W. Burchfield. 2 vols. Oxford: Clarendon Press, 1972.

Worcester, Joseph E. *A Dictionary of the English Language.* Cambridge, Mass.: H. O. Houghton & Co., 1860.

Secondary Books

American Folk Painters of Three Centuries. Edited by Jean Lipman and Tom Armstrong. New York: Hudson Hills Press for the Whitney Museum of Art, 1980.

Ames, Kenneth M. *Beyond Necessity: Art in the Folk Tradition.* New York: W. W. Norton for the Winterthur Museum, 1977.

Anderson, Clarita. *"No Man Can Better It": Maryland Coverlets and Their Weavers.* College Park: University of Maryland Press, 1981.

Andrews, Edward Deming, and Faith Andrews. *Shaker Furniture.* New York: Dover Publications, 1950.

Baltimore Museum of Art. *Baltimore Furniture: The Work of Baltimore and Annapolis Cabinetmakers from 1760 to 1810.* Baltimore, Md.: By the museum, 1947.

Bishop, Robert. *Centuries and Styles of the American Chair: 1640–1880.* New York: Bonanza Books, 1983.

Brown, Ann Eckert. *American Wall Stenciling, 1790–1840.* Hanover, N.H.: University Press of New England, 2003.

Carlisle, Lilian Baker. *Hat Boxes and Bandboxes at the Shelburne Museum.* Shelburne, Vt.: Shelburne Museum, 1960.

Cohen, Jeffrey A., and Charles E. Brownell. *The Architectural Drawings of Benjamin Henry Latrobe.* 2 vols. New Haven and London: Yale University Press for the Maryland Historical Society and the American Philosophical Society, 1994.

Colwill, Stiles Tuttle. *Francis Guy: 1760–1820.* Baltimore: Maryland Historical Society, 1981.

Cooper, Wendy A., with Tara Louise Gleason and Katharine A. John. *An American Vision, Henry Francis du Pont's Winterthur Museum.* Washington, D.C.: National Gallery of Art; Winterthur, Del.: Winterthur Museum, 2002.

Coysh, A. W., and Frank Stephano, Jr. *Collecting Ceramic Landscapes: British and American Landscapes on Printed Pottery.* London: Lund Humphries, 1981.

Curtis, John Obed, and William H. Guthman. *New England Militia Uniforms and Accoutrements—A Pictorial Survey.* Sturbridge, Mass: Old Sturbridge Village, 1971.

Davidson, Mildred, and Christa Mayer-Thurman. *Coverlets: A Handbook of the Collection of the Art Institute of Chicago.* Chicago: Art Institute of Chicago, 1973.

Decorator Digest: Chapters in the History of Early American Decoration and Its European Background Selected from the "Decorator." Edited by Natalie Ramsey. Rutland, Vt.: Charles E. Tuttle Co., 1965.

Denker, Bert, and Ellen P. Denker. *The Rocking Chair Book.* New York: Mayflower Books, 1979.

Denker, Ellen Paul. *Kirkpatrick's Pottery at Anna, Illinois.* Urbana-Champaign, Ill.: Krannert Art Museum, 1986.

Devoe, Shirley Spaulding. *The Tinsmiths of Connecticut.* Middletown, Conn.: Wesleyan University Press for the Connecticut Historical Society, 1968.

Distin, William H., and Robert Bishop. *The American Clock A Comprehensive Pictorial Survey 1723–1900: With a Listing of 6,153 Clockmakers.* New York: Bonanza Books, 1983.

Elder, William Voss. *Baltimore Painted Furniture, 1800–1840.* Baltimore: Baltimore Museum of Art, 1972.

Evans, Nancy Goyne. *American Windsor Chairs.* New York: Hudson Hills Press; Winterthur, Del.: Winterthur Museum, 1996.

_____. *American Windsor Furniture, Specialized Forms.* New York: Hudson Hills Press; Winterthur, Del.: Winterthur Museum, 1997.

Fales, Dean A. *American Painted Furniture 1660–1880.* New York: E. P. Dutton, 1971.

Foley, Paul J. *Willard's Patent Time-Pieces, A History of the Weight Driven Banjo Clock 1800–1900.* Norwell, Mass.: Paul J. Foley, 2002.

Fox, Eleanor J., and Edward G. Fox. *Gaudy Dutch.* Pottsville, Pa.: privately printed, 1968.

Frank, Robin Jaffe. *Love and Loss: American Portrait and Mourning Miniatures.* New Haven: Yale University Press, 2000.

Garrett, Elisabeth Donaghy. *At Home: The American Family 1750–1870.* New York: Harry N. Abrams, 1998.

Garrett, Wendell D. "John Adams and the Limited Role of the Fine Arts." *Winterthur Portfolio.* Vol. 1. Winterthur, Del.: Winterthur Museum, 1964.

Gerdts, William H., and Russell Burke. *American Still-life Painting.* New York: Praeger, 1971.

Gernsheim, Helmut, and Alison Gernsheim. *L. J. M. Daguerre: The History of the Diorama and the Daguerreotype.* 2d ed. rev. New York: Dover Publications, 1968.

Gibson, Michael. *Nineteenth Century Lustreware.* London: Antique Collectors' Club, 1999.

Godden, Geoffrey A. *British Pottery and Porcelain, 1780–1850.* London: Arthur Barker Ltd., 1963.

Gombrich, Ernst H. *The Sense of Order, The Wrightsman Lectures Delivered under the Auspices of the New York University Institute of Fine Arts.* New York: Phaidon, 1979.

Greaser, Arlene, and Paul H. Greaser. *Homespun Ceramics: A Study of Spatterware.* Des Moines, Iowa: Wallace-Homestead Co., 1973.

H. F. du Pont Winterthur Museum. *Glass in Early America, Selections from the H. F. du Pont Winterthur Museum.* Winterthur Del.: By the museum, 1993.

Heal, Ambrose. *London Tradesmen's Cards of the XVIII Century.* London: B. T. Batsford, 1925.

Heirlooms From Old Looms: A Catalogue of Coverlets Owned by the Colonial Coverlet Guild of America and Its Members. Edited by Mrs. Luther M. Swygert. Chicago: privately printed, 1955.

Heisey, John W. *A Checklist of American Coverlet Weavers.* Charlottesville: University Press of Virginia, 1980.

Hollander, Stacy. *American Anthem: Masterworks from the American Folk Art Museum, New York.* New York: American Folk Art Museum in association with Harry N. Abrams, 2001.

Hollander, Stacy, et al. *American Radiance: The Ralph Esmerian Gift to the American Folk Art Museum, New York.* New York: American Folk Art Museum in association with Harry N. Abrams, 2001.

Hughes, Therle, and Bernard Hughes. *English Painted Enamels.* Feltham, Middlesex, Eng.: Hamlyn Publishing Group, 1967.

Jacobs, Timothy. *The History of the Baltimore and Ohio Railroad.* New York: Crescent Books, 1989.

Kenney, John T. *The Hitchcock Chair.* New York: Clarkson N. Potter, 1971.

Lea, Zilla. *The Ornamented Chair: Its Development in America 1700–1890.* Rutland, Vt.: Charles E. Tuttle Co., 1960.

Lewis, John, and Griselda Lewis. *Prattware: English and Scottish Relief Decorated and Underglaze Coloured Earthenware 1780–1840*. Woodbridge, Suffolk, Eng.: Antique Collectors' Club, in association with Alan Kaplan, 1993.

Lighting in America. Edited by Lawrence S. Cooke. New York: Main St./Universe Books, Antiques Magazine Library, 1975.

Lipman, Jean. *Rufus Porter Rediscovered*. New York: Clarkson N. Potter, 1980.

Little, Nina Fletcher. *American Decorative Wall Painting, 1700–1850*. New York: E. P. Dutton, 1989.

_____. *Country Art in New England 1790–1840*. Sturbridge, Mass.: Old Sturbridge Village, 1964.

_____. *Floor Coverings in New England before 1850*. Sturbridge, Mass.: Old Sturbridge Village, 1967.

McClelland, Nancy V. *Historic Wallpapers from Their Inception to the Introduction of Machinery*. Philadelphia and London: J. B. Lippincott, 1924.

McConnell, Kevin. *Spongeware and Spatterware*. 3d ed. Atglen, Pa.: Schiffer Publishing Ltd., 2001.

McKearin, Helen, and George S. McKearin. *Two Hundred Years of American Blown Glass*. New York: Crown Publishers, 1966.

McKearin, Helen, and Kenneth Wilson. *American Bottles and Flasks and Their Ancestry*. New York: Crown Publishers, 1978.

Montgomery, Charles F. *American Furniture, the Federal Period in the H. F. du Pont Winterthur Museum*. New York: Viking Press, 1962.

Montgomery, Florence M. *Printed Textiles: English and American Cottons and Linens, 1700–1850*. New York: Viking Press, 1970.

Montgomery, Pauline. *Indiana Coverlet Weavers and Their Coverlets*. Indianapolis, Ind.: Hoosier Heritage Press, 1974.

Moss, Roger W. *Paint in America: The Colors of Historic Buildings*. Washington, D.C.: National Trust for Historic Preservation, 1994.

Nylander, Richard. *Wallpapers for Historic Buildings*. Washington, D.C.: National Trust for Historic Preservation, 1992.

Oberwager, Jerry. *Chalkware Tools and Methods, prepared as a complement for a talk by Jerry Oberwager before the Early Trades and Crafts Society*. Privately printed, April 1981.

O'Dea, William T. *The Social History of Lighting*. London: Routledge and Pue, 1958.

Of Consuming Interests: The Style of Life in the Eighteenth Century. Edited by Cary Carson, Ronald Hoffman, and Peter J. Albert. Charlottesville, Va.: United States Capitol Historical Society, 1994.

Orlofsky, Patsy, and Myron Orlofsky. *Quilts in America*. New York: McGraw-Hill, 1974.

Paulson, Ronald. *Hogarth's Graphic Works*. 2 vols. New Haven and London: Yale University Press, 1970.

Ring, Betty. *American Needlework Treasures: Samplers and Silk Embroideries from the Collection of Betty Ring*. New York: E. P. Dutton in association with the Museum of American Folk Art, 1987.

Rivard, Paul E. *A New Order of Things: How the Textile Industry Transformed New England*. Hanover and London: University Press of New England, 2002.

Roberts, Kenneth D. *Eli Terry and the Connecticut Shelf Clock*. Bristol, Conn.: Kenneth Roberts Publishing Co., 1973.

Ryser, Frieder. *Reverse Paintings on Glass: The Ryser Collection*. Corning, N.Y.: Corning Museum of Glass, 1992.

Schaffner, Cynthia V. A., and Susan Klein. *American Painted Furniture 1790–1880*. New York: Clarkson Potter, 1997.

Schoelwer, Susan P. *Lions & Eagles & Bulls: Early American Tavern & Inn Signs from the Connecticut Historical Society*. Hartford, Conn.: Connecticut Historical Society in association with Princeton University Press, 2000.

Schorsch, Anita. *Mourning Becomes America, Mourning Art in the New Nation*. Clinton, N.J.: Main Street Press, 1976.

Shuman, John A., III. *The Collector's Encyclopedia of Gaudy Dutch & Welsh*. Paducah, Ky.: Collector Books, 1991.

Spillman, Jane Shadel. *American and European Pressed Glass in the Corning Museum of Glass*. Corning, N.Y.: Corning Museum of Glass, 1981.

Sprigg, June. *By Shaker Hands*. New York: Alfred Knopf, 1975.

Swan, Susan Burrows. *Plain and Fancy, American Women and Their Needlework, 1700–1850*. New York: Holt Rinehart and Winston, 1977.

Tomlinson, Juliette. *Paintings and Journal of Joseph Whiting Stock*. Middletown, Conn.: Wesleyan University Press, 1976.

Van Zanten, David. *The Architectural Polychromy of the 1830s*. New York and London: Garland, 1977.

Weekley, Carolyn. *The Kingdoms of Edward Hicks*. New York: Harry N. Abrams, 1999.

Weidman, Gregory R., and Jennifer F. Goldsborough. *Classical Maryland 1815–1845 Fine and Decorative Arts from the Golden Age*. Baltimore: Maryland Historical Society, 1993.

Whitehill, Walter Muir. *George Crowninshield's Yacht "Cleopatra's Barge" and a Catalogue of the Francis B. Crowninshield Gallery*. Salem, Mass.: Peabody Museum, 1959.

Wilson, Kenneth M. *American Glass 1760–1930*. New York: Hudson Hills Press for the Toledo Museum of Art, 1994.

Zogry, Kenneth. *The Best the Country Affords, Vermont Furniture 1765–1850*. Bennington, Vt.: Bennington Museum, 1995.

Secondary Articles

Ames, Kenneth L. "Posture and Power." In *Death in the Dining Room and Other Tales of Victorian Culture*. Philadelphia: Temple University Press, 1992.

Andrews, Carol Damon. "John Rito Penniman (1782–1841): An Ingenious New England Artist." *Antiques* 120, no. 1 (July 1981): 147–70.

Barker, David. "'The Usual Classes of Useful Articles': Staffordshire Ceramics Reconsidered." In *Ceramics in America*, edited by Robert Hunter. Hanover, N.H.: University Press of New England for the Chipstone Foundation, 2001.

Carpentier, Donald, and Jonathan Rickard. "Slip Decoration in the Age of Industrialization." In *Ceramics in America*, edited by Robert Hunter. Hanover, N.H.: University Press of New England for the Chipstone Foundation, 2001.

Cummings, Abbott Lowell. "Decorative Painters and House Painting at Massachusetts Bay, 1630–1725." In *American Painting to 1776: A Reappraisal*, edited by Ian M. G. Quimby. Charlottesville: University Press of Virginia for the Winterthur Museum.

Deutsch, Davida. "Samuel Folwell of Philadelphia: An Artist for the Needleworker." *Antiques* 119, no. 2 (February 1981): 420–23.

———. "Collectors' Notes." *Antiques* 128, no. 3 (September 1985): 526–27.

———. "Collectors' Notes." *Antiques* 130, no. 4 (October 1986): 646–47.

———. "Collectors' Notes: A follow-up on our Man Folwell." *Antiques* 135, no. 3 (March 1989): 616–624.

———. "Jewelry for Mourning, Love and Fancy, 1770–1830." *Antiques* 155, no. 4 (April 1999): 566–75.

Endicott, F. Munroe. "English Lustre-ware: Two Inscribed Wares." *Antiques* 20, no. 3 (September 1946): 144–47.

Evans, Nancy Goyne. "The Christian M. Nestell Drawing Book: A Focus on the Ornamental Painter and His Craft in Early Nineteenth-Century America." In *American Furniture,* edited by Luke Beckerdite. Hanover, N.H.: University Press of New England for the Chipstone Foundation, 1998.

———. "The Genesis of the Boston Rocking Chair." *Antiques* 123, no. 1 (January 1983): 246–53.

Hebb, Caroline. "A Distinctive Group of Early Vermont Painted Furniture." *Antiques* 104, no. 3 (September 1973): 458–61.

Hosley, William N., Jr. "Wright, Robbins, & Winship and the Industrialization of the Furniture Industry in Hartford, Connecticut." *Connecticut Antiquarian* 35, no. 2 (December 1983): 12–19.

Hughs, G. Bernard. "Tricks in the Tavern." *Country Life* 121, no. 3138 (March 7, 1957): 424–26.

Humphries, Lance. "Provenance, Patronage, and Perception: The Morris Suite of Baltimore Painted Furniture." In *American Furniture,* edited by Luke Beckerdite. Hanover, N.H.: University Press of New England for the Chipstone Foundation, 2003.

Kane, Patricia E. "Samuel Gragg: His Bent-wood Fancy Chairs." Yale University Art Gallery *Bulletin* 33, no. 2 (fall 1971): 26–37.

Karmason, Marilyn G. "Shimmering and Brilliant: American Victorian Tinsel Painting." *The Clarion* 16, no. 4 (winter 1991–1992): 73–79.

King, Edgar Weld. "Painted Window Shades." *Antiques* 36, no. 6 (December 1939): 288–91.

Kirtley, Alexandra Alevizatos. "Survival of the Fittest: The Lloyd Family's Furniture Legacy." In *American Furniture,* edited by Luke Beckerdite. Hanover, N.H.: University Press of New England for the Chipstone Foundation, 2002.

———. "New Discoveries in Balti-more Painted Furniture." *Catalog of Antiques and Fine Art* 3, no. 2 (spring 2002): 204–9.

Lambeth, Deborah. "Rufus Cole: A Mohawk Valley Decorator." *The Decorator* 35, no. 2 (spring 1981): 4–11.

Lindsey, Jack L. "An Early Latrobe Furniture Commission." *Antiques* 139, no. 1 (January 1991): 209–19.

Little, Nina Fletcher. "William Matthew Prior: Travelling Artist and His In-Laws the Painting Hamblens." *Antiques* 53, no. 1 (January 1948): 40–44.

MacFarlane, Janet R. "Shades of Our Fore-fathers." *Antiques* 76, no. 2 (August 1959): 122–25.

Noël Hume, Ivor. "Through the Lookinge Glasse: Or, The Chamber Pot as a Mir-ror of Its Time." In *Ceramics in America,* edited by Robert Hunter. Hanover, N.H.: University Press of New England for the Chipstone Foundation, 2003.

Nylander, Jane. "Some Print Sources of New England Schoolgirl Art." *Antiques* 110, no. 2 (August 1976): 292–301.

Nylander, Richard C. "Prestwould Wall-papers." *Antiques* 147, no. 1 (January 1995): 168–70.

Parslow, Virginia D. "James Alexander, Weaver." *Antiques* 69, no. 4 (April 1956): 346–49.

Podmaniczky, Michael. "The Incredible Elastic Chairs of Samuel Gragg." *Antiques* 163, no. 5 (May 2003): 138–45.

Prown, Jonathan. "A Cultural Analysis of Furniture Making in Petersburg, Virginia, 1760–1820." *Journal of Early Southern Decorative Arts* 18, no. 1 (May 1992): 1–156.

Rickard, Jonathan. "Mocha Ware." *Antiques* 144, no. 2 (August 1993): 182–89.

Ring, Betty. "Memorial Embroideries by American Schoolgirls." *Antiques* 100, no. 4 (October 1971): 570–77.

Schorsch, David A. "Living with Antiques, A Collection of American Folk Art in the Midwest." *Antiques* 138, no. 4 (Octo-ber 1990): 776–87.

Skemer, Don C. "David Alling's Chair Manufactory: Craft Industrialization in Newark, New Jersey, 1801–1854." *Winter-thur Portfolio* 22 (spring 1987): 1–22.

Smith, Jane Webb. "The Wickham House in Richmond: Neoclassical Splendor Restored." *Antiques* 155, no. 2 (February 1999): 302–9.

Tarbox, Sandra. "Fanciful Graining: Tools of the Trade." *The Clarion* 6, no. 3 (fall 1981): 34–37.

Van Rensselaer, Susan. "Banded Cream-ware." *Antiques* 90, no. 3 (September 1966): 337–41.

Weidman, Gregory R. "The Painted Furniture of John and Hugh Finlay." *Antiques* 143, no. 5 (May 1993): 744–55.

Welsh, Frank. "The Art of Painted Grain-ing." *Historic Preservation* 29, no. 3 (July–September 1977): 33–37.

Zongor, Melinda. "Recommended Read-ing." *Newsletter of the Colonial Coverlet Guild of America* (fall 2003): 3.

Theses and Dissertations

Douglas, Ed Polk. "French Panoramic Wallpaper: Historical Background, Characteristic Development and Archi-tectural Application." Master's thesis, University of Virginia, 1976.

Jedlick, William. "Landscape Window Shades of the Nineteenth Century in New York State and New England." Master's thesis, State University of New York at Oneonta, 1967.

Index

Larcom, Lucy, 198
Latrobe, B. (Benjamin) Henry, 57–61, 232n32: card table, 61(fig. 99); side chair, 59(figs. 95, 96); window bench, 60(&fig. 98)
The Laws of Harmonious Colouring (Hay), 249n37
Lawton, George Robert, 87(fig. 144)
Lead-glazed earthenware: bottle, 183(fig. 324); bowl, 174(fig. 300); jug, 178(fig. 314); pie plate, 199(fig. 351). *See also* Earthenware
Leather buckets, xxii(fig. 4), 121(&fig. 205)
Leavitt, Joseph Warren, xxvii(fig. 13)
Leckey, W. E. H., 209
Leverett, Frances, 26(&fig. 52)
Liberty and Washington (transparent shade), 128(fig. 221)
Light: geometric patterns of, xxx; imagination and, 11; as visual stimulant, 10, 11, 16
Lighting devices: Fancy, 166–169(&figs. 281–289); replacement of Fancy, 215–216
List carpet, 163
Literacy, Fancy and female, 23–24
Literature, Fancy, 100
Livermore (Maine), chest of drawers, 72(fig. 118)
Lloyd, Edward V, 57, 232n29
Locke, John, 14, 226n32, 226n34, 237n42
Lockets, mourning, 31–32(&fig. 59)
Lodi (New York), coverlet, 165(fig. 279)
Lollipop design, 174
Lombard, Rachel, 28(fig. 55), 29
London Art of Cookery (Farley), 34
Longinus, Cassius, 225n17
Longworth, David, 148(fig. 253)
Longworth's American Almanac, New York Register, and City Directory, 148(fig. 253)
Looking glasses: Fancy, 37; painting on, 43(fig. 71), 67–68(&fig. 110), 69(fig. 115); transfer printing and, 127
Loom, Jacquard, 163–164, 243n8
Louis, Robert, 204
Lowell textile mills, 209
Lowndes, Joseph, 184(fig. 326), 185
Lugar, Robert, 212(fig. 366)
Lustreware, 178(&figs. 313, 314), 180(figs. 316, 317), 244n25

Mackenzie, Colin, 35(fig. 65)
Madison, Dolley, 58
Madison, James, 237n1
Maentel, Jacob, 117–118(&fig. 196)
Mahogany: card tables, 50(fig. 81), 53(fig. 87), 61(fig. 99), 62(fig. 102); Fancy painting and, 71; flame, 120; as graining, 101; secretary and bookcase, 40(fig. 69); shelf clock, 128(fig. 220); use of, 231n13; wall clocks, 68(fig. 111), 69(fig. 113); writing chair, 144(figs. 247, 248)
Mahogany veneer, 41: secretary and bookcase, 40(fig. 69)

Maine: dressing table, 28(fig. 55), 29(&fig. 56); rocking settee, 146(fig. 250). *See also* Livermore; Portland; Stevens Plains
Maine Charitable Mechanics Association, 114
Maine Enquirer, 123
Maltese Cross design, 237n32
Manheim (Pennsylvania), glass hunting horn, 189(fig. 333)
Mantel/mantelpieces, painted, 101, 102(fig. 167)
Mantel clocks, 127–128(&fig. 220). *See also* Clocks
Maple: armchairs, 47(fig. 77), 137(fig. 236), 150(fig. 256); box, 87(fig. 144); card tables, 47(fig. 75), 53(fig. 87), 61(fig. 99), 62(fig. 102); chairs, 44(fig. 72), 136(fig. 233); dressing tables, 28(fig. 55), 29(&fig. 56), 98, 99(fig. 165); Fancy chair, 45(fig. 73); Masonic chair, 141(fig. 242); pantry boxes, 108(fig. 179), 113(fig. 190), 173(fig. 298); rocking chairs, 139(fig. 239), 147(figs. 251, 252); rocking settee, 146(fig. 250); rush-seated side chair, 155(fig. 265); settees, 63(fig. 103), 64(fig. 104); sewing box, 27(fig. 53); sewing table, 113(fig. 187); side chairs, 51(fig. 82), 55(fig. 90), 56(fig. 91), 59(fig. 95), 61(fig. 100), 136(fig. 231), 154(fig. 263), 158(fig. 269); use of, 231n13; window bench, 60(fig. 98); Windsor armchair, 136(fig. 232); Windsor rocking chair, 145(fig. 249); Windsor side chair, 142(fig. 244); work tables, 27(fig. 54), 197(fig. 346)
Maple (soft): chair, 45(fig. 73); side chair, 135(fig. 230)
Marble, center table, 213(fig. 367)
Marbling, 70–72, 101, 106, 233n49, 238n8: on baseboard, 14(fig. 37); on ceramics, 78; on chairs, 137(fig. 234); distaste for, 215; on pier table, 71(fig. 117)
Martha Eliza Stevens Edgar Paschall (oil on canvas), 134, 135(fig. 229)
Martineau, Harriet, 147–148
Maryland: sconce, xxx(fig. 17); settee, 138(fig. 237). *See also* Baltimore
Masonic chair, 141(fig. 242)
Massachusetts: armchair, 47(fig. 77); chest, xxx(fig. 18); *The Dance,* 24, 26(&fig. 52); dome-top document box, 113(fig. 190); Fancy chair, 45(fig. 73); fire bucket, xxii(fig. 4); mourning piece, 33(fig. 61); rocking chair, 147(fig. 251); shelf clock, 68(fig. 112); trade sign, xxiii(fig. 6); Venetian carpet, 162(fig. 274). *See also individual towns/cities*
Master Chair-Makers Society, 151–152(&fig. 259)
Matteson, Thomas, 238n10
Maul, Gustave, 201(fig. 354)
McClellan House (South Woodstock, Connecticut), xxxi(&fig. 19)

Mechanics, 205, 247n14
The Mechanics Assistant (Tucker), 106
Medallions, 46
Megilp, 109, 238n13
Memoir Prepared at the Request of a Committee…(Colden), 152(fig. 259)
Memorial Hall Museum (Deerfield, Massachusetts), 241n7
Memorial pieces, 31(&fig. 58), 32–33(&fig. 61)
Memory, fancy and, 12
Men, in mourning pieces, 33
Middle-class Americans: decorative ceramic wares and, 183; Fancy and, xxii–xxiii, 99, 100; patterned carpeting and, 164–165
Militia matériel, 121–122, 239n24: drum, 121(&fig. 207); helmet, 122(fig. 208)
Milliners, 18, 159
Mind: deciphering workings of, 2–3; 18th-century British view of, 5; fancy as function of, 1–2
Mineral dyes, 203
Mineral pitch, 239n26
Miniature chest, 15(fig. 38)
Miniature footstools, 113(fig. 190), 139(fig. 240)
Mirrors. *See* Looking glasses
Mocha stone, 171. *See also* Mocha wares
Mocha wares, xvii, 171–172, 217, 244n18, 244n22
Modern: antique vs., 5; as term, 4(fig. 27), 5(fig. 28)
Moldings, painted, 101, 102(fig. 167)
Molds, glass, 191
Monkey Astride a Reclining Dog (figure), 217(fig. 373)
The Monkey Picture (oil on paper; Church), 218, 219(fig. 375), 250n49
Monkeys: figural, 217(&fig. 373); as visual image, 250n47
Montesquieu, Baron de (Charles de Secondat), 15
Montgomery (Fulton) County (New York), tall case clock, 120(fig. 203)
Monticello, 234n55: painted door, 73(&fig. 119); as window shade motif, 133
Moorestown (New Jersey), quilt, 94(fig. 157)
Morality: aesthetics and, 7, 212–215; Fancy and, 208; imagination and, 208, 209
Morse, E., 72(fig. 118)
Morse, Samuel F. B., 206
Morven (North Carolina), eight-pointed star quilt, 95(fig. 161)
Mosaic floors, quilt designs and, 237n29
Motifs: ancient, 41; balloon, 174; cable, 173(&fig. 299), 174(fig. 300); devil, xxxi–xxxii(&figs. 20, 21); diamond, 235n71; dipped fan, 174; egg-and-dart, 80(&fig. 135); egg and spinach, 175, 244n21; Fancy theorems, 197; floral and

𝒯HIS BOOK is set in Galliard, the typeface designed by Matthew Carter based on the 1503 drawings of Claude Garamond (1480–1561). The decorative script is Snell Roundhand also drawn by Matthew Carter and inspired by the early-eighteenth-century English writing master Charles Snell. It has been printed computer to plate offset lithography on a Heildelberg Speedmaster 102 F+L, on 170 gsm Magno Satin Text supplied by Sappi with Sun Chemicals Gibbons Finaset QS Sharp ink by Balding + Mansell in Norwich, Norfolk, England under the expert eye of Mike Boyce, January 2004. The first printing is 3,500 copies, case bound using handmade paste papers by the book designer, reproduced on sky extra matt 170 gsm text with Brillianta cloth by Skyline Bookbinders, Ltd., in Dorking, Surrey, England. Typeset by Mary Gladue, Aardvark Type. Book design by Wynne Patterson.

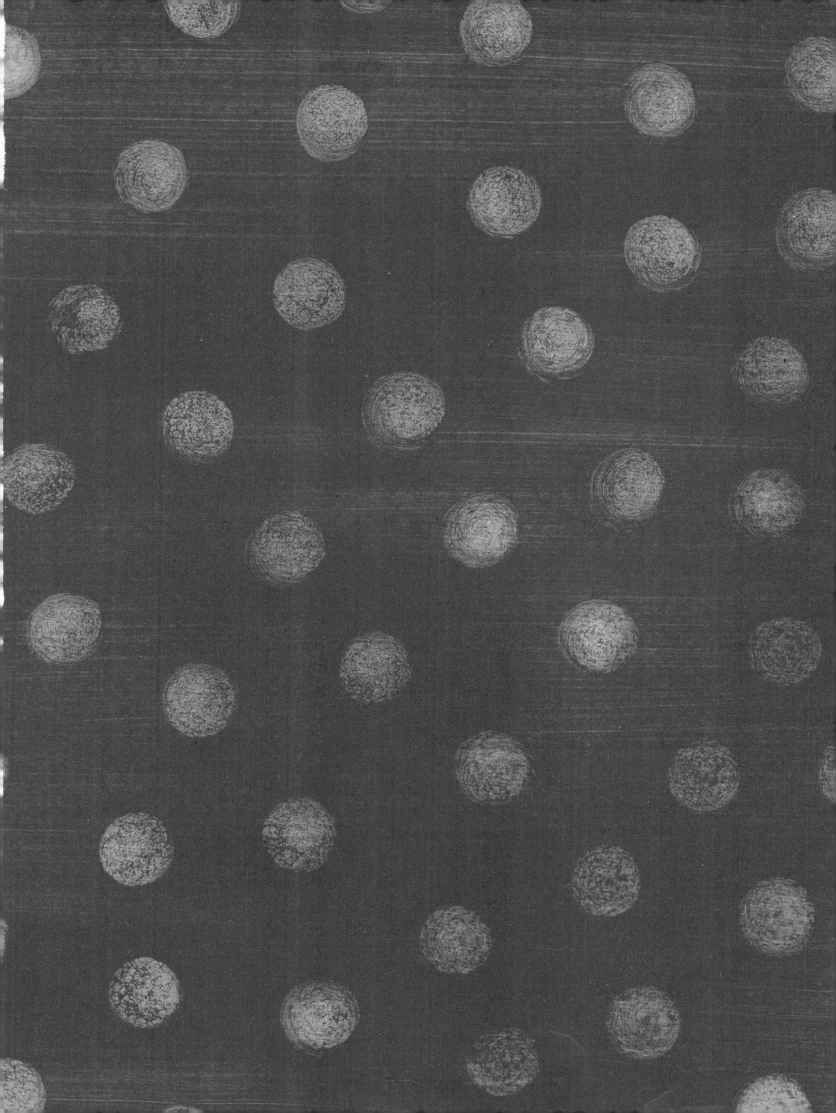